THE LOVE THAT DOES JUSTICE

Spiritual Activism In Dialogue With Social Science

Edited By Michael A. Edwards
& Stephen G. Post

D0980772

First Edition

TABLE OF CONTENTS

Introduction

For thinkers and activists across a wide range of contexts and historical experiences, unconditional love, spiritual experience, and the rigorous pursuit of justice in the world constitute a powerful path to social transformation, but only when they are strongly linked together. "Spiritual activists" draw on spiritual worldviews and practices to sustain an inner equilibrium of compassion and well-being while continually-engaged at the hard edges of social change (Horwitz, 2002). They practice what has come to be termed "engaged spirituality," in contrast to the spiritual practitioner who casts the world aside in favor of a socially-disengaged serenity. They take on the difficult work of organizing the downtrodden into groups capable of exerting social and political pressure through persuasion and protest, and do so with reliance on a background picture of a universe in which love and justice go with, rather than against, the grain of Ultimate Reality.

These activists have a defining voice in this book, and thereby offer a counterpoint to the widely-held view that forms of meditation, as practiced in the United States, lie mainly in the repertoire of those who are seeking personal happiness, self-realization, and alternative healing – but not social justice. It may be true that some contemplatives and mystics shy away from engagement in social and political issues, or advocacy with and for those who are the most marginalized and least powerful in society; but this cannot be said of the voices presented herein.

Our collection of essays—some of them in the genre of personal spiritual journey and some more analytic—presents the voices of American spiritual activists and social scientists who reflect together on how to deepen and advance our understanding of the role that spirituality plays in achieving social justice. Encounters between scholars and activists are never easy, but are often necessary to challenge each-other's assumptions, clarify the key issues at stake, and explore the transmission mechanisms that link love and justice in ways that are both conceptually rigorous and deeply-informed by concrete experience. In addition, we have deliberately included contributions from both the new and often younger American spiritual activists who draw so richly on Eastern traditions, and from their monotheistic forbears.

THE FORGOTTEN FACTOR

We suspect that the relationships linking love with justice are unlikely to be linear or universal, and certain to be complex. How do we define love and justice? Is religion the intermediary between the two, or spirituality, or can love and justice grow together in a humanistic framework that omits any reference to spiritual experience? We start from the position that love for a common humanity lies at the heart of the matter. "The essence of love," says the Institute for the Study of Unlimited Love at Case Western University, "is to affectively affirm as well as unselfishly delight in the well being of others, and to engage in acts of care and service on their behalf, without exception, in an enduring and constant way." Such love is universal, and therefore must consider the equal and general welfare of the whole. This means that love must consider and confront any factor that stands in the way of realizing the rights and dignity of every human being – whether rooted in personal prejudice and selfishness, or locked into the systems and structures of power that characterize all contemporary societies. This is our conception of justice, and it implies that the struggle for justice must encompass action at both the personal and the structural levels to create mutually-reinforcing cycles of change.

For some, personal change and social ethics have to be grounded in religious affiliation and/or spiritual experience. For others, these things are perceived as barriers to change, especially when religious communities are home to attacks on women's rights, homophobia, narrow-mindedness, a reluctance to enter into community-wide activities and concerns rather than intra-congregational commitments, and the substitution of individual acts of charity or service for a full and complete understanding of the structural factors that lead to oppression. Discrimination is rarely more dangerous than when it is cloaked in religious garb and cannot adequately be challenged by rationalist arguments for social justice because it assumes an other-worldly legitimacy. For the contributors to this book, love and justice are inseparable, for reasons we return to in a moment though do not fully understand, and spiritual experience is necessary for sustaining their capacity for a love that does justice. But membership in formal religious institutions is not seen as a necessary condition for either love or spirituality.

Spirituality in activism is not new, but it is too often ignored by those who do not see it as a driving dynamic. Yet many of the great social activists from early anti-slavery Quakers to the Civil Rights Movement were spiritual activists within a monotheistic framework. There is no need to remind readers of the prophetic tradition of Judaism, which exhorts, "and what does the Lord require of you but to do justice, and to love kindness, and to walk humbly with your God" (Micah 6:5). Perhaps we think of the classical Christian saint, in the style of a St. Francis, as far too ethereal to be interested in organizing the victims of ensconced group selfishness in order to establish a fairer balance of power through social and political suasion and coercion (Niebuhr, 1944). A pure love ethic has been deemed by saints-of-a-sort as above the acrimonious fray of the competing claims of classes, races, and nations, where rough solutions have to be achieved, usually with the help of form of some ultimate coercive threat. Yet what is the hard work of justice if not the first and most essential step on the ladder of unconditional love?

The spiritual background of so much social activism is often ignored by standard histories or the media. It is worth providing a few examples of this problem. Martin Luther King, shaped to his core by the notion of *agape* love and the prophetic call for justice, often invoked the Prophets of the Hebrew Bible. After being described on the news as "the son of a minister," rather than as the minister he himself was, he once responded with the following: "They aren't interested in the *why* of what we're doing, only in the *what* of what we're doing, and because they don't understand the why they cannot understand the what." Dr. King's poignant collection of sermons, entitled T*he Strength to Love*, (1963) describes how he made strenuous efforts to maintain the grounding of his activism in nonviolent love, even when he felt most weary, disappointed, and angered. In this book, Pastor Otis Moss, Jr., one of King's closest associates during the civil rights movement, articulates his own vision of the place of love in pursuit of justice in terms that are clearly influenced by King's writings and experience.

Another example of how spirituality can be easily ignored is the case of the late Dame Cicely Saunders. She was trained as a nurse, a medical social worker, and finally a physician. Since 1948, she was involved with the care of patients with terminal illnesses, and is best known as the founder of St. Christopher's Hospice in 1967, the very first research and teaching hospice linked with clinical care. She was a pioneer in the field of palliative medicine and has inspired the modern hospice movement worldwide. She fought hard to bring justice to the dying through the public health systems in the United Kingdom. One has to look a little more deeply into her personal memoirs to discover the spiritual experiences and divine calling she claims inspired her life work. At a conference in October of 1999 at MIT, she stated she would never have been inspired to invent the hospice movement without her sense of being called by God. She added that the spiritual aspect of her activism never quite makes it into the textbooks.

A third example of spirituality as a forgotten factor is the French Catholic social thinker and international activist Jacques Maritain. Maritain coined the modern notion of "human dignity," and was active in the drafting of both the United Nations Declaration of Human Rights and in UNESCO's statements on rights. He believed that dignity was conferred on human beings by virtue of the incarnation, and that, therefore, all human lives are worthy of those basic rights and entitlements that allow for a good and decent flourishing. How many of us know anything about Maritain, even as we invoke his terminology in justifying the contemporary human rights movement?

WHY LOVE DOES JUSTICE

Consider the following story from Jim LaRue, a former campus chaplain turned housing advocate, who has worked in Cleveland neighborhoods for many years: "There are millions who have had a 'memorable moment' with Dr. King. Mine became a 'formative moment' and occurred while a student at Bucknell University in the late 1950s. I was one of the student leaders who participated in a chapel service at which Dr. King spoke. But my memorable/formative moments came during a lengthy lunch with Dr. King, the other students on the platform that day, and several faculty.

"Having come from a small southeastern Pennsylvania town, I had no experience that would allow me to fully appreciate what was happening to him as the civil rights struggle he was leading started finding its way into the headlines of newspapers in the north. During our lunch he shared his great fear that his nonviolent approach would be met with such violence that his followers might feel they must finally retaliate with violence.

"But he said he was firmly convinced that only love could change the way the game of racism was played. *My formative moment came when he described the difference between love as expressed in personal acts of kindness and love expressed through social justice, and that one assumes the other. He said we cannot genuinely have one without the other. Helping someone in need fix their shelter can be a personal act of kindness, but if we do not address the poverty that created the conditions forced upon this person, we are not facing the whole truth. If I sympathize with a black friend who is being denied entry or access to something to which he is entitled, my personal act of support does not do enough unless I am also working to change the conditions that keep him from his due. But if I am fighting for social justice and do not treat individuals (especially the enemy) with the respect they deserve, my justice is hollow, it is without heart and I am at risk of starting to look like the enemy.*

"A seminary professor, Prentis Pemberton, Ethics Professor at Colgate Rochester Divinity School, helped me shape King's formative moment when he explained that our life mission as humans must be to find *how we can translate love into justice* structures. Every critical juncture in my life has been shaped by this thought and each time I return in my mind to that small room off the main cafeteria at Bucknell to refresh my heart and soul with the love twins, the Siamese love twins if you will, of personal acts of love and love as justice structures. They are joined at the heart, mind and soul, and cannot survive for long without one another."

As LaRue's story shows, the connection between love and justice is based on common sense. Consider the parent who loves a child, and discovers that there is no way to cover the costs of a necessary surgery. Love then quickly drives the parent to question the injustice of some children being treated more fairly than others when it comes to matters of life and death, and of his or her minimum wage that precludes a decent standard of living. Or consider the volunteer working in New Orleans after Hurricane Katrina, whose constant efforts, along with those of countless others, can achieve only a very partial alleviation of immense suffering. That volunteer inevitably begins to ask why it is that support and resources are unavailable from the corridors of power, and what forces are responsible for such neglect. Or consider the inner-city teacher who loves her students, and after immense frustration begins to ask why it is that the school is falling apart, without sufficient books to go around, while just a half mile away a shiny new football stadium is being built with every comfort imaginable? Or consider the family caregivers of loved

6

ones with Alzheimer's disease, who form a voluntary association to help one-another and quickly see the need to open a public policy office in Washington, DC in order to lobby for more research dollars and caregiver respite support.

These examples show how justice is *implicit* in love, and how justice seeking is the modulation or expression of love. "Doing unto others" does require the irreplaceable face-to-face interpersonal works of love, but it also requires the courage to confront larger, systemic unfairness. However much "random acts of kindness" can inspire, however much compassionate actions are trumpeted as "a thousand points of light," these invaluable works of love must not deflect attention away from the underlying problematic of injustice—the entrenched group selfishness that is blind to the common good. Love that does not "descend" into the struggle for justice is incomplete, if not irrelevant. Engaged spirituality, therefore, explicitly confronts social, political, and economic structures that are deemed unjust and contributory to the suffering of some needful group. Mahatma Gandhi, Martin Luther King, Abraham Heschel, and Bishop Desmond Tutu are obvious examples. Their moral appeal is to human dignity and human rights, and their endeavor is to effect structural change. The psychological dynamic involved in these efforts requires the persistent confrontation of entrenched powers that are recalcitrant to change.

In this sense, love is radical equality consciousness, a force that breaks down all distance and hierarchy. This is a love that respects the necessary self-empowerment of others, eschewing paternalism and romanticism for relationships of truth and authenticity, even when they move through phases of conflict and disagreement, as all do. This is a love that encourages us to live up to our social obligations as well our individual moral values, connect our interior life worlds to public spaces, encourage collective judgments, and create open networks of self-reflective and critical communication.

This love is active, not passive, explicitly considering the effects of oppressive and exploitative systems and structures on the welfare of others; it is not just focused on the immediate circle of family and friends, but rather on a deep and abiding commitment to the liberation of all. This is a love that seeks not to accumulate power, even in the face of oppression, but to transform it so that "victory" means more than a game of revolving chairs among narrow political interests.

This love forms an essential counterbalance to an excess of reason, adding in the discrimination, humility, intuition, ethical commitments, and emotional intelligence that are essential ingredients of wisdom. This love helps us to understand when and how to uphold and apply rationality, even in the toughest of circumstances, by increasing self-awareness of our biases, prejudices, and blind spots, and sustaining our objectivity about our own strengths and shortcomings. Love releases us from fear and insecurity, and our diminished sense of self. Love gives us optimism and hope, an expansion rather than contraction of our critical faculties, openness instead of closure.

Love does not generate ready-made answers to deep rooted and intractable problems of economic and social life, codified according to the conventional logics of Left or Right, Jewish, Muslim, or Christian. Instead, it provides a different set of motivations from which alternatives can grow, eventually producing a "social science of love" that can demonstrate how politics, economics, organizational development, social and international relations can be transformed through this radically-different form of rationality. The key to social transformation can be found in marrying a rich inner life dedicated to the cultivation of loving kindness and compassion with the practice of new forms of politics, economics, and public policy.

WHERE SPIRITUALITY FITS IN

Those spiritual activists who work for social justice and human rights are engaged in a contentious struggle and will be controversial – even hated and persecuted – for their actions. How do they deal with indifference, risk, hostility, imprisonment, and rage? The activist focuses a great deal of psychological energy on a sustained engagement with the powers that be. Essential character traits include courage in the face of threat, perseverance in the face of indifference, composure in the face of rage, equanimity in the face of hostility, and integrity in the face of imprisonment.

There are few internal challenges greater than sustaining love for those who would just as soon see the activist perish. King, Gandhi, Rabin, and many other activists with a vision of a common humanity have been killed for their views and actions; as an Indian saint once said when confronted by the bullet, "I will die loving you." The exemplar of compassion who sets aside the quest for justice is usually on no-one's hit list, and will generally be extolled by a society that looks to elevate its saints. It seems that society can easily forgive the personal flaws of these exemplars of compassion, but not the threats they perceive from the spiritual activist.

In part, spiritual practice is important to many activists because it helps to guard against the "thieves of the heart" – the greed, ego, anger, fear, and insecurities that will likely pollute or erode the success of even well-intentioned efforts to be a positive force for change in the world. This is why the transformation of the Self is so vital. Great inner strength is required to confront the structures of power in the world unselfishly, without demonizing one's enemies, alienating potential allies, or holding on too tightly to a particular vision of ends and means that can eventually become a prison. It is only by operating from the space where we are joined together in some deep sense that we are likely to find true common ground in facing up to the collective problems that confront us. How do activists, with all their human frailties, participate in love when engaged in actions that can easily give rise to bitterness and hatred? How does the spiritual activist refuse to hate the people who perpetuate injustice? How can an underlying love of all allow the activist to cope with adversity? How does the spiritual activist maintain a "higher self?" The answer is that they cultivate love, courage, and hope through spiritual practice in the face of indifference and weariness. Spiritual practice becomes both a spiritually- and politically-subversive activity.

We think that these insights are useful but preliminary. We need to go much further. How can the relationships between spirituality and social activism be better understood? Are there other links between spiritual practice, love, and the pursuit of social justice? And how do these relationships inform social activism today? It is best to begin, in *Section One*, with profiles written by spiritual activists who describe what spirituality means for their endeavors. We can listen and learn.

Section Two asks how the relationship between spirituality and social activism can be more carefully examined, conceptually and empirically. There are a number of ways to approach this question: through the experiential accounts of those activists whose lives are deeply shaped by spiritual beliefs and practices centering on love and justice; through the sociology of spiritually-engaged social activism; through the psychological study of the perseverance, effectiveness, and emotional qualities of such activists in the light of their spiritual practices and conceptions of love for humanity; and through new insights on leadership that show how and why spiritual values and practices are related to effectiveness in organizations (Reave, 2005).

Our purpose is to bring activists and scholars together to share their perspectives and experiences on the link between spiritual practice, unselfish love, and the rigorous pursuit of social justice, and on how these relationships inform social activism today. Through dialogue and sharing, we hope that activists can help scholars to develop future research agendas, and that scholars can contribute their perspectives on the work in which spiritual activists are engaged.

We note in closing that all those included in this book contributed to a conference entitled, *The Love That Does Justice: A Scientific Research Program*, that convened on the campus of Case Western Reserve University in Cleveland. The conference, convened on October 14 – 17, 2004, was sponsored by the Ford Foundation and by the Institute for Research on Unlimited Love-Altruism, Compassion, Service (supported through a John Templeton Foundation matching grant). Our thanks go to all these institutions for their support, and, most especially, to those who have participated in producing this book as contributors, advisors, editors, and publishers.

Stephen G. Post, President, The Institute for Research on Unlimited Love
Michael A. Edwards, Director, Governance and Civil Society, The Ford Foundation

Special thanks to the Seasons Fund for Social Transformation, which provided a generous grant for the publication and dissemination of this book.

References

Horwitz, Claudia. The Spiritual Activist: Practices to Transform Your Life, Your Work,   and Your World (New York: Penguin Compass, 2002).

King, Jr., Martin Luther. Strength to Love (Philadelphia: Fortress Press, 1963).

Reinhold Niebuhr, The Children of Darkness and the Children of Light (New York: Scribner's, 1944).

Reave, Laura. *Spiritual values and practices related to leadership effectiveness.* The Leadership Quarterly 16 (2005) 655-87.

SECTION ONE:
PERSPECTIVES FROM SPIRITUAL ACTIVISTS

1
PASTOR OTIS MOSS, JR.

The Reverend Dr. Otis Moss, Jr. is Past Chairman of the Board of Trustees at More-house College, Emeritus. Dr. Moss was called to the ministry at the age of 17 during his days as a student as Morehouse College. He received his Master of Divinity degree at Morehouse's School of Religion/Inter-Denominational Theological Center, and his Doctor of Ministry degree from United Theological Seminary.

During his early days as a minister, Dr. Moss was blessed to sit within the inner circle of many phenomenal persons, such as Dr. Benjamin E. Mays and Dr. Martin Luther King, Jr. Both of these persons provided friendship, leadership, and spiritual guidance, and helped to shape the thinking and model of leadership that Dr. Moss represents today. He served as co-pastor with Dr. Martin Luther King, Sr. at Ebenezer Baptist Church in Atlanta. He is recognized across the nation and globe as a charismatic and spiritually-oriented man of God, carrying the banner of justice and equality in civil rights for all.

Dr. Moss has served as Pastor of the Olivet Institutional Baptist Church, Cleveland, Ohio for 25 years. During this period, he has consulted with presidents and received a myriad of national honors for his work in civil rights. He is generally considered to be among the several most influential African-Americans in the United States.

I want address the context of prophets of love, apostles of justice, disciples of truth, ambassadors of peace and reconciliation.

When we look at non-violence in the context of the African-American communi-ty, we could examine aspects of African history prior to our experience in North America. Bennett's well known, highly recommended, and widely used sweeping history of the African-American journey before the Mayflower tells us that, 700 years before the Com-mon Era, there was an African leader by the name of Shabaka who initiated the end of capital punishment during his reign. It would be good to review some of those examples, including the reigns of other leaders who have subscribed to and been practitioners of creative love.

However, I want to look at a list of more modern examples. When I lift those examples up, they will not be exclusively African-American, but their lives and works and witnesses will be intertwined in our struggle. I maintain that each of us can be or can become, in our time and in our space, disciples of non-violence, practitioners of justice in the context of love, and peace makers, peace bearers, peace ambassadors, and apostles of reconciliation.

Now I would also strongly urge, within the context of the African-American experience, that we not look upon this as passive or meek—unless, of course, we are prepared to give a special and unique definition or an inscription to the word "passive" or the word "meek." And I am aware of the King James translation, "blessed are the meek for they shall inherit the earth." However, the use of that term has fallen among bad company for a long time. If we look upon that as being disciplined and using that discipline to tame the violent forces within ourselves and within our communities and within the wider scope of human existence, then we can use the word meek. But in the sense that we often grasp it, it has no place and certainly no way to be used as a substitute for non-violence. Not so long ago, I was reading a book by James Hillman, *A Terrible Love of War.* I have not finished it. But it was interesting to read the first page, first line, and first paragraph, where he quotes from the famous film *Patton.* There was a line in that book taken from the narrative or the words of General Patton as he walks across the battlefield of wounded, dead, torn humanity and says, "God I love it. I love it more than I love my life." And I've seen *Patton* several times, probably more times than is good for my spiritual health. But that particular line somehow escaped me in terms of its definition of how civilization and nations have fallen in love, not simply with war but with violence. We have romanticized it, we have theologized it, we have moralized it, and we have commercialized it—to the extent that we have made the non-violent love, the creative love, the unlimited love something of a strange abnormality.

Persons of love are to be watched carefully, listed on records of suspicious individuals, and carefully monitored lest they do damage to the body politic. These individuals we must report on the list of unpatriotic persons. In case of some continuing national challenge, they are the first to be rounded up. In the late 60s, I was told by an individual who had access to the records that I had been listed. I was serving a church in Cincinnati. You have been listed as a militant in the Police Department. Of course, that list was for reference in case of a civil disorder in the community. These are the persons who are to be among the first to be arrested or detained. It is an interesting phenomenon that you develop a pre-list of individuals and you can stretch that into a list of persons who are to either be detained or executed in the name of civil order. And this is the way we have turned the love epic upside down. However, I think we ought to study the writings and teachings of individuals such as Ghandi, Howard Thurman, Miss Sue Bailey Thurman, Clarence Jordan, and Martin Luther King, Jr. Or look at the foundation of the University of Tago in South Korea. When I visited that University as the guest of the president, Dr. Reed, a few years ago, I was amazed when he said that this university is founded on the principles and teachings articulated by Martin Luther King, Jr. We ought to look at the current work of Marian Wright Edelman, the life and services of Bishop Desmond Tutu. I think before you finish you ought to look at the life and work of Jimmy Carter, who is perhaps on one side of the ledger the most unappreciated prophet of our time. Despised by the religious right and demonized by both religious and political leaders, he was the one President who caused the news media to follow him to Sunday school. I think that was a part of their unhappiness. After sitting through a Sunday school class while the President was teaching a parable of the Good Samaritan, he would then not serve alcohol in the White House. He told all the members of the cabinet to catch a cab to come to work. I had an African-American call me a few years ago because Jimmy Carter took away his limousine. After all, it took him a lifetime to get to that position. Now it was interesting…we talked for about an hour, and he never said anything about any policy issues.

If we are to be fully informed, I think we have to study the movement led by Ghandi that began in South Africa. We need to look at the South African movement itself and see the violence on the side of the oppressors, as well as the violence sometimes practiced by those who were fighting against oppression. In looking at that, we will see who emerged in terms of the leaders during the transition from apartheid to a democratic society—Bishop Tutu and Nelson Mandela. If you go back to Mandela's speeches, one of the first appeals he made was to those who were fighting apartheid to take all of their weapons and throw them into the sea. I spent a whole day in South Africa one Saturday talking with some of the young men who had participated in that struggle as MK soldiers. They were not committed to non-violence, but they were raising questions such as, "How can we learn more about the life and work of Martin Luther King, Jr.?"

I do not want my children to grow up as practitioners of violence. I want them to have a different way of life. Now there are those who can and will argue that violence has brought progress, and you can point to the Revolutionary War. The Declaration of Independence has a paragraph that gives justification for violence under certain forms of oppression. It also has a section in the original version that condemns slavery. And Jefferson died a perennial slave owner. You can look at the Civil War. You can then look at the 14th and 15th Amendments, the Civil Rights Acts of 1866 and 1875, and say that out of the violence, out of the Civil War, came emancipation. John Brown himself said, on his way to his death, "I had believed that this conflict could be resolved and that the slaves could be freed without the shedding of blood." And of course he had changed his mind at that moment. The late Dr. Vernon John wrote an essay in which he referred to him as "good old John Brown, he made the war that made us free." You can name World War II. I was born in that era, and became caught up in watching our parents plant victory gardens, of gathering and taking scrap iron to elementary school to help defeat Hitler. If I had been an adult rather than a child during World War II, I can imagine that I would have been drafted or volunteered. I remember something that a colleague said after the march on Washington, after which we met in Cincinnati for a kind of debriefing and a community meeting to share our impressions from the march. Rabbi Goldman said, "I wonder how different the history of the world might be if we had marched in the 30s as we did yesterday in Washington DC."

We need prophets of justice, apostles of love, disciples of truth, and ambassadors of peace and reconciliation with the courage to give their lives non-violently, or in the context of unlimited love, if we are to create what Dr. King called the beloved community. It is no surprise that we have wars and wars and more wars. We have a curriculum of war in our entertainment industry, government, and education systems. We finance it. We have war colleges. If your son or daughter is admitted to West Point or to the Air Force Academy, they are assured that they don't have to worry about paying their bills. They do not have to worry about meeting the financial obligations of their education. We finance education for violence. But you've got to take a loan at a high interest rate, sometimes at low interest rates, but you've got to take a loan if you are in other schools. You might have the opportunity, depending on various grades and test scores and the school itself, to get a four-year scholarship. But the point I'm trying to make is that we finance the teaching of war. We finance the teaching of violence. Our actors in drama, movies, and videos of violence are paid well. And the whole toy industry is geared toward the promotion and sales of toys that teach violence…even if they are Christmas toys. Go and get an AK-47 and put it under the Christmas tree, so when your son or daughter wakes up on Christmas morning he or she can go around the room pointing the gun. In the name of Jesus.

Dr. Post, I salute your endeavour and your colleagues, and those who serve on your board, for endeavouring to look at the scientific side. It is coming up with a body of research that can say to the skeptical, to the scientific, to those who always want everything to be put in some "all of this is this, and this in that, therefore this." All men are violent. I am a man, therefore I am violent. In his book *Search for a Common Ground*, Howard Thurman questions to whether or not the human brain has matured enough to become a mechanism for love and peace in its thought process, or whether it is anchored in a paradigm of violence. We believe that there are and have been and will continue to be breakthroughs, but not enough and not fast enough. The African-American church has had the psalm, the sermon, the practitioner of love, of non- violence within its core commitment. "Gonna lay down my burden, down by the riverside… Ain't gonna study war no more…Gonna stick my sword in the sand of time and study war no more." And if you take that to an intellectual conclusion, it means that if we are going to change the paradigm of the human curriculum from a paradigm of violence and force to a paradigm of love and non-violence we need a new language. We need a language that teaches and counsels love.

Often our religious institutions will adopt the language of war in their quest for acceptance. "Onward Christian solder, marching as to war, with the cross of Jesus (and the bombs behind)…going on before." That's the crusaders' song. That is not the song of Jesus. For 300 years, the Christian church was a movement of creative love. But somewhere around year 325 of the common era, the Christian church put down the method of Christ and picked up the instrument of Caesar. It began to dress like Caesar, and talk like Caesar, and act like Caesar, and compete in being like Caesar. So 75 years ago Kirby Page was moved to write a book, *Jesus or Christianity.* And Ghandi remarked to Howard Thurman that, "I can embrace your Jesus but I cannot embrace your institutional church." Somebody put it another way… "Your Jesus I love, your church I hate." That is a tough indictment. I heard a lecture in which Hitler, Mussolini, and Ghandi were described. The person said Hitler in his brown shirt is leading Germany to a bloody grave, Mussolini in his black shirt is turning Hitler upside down, but when all of these have had their day there will stand Ghandi with no shirt on at all, leading his people to victory.

Several years ago, however, I was on a panel at Hiram College and a scholar from India was on that program. I was on the program dealing with the social vision of Martin Luther King. And after the program was over we had a chance to ask questions. I asked this scholar from India, "What is the position of Ghandi in the society and culture of India today?" His answer was, "We have forgotten him." And years later I was on a panel with the grandson of Ghandi, and he talked about how saddened he was that his nation had departed in such a dramatic way from the teaching of his grandfather. So there are times when we see love, unlimited love, make a breakthrough, and then we see a stepping back from that, as if to say put this epic on hold. We've got to invade Grenada even though they don't have an army. Put this on hold. We know that someone over there in the Middle East, Saddam Hussein, has got some weapons of mass destruction. We can't find them, we will get a committee to look for them, and while they are looking for them, we are going to war. We have lost our moral credibility. This war, this period in our nation's life, is worse than Watergate. And the media for the most part has gone silent.

Let me close by saying non-violence is not, as I see it, a tactic—although it does produce a methodology. It is a spirit of power, of force, of commitment that grows out of one's relationship to God, one's relationship to him or herself, and one's relationship to his or her family and community. Unlimited love or nonviolence or creative love--this is not safe, but it is saving. It will not keep you from getting killed, but it will keep you from being a killer. It can get you killed, and so can pork chops, cigarettes, the air we breathe, or the fish we eat, contaminated by all kinds of things that we have put in the environment. Unlimited love or non-violence has to do with the books I read, the songs I sing, and the art I produce.

When Rabbi Abraham Herschel introduced Martin Luther King, Jr. about 10 days before his assassination at a meeting of a congregation of Rabbis in New York State, he said this in his introduction: "Martin Luther King, Jr. is a voice, a vision and a way. I call upon every Jew to hearken to his voice, share his vision and follow his way." The future of our nation is dependent on the impact of Dr. King. Love needs a voice. Love needs disciples of vision. Love needs individuals who will follow the way of love and thereby create a new family, a new classroom, new toys, and new entertainment…a new nation, and ultimately a new world. And perhaps what Robert Kennedy often quoted in his days of campaigning is still true today-- "Come my friends, it is not too late to seek a new world." And then we can truly say we shall, we have, overcome.

2

REV. SAMUEL E. MANN

The Rev. Sam E. Mann has been Pastor Administrator of St. Mark Union Church in Kansas City & Executive Director of United Inner City Services for 33 years. Rev. Mann was a local preacher at the age of 15 at the First Methodist Church, Eufaula, Alabama. He was Associate Pastor at St. John United Methodist Church, Kansas City, and at First Methodist Church, Peculiar, Missouri. Rev. Mann was dismissed from both churches because of his views on race and peace.

He has been a long-time civil rights activist, and has marched in numerous demonstrations, including the march for the garbage workers in Memphis, Tenn., and the march against the war in Vietnam, led by Dr. Martin Luther King, Jr.. He was also with South African ANC Leader, Nelson Mandela right after his release from prison. Dr. Mann has been jailed on several occasions for his activity. He served as a key participant,along with his friend Dr. Mac Charles Jones, in the national effort to respond to the burning of Black churches in America. He is co-founder of the project "Reframing the Dialogue on Race in America." Through this national project, he attempts to address the problem of race by focusing on the issues of white supremacy and white privilege. He seeks to inspire White mnisters through training to address racism in their congregations.

I am grateful for the opportunity to participate in this gathering and dialogue on the meaning of "engaged spirituality." When I reflect on this topic, I am flooded with great energy that fills me with anticipation and joy. My reflections will be more along the lines of autobiography and stories about "engaged spirituality," love, justice, activism, and research. In the church, we call it "testimony."

I have never known spirituality that was not engaged. It has never "not been" engaged somehow to life in a real, tangible, and visible way.

There are three events in my life that embody most of what I know about our subject:

The first came at a very early age. I was raised in a working class family in Eufaula, Alabama, with a father who was a violent alcoholic throughout my childhood. My mother was the long-suffering woman who would not leave, and who stayed and took the pain. What I remember about this time and engaged spirituality is that she knew how to pray. Each night we knelt down by the bed and prayed to a God/Spirit to deliver us from our suffering, and anybody in the whole world who was also suffering. Some we called by name. We would pray, "Help Aunt Gussie and help Daddy stop drinking." Others we called according to their condition, the hungry, the poor, and the sick. My mother put me in touch with a spirit that I still talk to until this day. This was/is a (to use Tillich) connection with a loving, caring, acting, "ground of being" that when all else failed gave life meaning and strength and possibility.

Later I read of this moment in Howard Thurman's writings, when he spoke of the slave experience in America, "There is a bottomless resourcefulness in (humanity) that ultimately enables (us) to transform "the spear of frustration into a shaft of light." Under such a circumstance even one's deepest distress becomes so sanctified that a vast illumination points the way to the land one seeks" (*Deep River,* and *The Negro Spiritual Speaks of Life and Death*). Though my experience has not been nearly as grave as that of the African in America, I understand what Dr. Thurman means. This conversation with something so intimately close gave me strength to act and to continue to love and show compassion.

The second event was the Civil Rights Movement in America. Those years began for me in 1955, and continue until today. I have been guided by the issue of race as a determining force in my life and work as a preacher/minister. I believe it is as W.E.B. Dubois says, "The problem for America is the color line." The movement as I knew it was "engaged spirituality." Our activities, under resourced and totally out numbered, began in the "Church House" with prayer, singing, and preaching, and went into the streets with prayer, singing, and preaching. When the day was over, we returned either to the church house, jail, or hospital, with prayer, singing, and preaching. I remember many meetings that began with the conversation with that ground of being. Sometimes these conversations lasted long into the sunrise hours with violent exchanges, but we eventually emerged through prayer, singing, and preaching working together for the Beloved Community. Somehow, our struggle for justice and love and peace required a relationship with that ground, whatever the name—Buddha, God of Abraham and Isaac, Allah, Jesus, or "Black Power" or "Deep in my heart, I do believe."

The third event was another personal internal struggle. I came to a place in my life when I had exhausted my rational and emotional definitions/ feelings of the Ground of Being/ God. I literally had no cultural/definitions of this ground. Alone and away from everyone (literally 9,000 feet in the Carson National Forest), I faced suicide or insanity. In that moment, with nowhere to go, I surrendered (not gave up) to myself and to that ground that was not in just one culture or religion or nation or race, but in us all...engaged spirituality as I think we are naming it. This power to love creation and to seek the welfare of all creation is expressed so clearly in Howard Thurman's writings, "There is a spirit abroad in life of which the Judao-Christian ethic is but one expression. It is a spirit that makes for wholeness and for community;....it knows no country and its allies are to be found wherever the heart is kind and the collective will and the private endeavor seek to make justice where injustice abounds, to make peace where chaos is rampant, and to make the voice heard on behalf of the helpless and the weak. It is the voice of God and the voice of (humanity). It is the meaning of all the strivings of the whole human race toward a world of friendly (people) underneath a friendly sky" (*The Luminous Darkness*).

My relationship with the University, the primary research institution of our culture, includes a Bachelor's degree from Birmingham-Southern College with a major in History and Political Science, a Master's in Theology from Duke University, and Doctor of Ministry from St. Paul School of Theology. I say this to note that my relationship with the university, though not without some success, has been suspect when it comes to the issue of research.

I do claim a mentor, Dr. William H. Poteat, Professor of Religion and Comparative Studies, Emeritus, Duke University. He sought to reveal the wrong-headedness of western thought and epistemology as a culture "gone mad on Descartes." I refer to his essay/speech "The Banality of Evil: The Darkness at the Center" as an example of his thought. I will bring copies of this writing to the conference if there are those who would like to read it.

I am deeply encouraged that we are being called by the University to such a conference. I find hope in this endeavor and look forward to our dialogue. Here's to our continued STRIVINGS.

3
THOMAS F. BEECH

Mr. Beech is President and CEO of the Fetzer Institute in Kalamazoo, Michigan. Born in St. Paul, Minnesota, he received his B.A. from Carleton College and did graduate study at Union Theological Seminary and Columbia University, where he was a member of the International Fellows Program. In 1968, Mr. Beech joined the corporate staff of Apache Corporation. He was initially in an urban affairs position, and later became the Marketing Manager for that corporation's Oil and Gas Investment Division. He became Associate Director of The Minneapolis Foundation in 1974, and was Executive Director from 1978 to 1984. From 1984 to 2002, he was Executive Vice President and CEO of The Burnett Foundation in Fort Worth, Texas. He has served on the boards of directors of the Council on Foundations, Independent Sector and the Conference of Southwest Foundations. His work in philanthropy has focused primarily on early child development, youth leadership, and community revitalization.

What is engaged spirituality? The most honest and useful way for me to approach this assignment is to share some reflections from my own experience: during the 1960s, when I was working as a case worker and community organizer in East Harlem and playing a behind the scene role in the Selma to Montgomery March; thirty years of experience as a foundation executive supporting social justice and community renewal work in Minneapolis/St. Paul and Fort Worth, Texas; most recently, coming to know and be involved in the mission and work of the Fetzer Institute.

I will focus primarily on the following questions.

* What does "engaged spirituality" mean to you?
* How are love and compassion integral to the success of social justice work?

What stands out in my memory from my experience in East Harlem is how resilient the young people we worked with were and how committed their parents were to improved education, better housing, violence reduction, and economic opportunity—all in the face of urban systems and forces that were anything but hospitable. In the neighborhood where I lived and worked, there was a sense. and a reality of community that was deep and wide. A climate of trust developed among the residents of this community and my co-workers at the Good Neighbor Community Center; that enabled us to work together, develop common goals, and trust and support one another in the face of a range of forces that tended to create fear, distrust, and separation.

I traveled from New York to Selma in 1965. During the march from Selma to Montgomery, I was part of the support group to the marchers—setting up the campsites, working on food preparation, and coordinating housing for the thousands of people who arrived in Montgomery at the conclusion of the march. While pictures of violence and hatred, stirring speeches, and famous faces dominated the national news, my most power-ful memories are of the young people who were the inspirational leaders of the movement in Selma, and the families who risked their lives to provide hospitality to "outside agita-tors" and who each day demonstrated non-violently against the injustice and violence that was visited upon them.

What I witnessed in Selma and Montgomery was the same resiliency, the same commitment, the same sense of community and trust that I had experienced in East Har-lem. I didn't even know the term "engaged spirituality" then, of course, but I believe that this was the driving force behind what I experienced at that time.

I saw similar forces at work in both Minneapolis/St. Paul and Fort Worth. Be-cause my experience in both communities extended over a long period of time, I devel-oped deeper relationships, lasting friendships, and abiding respect for people living in urban neighborhoods and working in community agencies there. I've come to understand a distinction between those who become battle weary, cynical, and bitter, and those who find renewal and a sense of hope while dealing with persistent and pervasive racism and economic and social discrimination.

In both cases, commitment, courage, a sense of integrity, calling, and service are important motivators and a source of strength. Many of the people who have burned out, become battle weary, and cynical, however, tend to focus on their own anger, identify with their role as victim, and feel as though the weight of pursuing the cause of justice falls on their shoulders alone.

Those who seem to be more resilient draw their strength from relationships, being part of a community, and shared power and responsibility. They see their roles primarily as being facilitators of dialogue and relationships, building bridges across the lines that divide people from one another. They find their inner strength in being part of something greater than themselves: relationships; community; identification with a "higher power." They see their mission as one of rebuilding community and trust where it has become fractured or broken. They live "the love that does justice."

Truth be told, most of us experience being both of these kinds of people at vari-ous times. In my own life I go through cycles, sometimes moving toward burnout and despair and other times moving in the direction of resilience and hope.

In our work at the Fetzer Institute, we are discovering that the themes I describe here are enduring. As we examine the major problems and issues confronting our society and our world, it seems that the dominant forces are those that divide, separate, and create fear and violence among people, institutions, and nations. The search for ways to heal this separateness, fear, and violence calls us to look inward, to find the spiritual strength from which, as humankind has known throughout time, this healing power comes. And it calls us to reach out to one another across our separation from those we consider to be "other" to build relationships based on love.

The Institute's mission focuses on the power of love and forgiveness. We hope to discover effective ways to foster widespread awareness of the power of love and forgiveness as forces of transformation and healing in the lives of individuals, institutions, and communities. We are still in the process of developing our program strategy. Currently, we are approaching this work in four areas: lifting up stories of love and forgiveness; exploring how we can learn to be loving and forgiving; scientific research focused on love and forgiveness; understanding love and forgiveness through the perspectives and traditions of cultures around the world.

One of the many challenges we face in pursuing this mission is to find a vocabulary, a way of talking about love and forgiveness that invites dialogue and examination from differing perspectives and cultures. These words, "love" and "forgiveness," are significant and meaningful in some settings and cultures, and are irrelevant or even offensive in others. In this search for vocabulary, we acknowledge that talking about love and forgiveness in the abstract is, at best, sterile. This is why the sharing of stories is so powerful. When we share our own experiences with one another, communication, understanding, and trust emerge in spite of the limitations of vocabulary.

Another challenge for us is to understand the relevance of the power of love and forgiveness in institutional life. While the power of love and forgiveness has meaning for many people in their personal or individual lives, at least in western society, this seems less relevant to their lives as members or employees of institutions. Indeed, it is the presence of the "dominant forces" noted above in institutional life that gives rise to the injustice in our society and our world.

By bringing researchers and activists together, this conference recognizes that research and action are mutually reinforcing. It also holds promise for examining the institutional and cultural, as well as the individual, settings in which the "love that does justice" can flourish.

4
JUDY S. RODGERS

For the past twenty years, Judy Rodgers has worked with thought leaders such as Tom Peters, Peter Senge, and Walter Cronkite. She has also worked with organizations and networks as various as Appreciative Inquiry Consulting, The Port Authority of New York and New Jersey, and Green Mountain Coffee Roasters, a socially responsible business and Fair Trade leader in Vermont.

She developed and executive produced educational programming for the broadcast and corporate non-broadcast television markets for over 15 years. During the 1980s, she worked at Twentieth Century Fox Video and at CBS/Fox Video. During her tenure with CBS/Fox, she produced a number of award-winning programs, most with best-selling authors. She also was a stockholder and executive vice president of Video Publishing House, Inc., where she developed many programs with management author Tom Peters, some of which aired on PBS. In the 1990s, she joined New World Knowledge, a division of New World Entertainment, as executive vice president.

In 1997, she founded the Communication Architecture Group as a vehicle for a range of related work: organizational consulting; dialogue design and facilitation; management of communication projects; coaching; editorial consulting. She was founding director for Images and Voices of Hope, an international dialogue with media, journalism, and the arts co-sponsored by the Brahma Kumaris World Spiritual University, Case Western Reserve University, and the Visions of a Better World Foundation. Images and Voices of Hope seeks to strengthen the role of media as a constructive force in society. Since 1998, she has worked on the design and facilitation team for the Call-of-the-Time dialogues, a global dialogue series convened by the Brahma Kumaris for leaders in the field of world service. In 2003, she moved to the Weatherhead School of Management at Case Western Reserve University to help launch a World Inquiry and open a Center for Business as an Agent of World Benefit.

Over the past decade, dialogue has emerged as a way to bring those with disparate perspectives together for an exchange of thoughts and shared experiences in hopes of producing new awareness, new relationships, and new social networks to create possibilities for genuinely novel action. Some of the best known dialogues include the Public Conversation Project in Boston, which brought religious people on both sides of the difficult abortion issue together, and the World Faith Dialogues convened by the World Bank and the Archbishop of Canterbury to explore what the World Bank might learn from the world's faith communities.

A third dialogue, the Call-of-the-Time Dialogue, has sought to engage leaders in a deep consideration of their own spiritual identity and how spiritual understanding and practice might transform their work in the world. Over the past six years, I have worked on the design and facilitation of these dialogues. In this paper, I will explore how dialogue participants have changed, how the dialogues have changed, and how those of us working on the dialogues have changed as we sought to fulfill their original purpose.

Since 1998, the Call-of-the-Time Dialogues, convened by the Brahma Kumaris World Spiritual University[1], have engaged over 1,000 people on all continents around the question, "What is the call of this time?" The Brahma Kumaris (BKs) convened these dialogues for leaders in the field of world service who have a spiritual dimension to their lives and work. The organizing idea is to provide a space for spiritual reflection and dialogue that allows participants to reflect on themselves as spiritual beings and to locate ways to deepen the spiritual dimensions of their work. Dadi Janki, co-administrative head of the BKs and host of these dialogues, believes that the deep and transformative experience they provide opens the door for bringing spiritual principles to the field of action. Over the past six years, participants have included executives from the World Bank, faculty from universities, senior executives from business and media and civil sector organizations, heads of state, members of royal families, scientists, and artists.

Since the beginning, the same design team has worked on the dialogues. It includes six members of the Brahma Kumaris and a number of advisors, including Peter M. Senge of M.I.T., Alfredo Sfeir-Younis of the World Bank, Ragnar Angeby of the Swedish Foreign Ministry, and Tom Callanan of the Fetzer Institute, among others.

THE GENESIS OF THE DIALOGUES (1998- 2000)

The first dialogue was held at Oxford in August 1998 on the sprawling grounds of the Global Retreat Centre. Over 40 people from Europe and North America attended. The subject, "Self Sovereignty and World Transformation," attracted a wide range of participants, from management theorists to United Nations experts. While transformation was the topic of the dialogue, the focus was almost entirely external, remaining in the familiar territory of the world of outer action. Anything at the Retreat Centre that might have distracted dialogue participants from their intense conversation was removed. The music that normally plays at selected moments during the day to call people to a few minutes of silent reflection (called "traffic control," because it is an opportunity to stop the traffic of thoughts in the mind) was turned off so the dialogue could proceed uninterrupt-

---

1 The Brahma Kumaris World Spiritual University is a worldwide spiritual organization headquartered in Rajasthan, India, and located in 83 countries with 5,400 centers. The organization has general consultative status to the Economic and Security Council of the U.N. and to UNICEF. The basic beliefs of the Brahma Kumaris include an understanding that this time in the history of the world is unique and carries with it special opportunities for greater spiritual awareness and a greater inculcation of virtues and values.

ed. Participants were not invited to join the residents in their early morning or evening meditations. The three-day dialogue was lively and engaging; as it came to a close, many expressed a desire to return. Dadi Janki said, "The next time we get together, we will talk about time."

A second dialogue was convened in September 1999in Mt. Abu, India the world headquarters of the Brahma Kumaris. A group from all over the world seemed to pick up where it had left off in Oxford, focusing on social and political issues such as globalization and developing world crises. The conversation grew quite heated at times. In these moments, Dadi Janki would address the group and urge them towards the inner world of soul consciousness and reflection. Some wondered if she was hearing the issues they were raising and if she understood the complexity of the problems. She never raised her voice or grew impatient, but she also never abandoned her message – that spiritual methods do not look or feel like secular ones. The dialogue culminated in a meditation, with all 30 participants and three senior yogis of the Brahma Kumaris sitting in pin-drop silence for one hour. The time in silence was transformative, dissolving whatever vestiges of frustration had separated the group before. This was a turning point. As participants climbed into cars the next day to head down the mountain, they spoke most about this time of shared silence. They sensed that the political and social problems that proved so intractable in the outer world of action might yield to the gentle and powerful force evoked in the silence.

In 2000, the organizers of the State-of-the-World Forum in New York City invited the Brahma Kumaris to present a statement at the closing plenary. The design team of the Brahma Kumaris used the opportunity to invite participants in the Call-of-the-Time Dialogue series to collaborate on an oral presentation. The declaration expressed in a few pages the essence of transformation considered from a spiritual context:

If there is any conclusion on which we can agree from this week of presentations and workshops, it is that more of the same will yield more of the same. Even our very best intentions applied to the creation of imaginative new partnerships cannot provide us with the radical transformation we need at this time. Innovation in this context means looking beneath the material world to the non-material causes, beyond the outer state of the world to the inner state that generates it. It means recalling not just the treaties and pacts by which we mandate fairness, but reflecting deeply on the universal values that are the very DNA of the human family…Since the inner world and the outer world are parts of the same wheel of life, for the outer state of the world to be utterly transformed, the inner state of the world must first be transformed. If peace is to be attained, we must start with inner peace. …for the kind of sweeping transformation we are seeking in the world, each of us must stir ourselves from the numbing effects of a world obsessed with materialism. We must take responsibility for recovering our own inner strength and wisdom, which happens when we link ourselves to the divine intelligence…

Members of the design team did the primary drafting and circulated drafts to dialogue participants for input. The process of creating the document seemed to clarify several of the most basic ideas we had been struggling with as a group.

THE SHIFT TO A "DEEPER TRACK"

In preparing for the 2001 dialogue season, Tom Callanan of the Fetzer Institute proposed what he called "a deeper track," a consideration of deeper spiritual issues relative to transformation. Others on the design team echoed Tom's suggestion. Clearly, the real yearning was for deep spiritual experience and for the very different quality of conversation that such deep experience creates. When we planned for the 2001 dialogues, we decided to consider the deepest spiritual roots of transformation. The subject for the season was *Transformation of Sanskaras*. ("Sanskaras" is the Hindi word for impressions on the soul, the patterns of the spiritual being.)

This request for a deeper track for the dialogues prompted us to rethink some of our other assumptions about the dialogues. Perhaps we had gone too far in adapting our retreat spaces to incoming participants. Perhaps what they most wanted was to put the pace and habits of the world behind them for a few days and to immerse themselves in a spiritual experience. So we returned to the daily practice of "traffic control." We invited Dadi Janki to begin each dialogue by setting a spiritual context. We also invited those participants who were interested to join the residents for 4 a.m. and 7 p.m. meditations, and we added a day of silence to the dialogue design.

The decision to add significant time for participants to be in silence required a good deal of thought. Some told us that time in physical silence sometimes amplifies their inner dialogue of worry and fear. In redesigning the dialogues, we added time for one of the senior yogis of the BKs to set a context for the time in silence, explaining that the soul originally comes from a place beyond sound, and that silence is the natural language of the soul. Participants were offered a question or an idea on which to focus their thoughts in silence, and had time to ask questions. They were encouraged to have lunch in silence, to walk, to journal, and to notice, when they encountered one another, how much can be silently communicated with the eyes.

These changes had a profound effect. The dialogues that took place that season produced a markedly different experience. Participants spoke less of the issues "out there" and more of their own internal work. On Sundays, the conversation turned to the preparation to return to their work and how their deep experiences of the dialogue and silence might inform the way they work in the world.

That same season, we accepted an offer of support from the Fetzer Institute and began publishing a journal called *Experiments in Silence* to capture the voices and the experiences of those in the dialogues. Our hope was that this journal would help participants convey their experiences to others with whom they lived and worked – that it would extend the impact of the dialogues beyond just those in the room.

The 2001 dialogue season ended abruptly with the shattering events of 9/11. Shortly after this, we heard from many participants about the strong need they felt to deepen their service to an increasingly fragile world. We decided to take up the subject of service, while continuing with our deeper track of spiritual consciousness—i.e., to look at serving through the mind – not instead of serving through the physical body, but as the essential state for all service. We called the season's subject "Mansa Seva: Serving through the Mind." We decided to convene seven dialogues that year in Oxford, Mauritius, Chile, the U.S., and Malaysia. Dadi Janki, notwithstanding her 86 years, committed to be at six of the dialogues. I decided to set aside my paying work for seven months and to work exclusively on the dialogues for that year.

It was the most powerful season of dialogues we had convened to date. The provocative question for the season was raised at the very first dialogue in Oxford by Alfredo Sfeir-Younis of the World Bank: "What does it mean to have a mind that is qualified to serve?" This question took us into the depth of the questions we had begun to consider the previous season. Participants reported very moving personal experiences. One of the moments that stands out most for me took place at the beautiful island state of Mauritius, where the dialogue was co-facilitated by Thomas Odhiambo, Chairman of the African Academy of Sciences.

The African dialogue proved especially powerful. It had a title of "Harmony, Honesty and Respect." On the opening evening, Dadi Janki took up the subject of "Harmony." She spoke about the Hindi word "haar mani" as a point of departure. "Haar mani" she said, "means to accept defeat." She explained how many times we feel we have found "the truth" and proceed to press it on others, insisting that they accept our way of understanding. When we are doing this, we are not respecting and honoring the other. If it is the truth, she counseled, it will eventually reveal itself to be the truth and there will be no need to press it on others. The right thing in that moment may be to "accept defeat"—to withdraw from your position and to listen closely to others. Her talk caused quite a stir. Several people came up to her to challenge her. How could this be true? If one has "the truth" isn't it important to share that truth with others?" She was delighted and promised to take up the subject more completely the next day. On Friday, she explored it in more depth – this time focusing on the quality of mind that is produced when one insists on a certain position, as compared with the quality of mind that allows one to listen deeply to others and to be at one with the truth. A spirited dialogue ensued, culminating in an address to the group by Dr. Thomas Odhiambo. Dr. Odhiambo had spent the previous two years serving in a structured forum, consisting of the heads of state and thought leaders from different parts of Africa considering the most serious issues affecting the African continent. Part of their conversations revolved around the issue of restitution to Africa by the "northern nations" for the injuries Africa had sustained from the practice of slavery. Now, he carefully framed his thoughts in a spiritual context and said, "as I have thought about *mansa seva* and the kind of mind we must have to serve the world, I have become convinced that we in Africa are putting too much energy into the past, that we need to use our powers for the present and the future. We need to forgive and forget." The room was stunned. Many felt passionately about this issue of the restitution to Africa, and saw it as a key piece of the way forward. Dr.Odhiambo addressed the subject directly: "I have come to believe that asking the North to pay won't bring about any transformation for them or for us. We are on a memory lane, re-constituting the pain of our ancestors, creating an environment of revenge. We need to get out of this memory lane and be in the present lane. The past is an episode of the past. Accept defeat, forgive, and begin to heal the scars. Only this, I believe, will remove the most significant blockage to our development. After that, we will move very fast because a sacred place will have been created in our hearts and minds." The dialogue that ensued over the next three days was extraordinary, leaving no one untouched.

Thomas Odhiambo's epiphany signaled how far we had come from the early dialogues in connecting spiritual understanding and social action. We went from Mauri-tius to beautiful Puerto Octay in the South of Chile, where cognitive biologist Humberto Maturana joined the dialogue as a science resource, complementing Dadi Janki's role as a spiritual resource. Together they engaged with each other and with those present on the subject of love, and how it is a precondition for creating the kind of world that we want.

The dialogues had passed some kind of a threshold. Participants were no longer speaking of their work in the world as separate from their deepest spiritual understand-ings, but as emerging from those understandings. Since then, Peter Senge has spoken and written about how we might create safe spaces for the leaders of the world to meet prior to their political summits, where they are to consider issues with far-ranging impact such as the Kyoto Accords. Joseph Jaworsky has created a retreat /seminar for the most senior business executives that combines meditation and extended time spent in nature. At a recent Global Leader's Summit at the UN, two Brazilian business leaders approached me, saying, "Brazil is ready for a Call-of-the-Time dialogue so that we can look in new ways at the issues raised by President Lula around eradication of poverty and hunger in Bra-zil." In August, an under-secretary of the U.N. proposed a subject for a 2005 dialogue in the South Pacific Islands: "Vulnerability," he said, "The small island states in the South Pacific are in a state of vulnerability." So, in 2005 we will ask, "What are the spiritual understandings we must have about poverty and hunger, and about vulnerability? What is the quality of awareness that will allow us to respond to the inner phenomena that are driving the outer manifestations of these conditions?"

IMPLICATIONS FOR FURTHER CONSIDERATION

After being with so many inspired leaders in such increasingly fragile times, I find the questions that move me most deeply are about fusing inner spiritual experience with outer social transformation agendas:

- How do we introduce spaces of silence and reflection into public forums?
- How do we broaden the frameworks of business to allow those who work in business – in the words of the U.N. Secretary General, Kofi Annan, to "choose to unite the power of the markets with the authority of universal ideals?"

- How do we cultivate individual experiences of deep peace and expand them to create cultures of peace?
- How do we engage the world's media community to shift the world's attention towards the examples of moral acts of beauty, courage, and generosity that can instill an elevated sense of hope for the future?
- And how do we create forums for "applied spiritual understanding" that are not limited to 20, or 30, or even 40—but which create powerful transformative experiences for hundreds or even thousands of people?

5
ESMERALDA SIMMONS, ESQ.

Esmeralda Simmons is a long-time social justice activist from Brooklyn, New York. She was a leader in the New York City Student Rights Movement in the 60s. She went on to become a political activist and professional advocate as a civil rights and human rights attorney who specializes in racial justice work in the United States. Esmeralda is the founder and executive director of the Center for Law and Social Justice, a 19-year-old community legal advocacy institution at Medgar Evers College of the City University of New York, located in Crown Heights, Brooklyn. She formerly served as the First Deputy Commissioner for Human Rights for the State of New York, a member of the Board of Education of New York City, and as the Vice Chair of the <u>New York City Districting Commission.</u> Because of her involvement in pressing racial justice issues, Ms. Simmons has appeared on numerous television and radio talk shows, and is the recipient of dozens of community service awards. During her successful career, she also served as a civil rights attorney for the state, city, and federal governments, and clerked for a federal judge. Ms. Simmons is a graduate of Hunter College, CUNY and Brooklyn Law School. She is married to Lesly Jean-Jacques, and is the mother of two sons and the grandmother of three young jewels. Esmeralda Simmons is initiated in the Yoruba religion, and resides in Bedford-Stuyvesant, Brooklyn.

While I do not use the term "engaged spirituality" to describe my methods or actions, I relate to its connotation. When approached about my working practices and guiding principles, I generally state that, "I let the Spirit lead my work." I believe that the phrases are synonymous. The term "engaged spirituality" generally refers to the actions of one person or a collective toward the intent of spiritual beliefs, philosophy, or practice. Engaged spirituality, as applied to me and my work, means to use spiritual practices regularly and consistently to guide social justice actions and work. I do not actually distinguish between spiritual practice and my work. I am employed in my life's work – my vocation, my purpose for being on the planet, God's intention for my time on earth. The work I do as the leader of the Center for Law and Social Justice and all of my volunteerism are actions I do for God. They are a form of worship or spiritual practice. I use specific "spiritual practices" to strengthen, focus, intuit, maintain balance in the actors, heal or restore balance, and aid in my decision making. Essentially, the practices are used to maintain the alignment between the goals of my social justice work and the actions, methods, and means employed both individually and collectively.

My major spiritual practices include: multiple consultations per day for guidance and direction with my ancestors, Orisas and God (by means of conversations and listening for the inner voice); sitting meditation (Insight and Yogic); oral and silent ritual praying and chanting; Yoruba ritual singing and dancing; periodic fasting; divination; the general practice of Yoruba religion.

Social justice work is premised on striving toward "justice"—i.e., balance in society. "Balance in society" is a political term that stands for providing a fair social system so that all people in the society can have an equal or equitable opportunity, even those persons who have been historically underprivileged. Such work is based upon strong feelings of compassion, or empathic or sympathetic love, as Martin Luther King, Jr. spoke of in his *Beloved Community*. Social justice workers toil for innumerable persons, most of whom they never meet. Almost every goal of the social justice worker, whether he/she is doing casework or impact public policy, implies acts of unselfishly doing for others out of love and compassion. Not every social justice worker is loving and compassionate; some are just earning a paycheck. *The culture of the work, however, presumes that they care and want to assist the downtrodden, and right a social wrong.* Social justice culture requires those who are not in it for love or concern to pretend that they care about people, at least at the beginning of their tenure—in order to be hired and meld with coworkers and those whom they serve.

Any culture, belief system, or spiritual practice that calls upon its adherents to practice charity, in turn, fosters activism. Many indigenous religions and all of the world's major religions call for charitable work; likewise, they urge their followers to work against injustice within their societies. Indeed, many philosophical systems and political thoughts make the same argument independent of religion.

These systems posit or theorize the interconnectedness of all humans (and often all things) and our responsibility for each other's welfare. While they most often encourage respect for social order and public authority, they also urge social upheaval in the face of continued injustice. One need only examine the great religious texts and oral traditions for ample evidence: the Holy Koran; the Holy Bible; the Book of Coming Forth by Day; Sanskrit texts; the teaching tales of Africa, Asia, and South America.

Entire cultures (imagined communities) have evolved in the history of humans on Earth, each with a major theme of social activism. Most recent examples in the twentieth century include the South African Anti-Apartheid Movement, the Indian Independence Movement, the Civil Rights Movement of Africans in America, the numerous anti-colonial Liberation Struggles, and obviously, the Socialist Movement.

I am curious to know what sustains long-term social justice activism among the underprivileged as well as the privileged. Where did their acculturation into "the Movement" occur? Are there any elements of propagation of the Movement or organizing in their activism?

I also want to know how many activists are at this point professed spiritual practitioners?

- Do they view their work as being based upon love and compassion? If so, do they believe in violent methods of social activism? How do love and compassion align with violence towards others?
- Are many of them socialists? If so, how do their spiritual practices meld with the overt materialism of Marxist socialist philosophy?

There is a growing social justice movement for rights for persons who were formerly incarcerated. Does the compassion of most social justice workers extend to these persons (non-innocents)?

Both activists and researchers can tremendously profit from deep and sustained dialogue and the development of personal relationships around social justice work and the source of that inspiration. Activists seldom record in depth the extent and the impact of their work on society. Rarely are the compelling personal, altruistic reasons for their actions discussed. Instead, rhetorical, often political expressions mask the depth of their compassion. Thus, the inspirational "stories" that may give birth to a new generation of social justice activists are lost, as are the records of vast dimensions of society.

I believe that one of the best sources of knowledge is practice: those practitioners in the "field" often have a deeper appreciation for the reality of a subject than is often experienced in the academy.

Conversely, researchers often observe contradictions between creed and practice that have long been accepted into the cultures of social justice workers. Raising these buried issues (e.g., racism and sexism) often reinvigorates an entire movement toward its professed social justice vision.

6
SUE HUTCHINSON

Sue Hutchinson is a Senior Program Officer with the Common Counsel Foundation in Oakland, California. Common Counsel manages grantmaking for several family foundations and two retreat programs; its grantmaking and retreats support a broad range of progressive social and environmental change activities. Sue serves as a program officer with the Penney Family Fund and the Abelard and Acorn Foundations. In addition to serving as a program officer for grantmaking, she also serves as the outreach and selection coordinator for the Windcall Resident Program, a reflective retreat program for social change organizers and activists. Sue is currently coordinating the work of the Windcall Futures Project, to plan for and build more programs like Windcall. She participates in grantmaker affinity groups, such as the Neighborhood Funders Group and the National Network of Grantmakers, where she worked with the 2001 Program Committee to create and plan a successful youth organizing plenary session. Sue also served on the grantmaking committee of the Funders Collaborative on Youth Organizing. In her volunteer work, she currently serves as the elected chairperson of the Tenants of Preservation Park, a non-profit office park in Oakland, where Common Counsel is located. She has 23 years of experience, including grassroots organizing in racially diverse low-income communities, strategic planning, and nonprofit and business management. Sue previously worked with the Center for Third World Organizing, the Association of Community Organizations for Reform Now (ACORN) for 10 years as a lead and head organizer, the Applied Research Center, Californians for Justice, the Center for Ethics and Economic Policy, and Fern Tiger Associates. She attended Swarthmore College for two years and holds a BA with Honors in Community Studies from the University of California, Santa Cruz.

As an introduction, I started some 25 years ago as a social justice activist around women's, United States imperialism, and racial justice issues. I evolved into becoming a grassroots community organizer in low-income, racially diverse communities for more than 11 years. I now live with this community organizing experience, rooted in the "power in numbers" concept, profoundly coloring all of my work. Since 1997, I've been a program officer with the Common Counsel Foundation, an Oakland, California-based nonprofit that assists several progressive family foundations in strategic social change grantmaking. It also manages two retreat programs, one for writers examining the relationship of the economy and the health of the environment, and the other, Windcall, which is a contemplative and healing retreat program for social change organizers and activists. In addition to spending part of my time as a grantmaker, I am also the primary coordinator for Windcall outreach and the selection of residents. I have now worked with Windcall for about half of its lifetime. This work has been deeply moving and rewarding, both for the Windcall staff and for the 375 residents and their organizations. And now, through Common Counsel, I'm coordinating the Windcall Futures Project, a new effort led by over 30 past Windcall residents to continue this valuable program in a new location after the current location in Montana closes in a few years.

I write this presentation after returning from ten days of traveling solo in far northern California, spending a good part of that time in the wilderness on a contemplative and spiritual retreat. During this trip, I was ecstatic to find great expansion in my awareness and understanding of the universal "All is One" concept. Through hiking in redwood forests and mountains, listening to stillness, exploring unknown places, sitting and staring at rivers, wetlands, and the ocean, watching birds, swimming with fish, co-existing with insects (mostly peacefully!), meeting and talking with new people, touching rocks, visiting sacred places revered by local Native American tribes, reading, writing, painting, singing, and practicing shamanic journeying – all roads seem to lead to this point. And yet this trip was not removed from that part of my soul that is deeply dedicated to working for justice and a better world, indeed universe, for all beings. Because all beings are One, are me, are us. God(dess) is Life, Life is God(dess), we are One, we are Life, and we are God(dess). And once we have this understanding, we cannot simply sit by while hate and destruction threaten to dominate our world. We are all connected, and we all have power – it's a matter of how we harness and use our individual and collective power. And the other profound and key component is that we must all *love ourselves deeply first* in order to love the whole of Life. For if we judge ourselves harshly, then we punish ourselves, and this in turn punishes the world.

As I said, I come to this conference looking forward to delving into ideas and questions that I have pondered for quite some time. A key question I've considered for years is: How do we weave an inclusive spirituality into our work for social justice? I want to know this because I think it's the only way that we'll make profound and lasting changes in the way our societies function in a healthy way on the planet. When I look at the past movements that have had great success, it seems that a unifying spirituality or faith in a greater power was a key part of most of them. Two stand out for me as prime examples: the Civil Rights movement and the United Farmworkers movement. Though I am too young to have been in the thick of them, I feel that a key factor that brought in the large numbers of people required to gain enough power to make real change – and kept those people in the struggle, despite great odds, extreme poverty, threat of loss of livelihood and family, and even very real threats of death – was a strong spiritual base. I sense that the individuals in these movements knew that their struggle was bigger than the immediate issues, that "right" was on their side – and that there was a deep well of spiritual strength that they could go to for replenishment, faith, and encouragement. Yet the problem I see in looking to the future use of this power is that both of these movements were largely homogeneous in terms of their Judeo-Christian religious roots. So how do we figure out an inclusive faith system that has a place for and respects Christians and Jews—but also Buddhists, Muslims, Wiccans, Hindus, practitioners of Native American spirituality, Vooduns, atheists, agnostics, and everybody else?

The second big question relates to the balance between individual healing and community healing. Some say you can't even begin to heal society until each person heals him/herself, while others contend that individuals who only "work on themselves" will never lead to the building of collective power to bring about social change. They say, "Change the world first, then you have the luxury to change yourselves." There are clear dangers in taking an exclusive approach either way. In the first scenario, people may "stick their heads in the sand" while exploring inner worlds and never engage in collective action for social change. In the second scenario, which we often see in the social change arena, activists and organizers use their time-intensive work to escape or avoid actually getting to know themselves and figuring out their own wounds; this hampers their ability to go about their work from a place of love, forgiveness, and compassion instead of a place of anger, hatred, and "victimhood." For example, the internal "martyr" is a common archetype in many activists and organizers (I should know, I used to have her running my own show much of the time!). But the martyr is, by definition, ultimately completely destructive to the self, and thereby to the organization and the whole of Life. These common unhealthy patterns often lead to frequent problems of conflict within organizations that, unfortunately, more often than not lead to the eventual disintegration of organizations. The third, or middle road, says that these two things – individual spiritual growth and organizational or movement growth – need to happen simultaneously. But how do we figure out models so that those personal journeys of healing and growth also feed into powerful collective action for social change?

I think that many of the lessons we have learned over the past 15 years of running the Windcall Resident Program can help in figuring out this second question. Windcall was founded in 1989 by social change philanthropists Susan and Albert Wells, with the assistance of the Common Counsel Foundation. Windcall's mission is to strengthen the work of social change organizations by offering long-term social change leaders and organizers a two- or four-week cost-free, reflective retreat on a beautiful ranch in southwestern Montana. Since 1989, more than 375 social justice leaders have attended Windcall and have found the experience to be transformative for themselves and for their organizations. Individuals who do social change work are under enormous pressure. The chance to take time away from work to rest and revitalize themselves and to evaluate their work and organization comes rarely, if at all. The opportunity to be in a new and beautiful natural environment, free from the constant demands and pressures of work, offers residents the possibility for deep rest. And it offers the rarest treasure of all:

unstructured time for creative and inspired reflection. Long-term benefits from such time away find expression in the individual as well as the organization in which he/she works. Strengthened and revitalized leaders bring new creativity and a renewed commitment to their social justice work. In fact, many new organizations, campaigns, and programs have been started as a result of a Windcall residency.

Windcall is currently located on a small working ranch near Bozeman, Montana. It lies on the western slope of the Bridger Mountain Range, and borders a National Forest. A spectacular array of wildlife and plants lives in the area, and the weather can change from moment to moment—but it is always dramatic and beautiful. Four residents stay at Windcall at any one time; each is provided with good food, comfortable lodging, and a natural and deadline-free environment. According to alumni, one of Windcall's greatest gifts is that there is no set program and no expectations of residents. Nothing is required of them other than showing up for the daily evening meal prepared by a local chef. Women residents, who often find they have the burden of housework and food preparation on top of their daily organizing work, have reported that the simple fact that someone else is taking care of them (for the first time ever in many cases) is one of the most profoundly moving aspects of the Windcall experience. Along with outdoor opportunities for hiking, fishing, swimming, and horseback riding, each resident has the use of a personal quiet room for reading, writing, meditating, and reflecting. There are also two fully equipped art studios, and yoga and ceramic classes are available when requested. Residents have found that activities that require balance and "centering" – such as horseback riding and throwing clay pots on a potter's wheel – have contributed greatly to their healing experiences.

Residents can choose to spend time with peers, or alone. While solitude is a moment's walk away, many residents have stated that one of the most powerful benefits of their residency has been the opportunity to spend real time with other social change leaders. They find house mates who have also invested years of their lives working for social change, and who grapple with common issues of balancing work and family, spirituality and social action, and working for their heart's passion – social justice – without sacrificing their health and resolve. And at the same time, there is no pressure to socialize. Residents find they can easily set boundaries and spend as much time alone as they need.

The results of this 15-year experiment have been dramatic. The vast majority of residents report that the experience profoundly changed their livea. Some even say it saved their lives. Others report that they were on the brink of quitting social change work completely, but found inner resources to continue while at Windcall. And so the founders, staff, and other stakeholders have asked themselves, "How? How can just two or four weeks have such dramatic results?" Susan Wells, who holds graduate degrees in both education and psychology and was in private practice as a psychotherapist for fifteen years prior to founding Windcall, says that colleagues in her field will work with clients for many years to achieve the kind of results that are seen in just a few weeks at Windcall. So several years ago, Susan started writing a book about Windcall (<u>Bringing the Moun-</u>

tain Home, to be published next year). Around the same time, a group of us came together as the Windcall Futures Project to explore the idea of continuing this valuable program in another location once the current ranch is no longer available. These two projects have led us to hundreds of interviews with past residents to try to figure out how the experience works.

We've been able to boil it down to its essentials. Overwhelmingly, the residents we have spoken to say that the **unconditional love** that is offered them by the hosts and staff of Windcall, verbally and through the gift of this cost-free retreat, is one of the most powerful factors in their experience. Many residents have profound spiritual experiences while at Windcall. One resident stated, early on, *"I know several things – by opening Windcall to us, which goes well beyond your support for organizations to do social change work, you've ventured into something I would call the spiritual – assisting us to find deeper spiritual ground to do our work."*

As part of the Windcall Futures Project, we have figured out that we can do this program elsewhere if we have the following things in place:

- A host (or hosts) that offers the gift of unconditional love, thanks to the residents for the work they have done, and who can quietly "hold the space" for healing and refection.
- A place of great natural beauty that has a special sacred "feel" to the land. In addition, the site should feel "removed" – but not be too remote, so that affordable access is available for people traveling from long distances. (Windcall currently pays for 2/3 of residents' travel costs, and it is hoped this assistance can continue.)
- Only a few residents at a time (three to six maximum – although most people feel that four is a good number).
- A "non-program" program – no expectations of the residents, including minimal phone and e-mail.
- Comfort – good food, prepared meals at night, outside cleaning service, comfortable surroundings. Residents report that the feeling that they are being taken care of (often for the first time in their lives) is a crucial element.
- Access to creative endeavors, such as art supplies, and private reading and writing areas.
- A similar outreach and selection process as is in place now (a national selection committee, staff for outreach and recruitment).

And so, for the next two years, we will seek out a great new location, or partner with other similar organizations that already have a beautiful place. I trust that if we hold strong to our vision, we will create this reality and make it happen.

Upon returning to the Common Counsel office from my own retreat trip, I was moved today to read some impressions from a long-time organizer who was a Windcall resident for two weeks this summer. The only thing we ask of residents (although it's not required) is that they share, if they feel moved, some "impressions" of their experience at Windcall when it's time to leave. His words really spoke to a common experience of many Windcall residents. So I wish to share with you a few paragraphs from this man, who put it better than I ever could:

"As advertised, my time here has been my own – almost entirely a blessing, but carrying its own weight as well. Our issues and challenges don't abandon us on the way to Windcall. What the place has given me, and I suspect most residents, is the ability to pare away at the usual stresses and pressures, allowing space and time to process things intellectually, emotionally, and spiritually, and also connect with personal and universal forces that nurture and sustain me. The dictionary defines 'retreat' as not only a strategic withdrawal, but more importantly as a place of seclusion or privacy, or the act of withdrawing into such a place, as for meditation. Retreat raises images not so much of failure but of regrouping and renewal. Too often we and our organizations insist on pushing forward without respite or reflection, and we pay both personal and organizational costs for that failure.

"I've spent part of my time here reading about relativity and quantum physics, and also about Tibetan Buddhism. Both concern themselves with perception and reality, connections between things, and the consequences of actions. The creative energies of the universe, our selves and our spirits, our actions, and our families and organizations are all inextricably linked. We ignore our connection to others and to the fundamentals of natures and life and the universe at our peril. Windcall allows us – or at least allowed me – to experience those connections in deeper, visceral, and hopefully more lasting ways than I have in some time.

"How do we sustain ourselves, and by extension our organizations and our movements? I was struck by how many residents' 'impressions' mention internal organizational tension and conflict. I shouldn't be surprised: my own career has seen all too much of that. Why don't more organizations value retreat, reflection, and rejuvenation more highly? Why isn't it mandatory, or at least more strongly encouraged and supported financially? Plenty of us are familiar with working retreats and strategic planning. Clearly Windcall – and more generally the need for unstructured, restorative, creative times, places, and spaces – is something very different and equally necessary. What are we all going to do to make it more of a reality for more people and organizations? Rhetorical questions, mostly. But I do hope that we will all help build movements more appreciative of restorative and reflective practice and leadership."

ACKNOWLEDGEMENTS

In addition to the deep teachings I have gleaned from the experiences of Windcall residents, I have been greatly helped in my own individual work and study by teachers and therapists in healing and energy work, Native American spiritual practices, non-dualistic meditation practices, Tai Chi, yoga, eastern medicine, as well as my ancestors and spiritual guides. On top of that, the following authors, artists, and teachers have helped me a great deal in the last several years:

Caroline Myss, Ph.D., <u>Anatomy of the Spirit</u>

Don Miguel Ruiz, M.D., <u>The Four Agreements and The Mastery of Love</u>

Clarissa Pinkola Estés, Ph.D., <u>Women Who Run With the Wolves</u>

Thich Nhat Hanh, <u>Peace is Every Step</u>

Neale Donald Walsch, <u>Tomorrow's God</u>

Susan Wells and Sally Lehrman, <u>Bringing the Mountain Home</u> (unpublished manuscript)

Gary Snyder

Peter Matthiessen

Angeles Arrien, Ph.D.

Michael Harner

Marge Piercy

Patti Smith

Joey Ramone

Bob Marley

The recent film, *"What the #!% Do We Know?"*

7
REV. ANGEL KYODO WILLIAMS

A spiritual teacher, activist, artist, and founder of **urbanPEACE**. *Angel Kyodo Williams recently opened the* **New Dharma Meditation Center for Urban Peace** *in Oakland, CA, as a living laboratory for exploring the potential of integrating individual, community, and social transformation as spiritual practice. Trained in Zen Buddhism, interfaith, modern consciousness and, recently, First Nation Ways, Angel has an intense interest in the universal truth, self-responsibility, and authenticity of liberation spirituality. She is a dynamic thinker and communicator, who sets forth the challenge of why authentic being, abiding love, and transformation of the spirit are the only possible catalysts for lasting, revolutionary social change, and how we can abolish prisoners rather than prisons.*

Angel has created **Warrior-Spirit Training,** *an "alloy of consciousness" of the world's wisdom traditions that invites living, loving, and leading from the heart. While it was initially a year-long training, it is now the foundation of her work cultivating the wholeness of spiritually-based leaders, activists, and change agents. She offers and teaches intuitive coaching that calls forth what is already known to inspire deep, sustainable life change. She leads virtual and nation-wide retreats, workshops, and trainings.*

In past lives, she's been a founding board member of Third Wave, opened the first black-owned, women-owned Internet café, and sat on the board of the Institute for Women, Spirituality and Justice. Dubbed "the most vocal and most intriguing African-American Buddhist in America" by Library Journal, Angel is the author of Being Black: Zen and the Art of Living with Fearless-ness and Grace,which has been hailed as "a classic" by Buddhist teacher Jack Kornfield, and "an act of love" by Alice Walker. It continues to make Universal teachings accessible to thousands of people of color and white folks. Her book inspired a conscious hiphop CD, and her work has been covered in the New York Times, Essence, Village Voice, O: The Oprah Magazine,and on the Oxygen Channel (www.urbanpeace.org).

THE THIRD SELF: ON WISDOM, CONFLICT, AND THE CONQUERING SOUL

I will begin with what stirred me in writing:

* First: **resistance** to writing about that which I so deeply know is a living process

and, as such, how could I possibly capture it in a fixed set of rambling thoughts strung together on a page?

- immediately followed by: a **sense of absurdity** about entertaining my thoughts and subsequent scribblings about a thing as even remotely grasping the thing itself,
- and then: a **chafing feeling of self-importance** that I am being asked to write about something I feel "just is" and have as little choice about, if I heed my internal compass, as which feet to put my shoes on in order that they feel all right,
- quickly engulfed by: **a tangled knot of inexpressible emotions** altogether fleeting and unintelligible, individual and transgenerational, ancient and beyond time: grasping—aversion—arrogance—fear—lack—pride—self-hatred—and more fear. These emotions are deeply embedded, psychically and physically, in many, many layers of personal and collective years of experience: joyful, tragic, and disturbingly indifferent, each subtly and imperceptibly shifting the current of my stream of consciousness,
- and finally: **a relieving flash of purifying laughter** showing up only as a crinkling eye and knowing, muted smile

Two, maybe three seconds have passed that beheld lifetimes. I've once again been spared the protracted agony of acting out each of these emotions on myself, unwitting loved ones, assorted strangers, and supposed enemies by a deep and abiding practice of love and fierce, unwavering compassion for the apparent complexity of being human—with all of its attending afflictions.

Even as I opt to navigate steadily beyond each of these doorways, leaving them unopened and unindulged, I hold in my consciousness a simultaneous awareness of the wellspring of potential for unmitigated suffering each one had in store had I defaulted to the behaviors prescribed for the role I should have played in life—i.e., that of a stumbling, aimless, and sometimes blissful sheep.

As each moment arises in an ever-interdependent chain of this causing that, and then that, and then that, there is present a Witness that observes the unfolding drama in its entirety with formidable and humbling dispassion.

I've taken notice of Life's play from the seat of the Watcher, and self liberated the wretched limitations of the part I'd been handed. I've been awakened to the Truth of the inherent cycle of suffering written into the scene and, as simultaneous Player and Witness, I rest in the *in it but not of it* land of the relatively free. Still, I'm not quite satisfied.

Aloof, pervasive, ineffable and palpable, this Witness is non-interfering as is the Moon, casting light without discrimination on all that Is, just as it Is. The Witness neither beckons things to grow nor shrink, aspire nor retreat, harbor faith nor despair. As such, cultivating an awareness of the presence of the Witness is not enough, for the gift of the Witness is only Wisdom.

I question this myself: Isn't wisdom what we want? Isn't that our highest pursuit? We're not speaking of plain-old knowledge. We've already deconstructed the Altar of Information and reduced the budget for the Department of Intelligence Acquirement. *I Know* lost to *I Am* and the votes counted this time. We might even say that East edged out West, though this is a game of non-competition. Don't we need an array of model examples of 100% pure, certified organic Wisdom? Even locally-grown? Wisdom is the apex of our aspiration and panacea for the pain caused by our constant entertainment of millennia-old habit-patterns, able to cut through delusion in a single slice...or is it?

PERFECTING WISDOM

> *"No eye, ear, nose tongue, body, mind; no color, sound, smell, taste, touch, thing...*
> *Overcoming all delusion, realizing Nirvana."*
> — Heart of the Perfection of Great Wisdom Sutra

Alone, wisdom is cool, distant, and choiceless. It simply reflects the Truth of as-it-isness with an unflinching clarity and objectivity that is sullied only when cast (as it must be) through the veil of the small, egoic, Lower I. And in a cruel and predictable backstretch towards our culture's allegiance to rugged Individuality, Wisdom seems to lord over the realm of Spirit. There is a danger here. Observing and unobserved, Wisdom as Higher Self falls prey to passive indifference and, like mega-corporations, is responsible to and invested in only itself and its own growth and manifestation. At its best, surgical, skillful and precise; and at its worst, cutting, steely, and sharp.

And what about that Lower I, Ego, Small Self that we've been advised time and time again to avoid, let go of, surrender, even kill should we find it in the form of a Buddha? Is there any redeemable value in it at all in the great rush towards Self-lessness, No Self, Non-Self? Further and perhaps seemingly more improbable, does the Self with its coarseness, clinging, craving, and general crankiness have in it some seed of usefulness that can serve, indeed enhance, the High seat of wisdom?

While wisdom seems to hover high in the vast, all-encompassing realm of Spirit, what enlivens the lower, rooted, Earth-Bound Self is Soul. Anything but choiceless, Soul is chocolate ice cream-loving, ideas and ideals, art as revolution, double-shot latté-having, power to the peaceful, making Love not war.

Our Soulful Selves see our own children in theirs, mothers in women, sisters in girls, and lovers in 10 and 10,000 lost men of war. Our hearts are wrenched by the Soul's communal beating that feels every death in a minute skipping of the breath. 3,000 inconceivable deaths and we gasp uncontrollably for air.

Thus, it is soul's flaming passion that takes it to heart, takes it to the street, and eventually even takes up arms. Because Soul is **also** needing and nurturing, family and familiar, fearful and fiery, safety and security, securing and protecting, propositioning and propagandizing, high-hand and Homeland. It is, in direct paradoxical proportion, what makes us human beings and what makes us need to practice becoming human.

Don't be disheartened because it is exactly herein that lives the hearty seed of compassion: From the very dark, muddy, contemptible earthfulness of our frail conditioning, we are, with impassioned intention and practice, capable of ushering forth the unstained white lotus of peace and pure, Loving action. It's no mistake that in ancient Buddhist texts, The Conqueror that practices perfect Wisdom is the Lord of Compassion. Compassion is directly cultivated from forming the habit-practice of *being with* Soul.

THE GRACE OF CONFLICT

It is the practices of *being with and bearing witness* to that most avail themselves to birthing and sustaining action and activism tempered by compassion. Practices of *being alone in the company of others* invite the transparency needed to strengthen integrity. Bearing witness is the courageous intention to have one's heart broken and eyes open to another's suffering with nothing to do but be there.

The forms of these practices are at once varied and specific: community-rooted meditation and prayer; councils of the collective; exchanging self for others with others; looking steadfastly into the lovingly-held mirror of a spiritual friend's heart/mind; vision-seeking held in a container of family & friend's support; singing heartily, dancing wildly, breathing deeply and conflicting willingly.

This last one is often overlooked and is the source of a great deal of our confusion: we seek peace through the avoidance of conflict when it is the willingness to be in conflict gracefully that most fertilizes the field of unconditional, unlimited, unassailable Love for all involved.

> *"We are desperate to have the answers to every question, to always know what to do and how to respond. It is obvious that there is so much that we don't, but what we do know is that the way it has been done is not working... You have permission to not know."*
>
> — from "Courage to Be Human"

We need to believe, first and foremost, that a new world, a new Way of being, is possible and that we don't have to have a snapshot handy before we've lived it. That we can dream of colors and shades not yet seen. And that not only is there a place of dignity, respect and wholeness for each of us, but that it would be nothing but a thirst-driven mirage without all of us.

We need to believe in Purpose as the director of our Power, but we also need to honor and support purposelessness: time and space for activity with neither goal nor intention other than exquisite attention to the activity itself. We have to exalt in planting seeds and bristle with excitement as the first small shoots peer above ground, but we also need to protect the sacred time of gestation, cocooning, metamorphosis that appears as not doing.

I want to articulate something about what I believe an engaged spirituality actually IS, rather than what we may be witnessing as our fumbling attempts at it:

- Engaged spirituality is our very human effort to begin to minimize the desperately gnawing feeling of alienation we've nurtured into a disproportionate chasm with our tired strategies of herding people like cattle to divide and count(er) under the guise of organizing.
- It's our confusing and sometimes confused attempt to rectify the discordance and mistruth that we hear in every "us vs. them" politic and persuasion.
- It's the expansion of our hearts for that most noble effort of becoming spacious enough to allow for what is while keeping an eye towards what could be.
- It's finding the balance between things perfect just as they are, the awareness of incalculable suffering and injustice, and the bittersweet middle path that we must walk in the meantime, the between time of the reality of Now and promise of Then.
- It's the continuous, unwavering march forward in an endless and seemingly futile battle in which, paradoxically, that futility manifests only when we deign to cease walking.
- It is the hard-won marriage of Spirit and Soul, forged in silence, that gives birth to Loving Action. A creation borne from the deep practice and learning of how to hold space with a broken heart and still show up again and again.

AUTHENTICITY & THE THIRD SELF

"Take your practiced powers and stretch them out until they span the chasm between two contradictions...For the god wants to know (her)self in you."

— Rainer Maria Rilke

Practice that aligns our inner and outer worlds is the bridge and balance between Wisdom and Compassion, Spirit and Soul, Silence and Action, Being and Doing, Impersonal and Transpersonal. But we need more than just one-shot deal, weekend Better Person boot camps. We need to locate the energetic leaks coming from the incomplete and unattended areas of personal spiritual growth so that we can harness that lost fuel into the drive towards real and sustainable social transformation.

We'll want to do it with less of the drag of a stuck Ego Self, and not much of the disinterest of a too-lofty Wisdom Self. For that we need the reflective, flexible container provided by sustained, contiguous practice within the safe and nurturing walls of a richly diversified community. It is from here that we are able to embody that elusive but infinitely generative Third Self, wise in its stillness, compassionate in its action, authentic in each moment to the next.

It is this Third, Authentic Self that I believe holds the key to our salvation. It is, by its nature, holistic, integrative, collective-minded, and self-responsible. It is not manufactured outside, but called forth from within. When truly invited, the Third Self lives in service to the liberation of all, drawing from the endless energetic source of Spirit, committed to the Earth Mother and all her wounding and wounded children.

I have been both witness and guide to ceremonies, rites, and practices of individuals and even organizations striving to make the reconnection to their Authentic Being Selves. They pray to find a Way so that they can act more cleanly each time they bravely face down injustice, and treat themselves more kindly when they cannot.

What I pray for is their support, and even my own, as we earnestly spread the pieces of this world in front of us so that we can rearrange them to fit more of us in a fulfilling way. As activists, we need and welcome support and collaboration with researchers who can help us expand our language for what we deeply know; we can, in turn, provide more faces and stories for what's been deeply thought of. We need time to re-search our own actions, and craft new, revolutionary forms while living our lives in ecologically sound ways: less isolation, more collaboration, in ongoing conversation about our hard-won discoveries with our peers and the world.

Time isn't running out, but it is always running. If we're to have any sustainable social transformation, sometimes we need to simply sit on the side: to catch our breath, watch our thoughts, and invite the Third Self to come home to serve.

— *to all my relations.* © MMIV, Angel Kyodo Williams

8

CLAUDIA HORWITZ

Claudia Horwitz is captivated by the intersection of spiritual practice, community experience, and social change. This is the underlying foundation for her work with Stone Circles, a small nonprofit organization that works to sustain activists and strengthen the work for justice through spiritual practice and principles. Stone Circles is based in Durham, North Carolina, in a cooperatively shared space for nonprofits in the newly-enlivened downtown.

Stone Circles works with people all over the country through training, workshops, conversations, organizational development assistance, and interfaith gatherings. Claudia has had the opportunity to work with a broad range of people, from front-line activists to leaders in the non-profit sector to students here in the U.S. and in Eastern Europe. Her previous work includes developing youth leadership, supporting struggles for economic justice, and strengthening nonprofit organizations. She lives in a converted tobacco warehouse with her dog, Zak. Still connected culturally to her Jewish roots, she practices meditation and teaches Kripalu yoga.

It's the third night of the Republican National Convention. I turn the television on reluctantly, kind of like sitting down to my physics homework in twelfth grade. Pep rally chants of "USA! USA!" fill the room and I remind myself the Olympics are over. Dick Cheney describes George Bush using these phrases: "Loyalty and kindness... he means what he says... he's a man with a heart for the weak..." I drift in and out of consciousness. Is he talking about the same guy who brought us the invasion of Iraq and the Patriot Act? The gutting of the social safety net and immigration crackdowns? The "free speech zones" and the initial stages of New American Century? My heart speeds up. What level of delusion makes this rhetoric possible? How could my own world view, and that of so many people I respect and love, be so drastically different? There is a story being spun here that I don't recognize at all. And it is one that seems to leave out most of what I know to be true and real.

Staring at the scene I just don't know where to place myself. I breathe deeper and, for brief moments, I can imagine a story behind a face, the yearning behind the cheers. The pit in my stomach shrinks a little. I'm trying to practice compassion, but truthfully, nothing about this makes sense or seems right. The television convention coverage is drawing to a close and we hear briefly about the woman who crashed the convention and protested Cheney's relationship with Haliburton. I exhale and say a prayer of gratitude and safe-keeping for her. A small edge of something feels familiar.

Liberation spirituality is a moment-to-moment enterprise. And it calls for the development and joining of two phenomena of consciousness: first, a transcendent, pluralistic narrative of collective liberation – a vision that speaks to both reality and possibility, one that both acknowledges and transcends dichotomies; second, it requires the ongoing cultivation of individual liberation – an internal freedom that helps us to function as wise and compassionate beings when all the odds are against it.

COLLECTIVE LIBERATION: SOME PRESSING QUESTIONS

Somehow, we all fit together. There are inextricable links and salient differences in our stories and histories, our practices and rituals, our beliefs and values. A global community based on truth, justice, and love demands an interwoven set of stories, a pluralistic picture of what real freedom looks like, and integrated blueprints for how we get there. It matters too that climate change is having dramatic effects on nearly every corner of life for Alaskan and Canadian natives. It matters that we know little about the Iraqis who have died since the war began. It matters that we are without socialized medicine, that minimum wage is $5.15/hour, and that some cities in the U.S. have an equal number of abandoned homes and homeless people.

These things that matter don't fold in neatly together, don't stack easily into one deck; this is partly why the progressive left has had a harder time devising truly winnable strategies that keep people happy, healthy, and *alive*. We are spectacularly diverse in terms of ethnicity, race, class, and sexual identity. How do we begin to understand this array of cultures and traditions, legacies, and habits? And how do we do it without watering down any of the particularities, without whitewashing the distinctions? We've got dissimilar ideas about methodology and even have contrasting ideologies. How can we do a better job of knitting these together tightly enough to create strong, cohesive, and lasting initiatives for change?

We're dramatically different, too, in our religious and spiritual beliefs. As more people embrace spirituality in this post-modern era, it takes on a hybrid quality that makes the spectrum more beautiful and all the more complicated. We are exploring alternative rituals, looking outside of the tradition in which we were raised, and engaging in cross-disciplinary practices. Jews are meditating, Black Baptists are practicing Yoruba, Catholics are leading Sufi Dances of Universal Peace. We have this diversity among activists, and, of course, more secular expressions of love. "Organizing is my religion," as one labor organizer told me recently.

With increasing variation in our practices, a depth of connection becomes more challenging. As our eclecticism grows, the ease of finding places we can collectively call home diminishes. So, how does solidarity and community build amidst these varied motivations, without one defining story or text or set of rituals? How can we turn towards the pluralism, create spaces where all are welcome, where the "other" becomes less other? We need to learn to build community across spiritual lines of difference without watering down the particulars. Issues of spiritual protocol present some wonderfully juicy challenges, which can easily become land mines. But we need to keep gathering across lines of spiritual difference in ways that maintain integrity and rigor. The Christian right has been able to effect enormous political change at the local, national, and international levels. How will we organize ourselves around collective commitments and harness the power of our collective beliefs? And what will happen if we don't?

INDIVIDUAL LIBERATION: FINDING FREEDOM WITHIN

There will never be justice anywhere until you yourself are justice now.

– Marguerite Duras

Individual freedom is the seed of collective liberation, the building block. Freedom unfolds in the silences we keep and the relationship with the divine that we cultivate. Freedom is what happens when we turn to wonder instead of worry in times of crisis. Freedom is the spaciousness that allows us to stay and sit and listen when things get hot. The growing affinity for Eastern tradition here in the U.S. must be related to some potent conditions of our current climate: anxiety levels are high, the drive to produce is intensified, we have more choices to navigate,and more information to process than ever before. In this light, the hunger for renewal, pause, and ease makes sense. As a result, we wisely seek out practices that lead us to greater peace and a calmer existence. Judeo-Christian frameworks offer us different gifts. We are confronted with ideas such as the kingdom of God. We receive stories of redemption and reconciliation. We find traditions of prayer and prophetic witness. I recognize the polarity between East and West is a false one in many ways, but I think it's a useful one to consider for this dialogue. Perhaps we will find a way to harness the best of both realms, without having to demonize one or exalt the other.

For myself, I have noticed that Eastern traditions are teaching me how to be with what is, and Western traditions continually challenge and inspire me to imagine what could be. It's the Jewish tradition I was raised in that taught me how to see possibility, how to understand my responsibility for repairing the world, how to appreciate the ritual rhythms of the year. And it's the experience on the yoga mat and the meditation cushion that gives me a taste of a deep, abiding presence that is beyond personality. This is the energy that nurtures compassion and non-judgment, illuminates authenticity and wisdom. From this place, I find it easier to deal with complexity, to hold two seemingly conflicting ideas at one time, to take risks. These are the reasons I practice, the reasons I teach and train, the reasons why I believe in the idea of liberation spirituality.

THE POSSIBILITIES WE MISS

I was part of local anti-war organizing efforts in Durham surrounding the invasion of Iraq. Our local group, the Durham Peace Coalition, planned a 24-hour vigil to begin immediately after Bush launched the initial attacks. By 11:00 pm, we gathered on the street corner, where we'd done many other protest vigils, to set up camp for 24 hours. A group of folks were busy setting up a makeshift altar on the curb, and someone had just dropped off a crate of orange juice and snacks. In the midst of this, two young people came out of a local bar just a couple of doors down and began to heckle us.

We were used to this by now, but this one young woman was particularly distraught. A couple of older, seasoned activists in our group began to take her on, yelling arguments back at her. She and her companion were clearly outnumbered and her hysteria rose. As she swaggered down the street, she screamed into the night air: "He has weapons of mass destruction! Biological and chemical warfare! Are you people crazy?" Even now I can feel her anguish in my belly and my heart—a visceral memory of her intense fear.

Remembering my training in non violence, I moved my body to create a buffer between her and the folks on from our group who were egging her on. I tried to talk to her, in a calmer, quieter voice, but I was tentative at best and it was clear she couldn't hear me. I began to follow them down the street just a few steps. I wanted to reach out to her, to ask her if she was afraid, to engage her. Isn't this how waves of collective liberation begin to swell, across lines of significant ideological difference? I didn't do any of that. The emotions of the months preceding the start of the invasion had caught up with me. I couldn't think straight, couldn't engage my practice, couldn't manifest my love. Instead of expanding, I contracted.

WHERE WE ARE HEADED?

We are human. We can, might, and sometimes do inflict pain on each other. And we have grooves of susceptibility to pain that are well worn, from the karma of past lives, the traumas of childhood, the cultural legacy of ancestral realities. We have to work through this, not around it. Our pain, our rough edges, and our mistakes hold the keys to the liberation work left to do – both within and around us. The body offers us a vital new leading edge for this exploration. It offers such an accurate barometer of what is real and what is meaningful. In seconds, my mind can take elaborate trips to the distant past or a far away future, but the body always exists right here in the present.

There is a dynamic tension between individual practice and the community cohesion needed to effect change. If we're doing the work of our own inner liberation in isolation, without the reflective mirror of a community, then we run the risk of bolstering individualism and attachment to identity. We forsake our part in the development of the narrative. Things become too self-referential and we lose the opportunity to contribute to collective growth. And if we engage in the collective without some practice of individual consciousness, we're more likely to get caught up in group think and only use a fraction of our human capacity. Without consciousness, there is no choice. That is what makes engaged spirituality so exciting and so critical. What we're really saying is that we're not settling for old beliefs and thought patterns. Instead, we are entering the realm of infinite possibility.

9
JAY EARLY

Jay Earley, PhD, is a psychologist, group leader, coach, social theorist, and change agent. A former computer scientist, he has been practicing psychotherapy for over 30 years. During the 1980s, Jay was active in the peace movement, when he led workshops that integrated psychological, spiritual, and planetary concerns. Nationally known for innovation in the group psychotherapy field, he was formerly Director of the Group Therapy Center of Long Island. Jay has created the Pattern System, a method for understanding interpersonal behavior and its underlying psychological issues. In addition to individual, couple, and group psychotherapy, Jay offers Life Purpose Coaching, Change Agent Coaching, and coach training (www.lifepurposecoaching. com) to help people find their deeper purpose in life and make a difference in the world. He is a long-time student of the Diamond Approach to spiritual realization, and is in training to become a Diamond teacher. He is director of Conscious Action, a non-profit organization dedicated to helping people engage in social action from a place of greater consciousness. He is the author of Inner Journeys: A Guide to Personal and Social Transformation, Transforming Human Culture: Social Evolution and the Planetary Crisis, Interactive Group Therapy, and Finding Your Life Purpose. For more information, see www.earley.org.

THOUGHTS ON LIFE PURPOSE, SPIRITUAL DEVELOPMENT, PSYCHOLOGY, AND SOCIAL TRANSFORMATION

SOCIAL TRANSFORMATION

If we truly want social justice in the world, it is not enough to work for the kinds of changes in social, political, and economic structures that are usually pursued by social justice activists. We need a more fundamental transformation of our entire society, as Martin Luther King realized near the end of his life.

At the current time, our world is in the midst of a planetary crisis. The modern/industrial world view and social structure are no longer able to handle our current problems. Therefore, the world is undergoing a whole-system transformation affecting all aspects of society, from our consciousness to our economy, from our values to our politics, from our technology to our organizations. This is a historical transition of a scope as has happened only a few times in human history. We are moving to the next stage in the social evolution of humanity (Jay Earley: *Transforming Human Culture*; Duane Elgin: *Awakening Earth, Promise Ahead;* Thomas Berry: *The Great Work;* Ervin Laszlo: *Macroshift)*.

Though social injustice has been around for thousands of years, this transformation provides an opportunity to finally overcome it on a large scale. For the first time in human history, we have the knowledge and power to choose our overall direction with foresight. We have the opportunity to construct a planetary society that will provide security, health, and prosperity for everyone, and that will foster love, harmony, and creativity. And we will be forced to do this in order for our civilization to survive intact.

For this reason, I believe that social justice activism should be pursued within the larger context of this whole-system transformation. Too often, an activist group will focus on one narrow political issue without recognizing what is truly needed for that issue to be resolved.

DEVELOPMENT PERSPECTIVE

Psychologists who study adult development have learned that there are levels of development that extend beyond the well-known stages of child development. They have studied how we develop along various lines—e.g., cognitive, moral, emotional, interpersonal, representing different human capacities. In addition, they have studied the development of consciousness. Some have concluded that the highest of these stages reflect the noblest spiritual aspirations of the world's religions. It seems to me that a person's moral and spiritual development will be directly relevant to his/her becoming a social activist. Therefore, I recommend that research into activism include a development perspective (Ken Wilber: *Integral Psychology*; Robert Kegan: *The Evolving Self* and *In Over Our Heads*; Lawrence Kohlberg: *Collected Papers on Moral Development;* James Fowler: *Stages of Faith)*.

PROGRAMS FOR SPIRITUAL DEVELOPMENT

I believe that spiritual beliefs and attitudes tend to encourage the kind of love and compassion that lead to effective social activism, especially when we are encouraged to be open to people outside our religious tradition. However, I don't think this is enough for most people. Too often, our spiritual beliefs don't really reflect the way we actually live, especially when confronted with the often difficult situations involving race and poverty. In addition, even when our spiritual attitudes of love are genuine and deeply felt, our love is often restricted to people similar to us in identity or political stance.

Therefore, I think that it is important to have programs of spiritual and psychological practices that foster spiritual development in a way that includes the social and political dimensions of our lives.

PSYCHOLOGICAL PERSPECTIVE

Spiritual practices may lead to powerful spiritual experiences, but too often they are hard to integrate into our lives. This is because there are usually entrenched psychological issues that block us from realizing the spiritual insights on a permanent basis, and then living from that place. Spiritual practices can overcome or bypass these psychological issues on a temporary basis, which is extremely useful, but the issues usually return. This is even more likely when we are struggling to live our realization in the hotbed context of social activism, which can trigger strong fear and anger.

Therefore, I believe that psychological work must be a central component of programs of spiritual development for activists. My own spiritual path is the Diamond Approach (www.ridhwan.org), which incorporates psychological understandings and methods as a central aspect of its spiritual practices. I am also an experienced psychologist who is knowledgeable about the leading methods in the field of psychotherapy, especially those that are spiritually oriented (Internal Family Systems Therapy www. selfleadership.org).

I am incorporating these approaches into a new personal growth program aimed at facilitating the development of personal attitudes and capacities for social transformation. These include:

- Feeling empowered to make a difference;
- Being consciously in touch with the spiritual calling that motivates your work for change in the world;
- Having a self-reflective attitude, so that any difficulty or challenge from others leads you to inquire into your own consciousness;
- Working through reactivity, so that you are less likely to react from unresolved psychological issues and more likely to respond constructively and creatively;
- Embodying hope, vision, inclusiveness, passion, participation, self-organization, collective intelligence, and other transformational capacities;
- Being open to learning better ways to operate and new creative ways to proceed;
- Dialoguing with others and learning from differences;
- Leading in a way that empowers others while not holding back your gifts;
- Recognizing that your best contribution to social transformation comes from manifesting your life purpose;
- Manifesting compassion, oneness, love, openness, mindfulness, and other spiritual qualities in your work for the world.

LIFE PURPOSE AND SPIRITUAL CALLING

For the last 20 years, I have been in touch with a spiritual calling to contribute to transforming society, and it has inspired much of my work during that time. I believe that many people can tune into a sense of the deeper purpose of their lives, which sometimes takes the form of a spiritual calling, and that this can foster passionate engagement in altruistic work. I think this is a key component in motivating people toward social activism. For years, I have been offering Life Purpose Coaching (www.lifepurposecoaching.com) to help people do this. I have especially enjoyed helping people whose calling relates to social transformation.

I believe that research must be practical if it is to be truly useful in promoting social justice and transformation. This means:

(1) Research should discover information we didn't know before. Too much empirical research is designed simply to prove things that we already know or can guess intuitively.

(2) Research should point toward actions that we can take to foster effective social activism, not just give us information. For example, finding correlations between personality variables or life situations and social activism may not tell us how to promote greater activism.

RESEARCH QUESTIONS

The following research questions would be very helpful in advancing our ability to transform society:

1. *When people hear a spiritual calling to contribute to social transformation, what forms does this take and what are the ways in which it is experienced? What psychological issues block people from hearing and responding to their calling, and how can these issues be resolved?*

2. *What capacities (psychological, spiritual, and social) are most useful in helping social activists to be effective and spiritually oriented in their work? What psychological issues block people from manifesting these capacities, and how can they be resolved?*

3. *What are the development stages that people go through in their attitudes toward justice, the suffering of others, the state of our society, and the need for social transformation? What enables a person to advance to a higher stage?*

4. *What psychological issues block people from recognizing injustice and other societal problems and responding to them in an active, constructive way? How can they be resolved?*

5. *What psychological issues lead activists to respond primarily from anger and fear, rather than from love, compassion, and vision? How can they be resolved?*

6. *What factors lead social justice activists to broaden their understanding so they understand the importance of social transformation in achieving social justice?*

10
SIMON GREER

Simon Greer is President and CEO of the Jewish Funds for Justice in New York. He was previouslythe Co-Director of New York Jobs with Justice since April 2002. JwJ is a city-wide coalition of labor, community, religious and student organizations. Simon has been responsible for building the organization's staff from 2 to 15, restructuring the Board of Directors, and overhauling the organizational structure. The organization has won significant workplace democracy, economic development and access to higher education victories, has rebuilt strategic partnerships with labor, community, student and faith-based organizations, and has developed innovative policy campaigns around subsidy accountability and health insurance reform. Simon has also implemented innovative management and leadership programs within the organization.

WHAT CAN I TELL YOU . . .

"A South Carolina Sea Island housekeeper says Jesus Christ is her hero and he gives her the courage to organize with her co-workers, against historic odds, to gain dignity, respect and a family-supporting wage. Collectively they risk what little they have, for the against- all-odds chance to leave the world a little bit better for their children. With the first step they act as free people and so they are."

"A Bushwick community organizer utilizes a leadership mantra to ground himself before each significant leadership opportunity. In reflecting upon this practice he observes that less important than the content of the mantra is the silent pause that it precipitates and the resultant wisdom that may be gleaned in the quiet."

"A Rabbi stands before an owning-class suburban congregation and introduces them to the concept of County Living Wage legislation. Rather than explaining why the congregation should care through frequently sited Jewish texts on healing and repairing the world he describes the legislation as a pro-Shabbat ordinance. A law that will allow a hard working family to rest on the 7th day."

These vignettes are my gut response to the question, "What does 'engaged spirituality' mean to you?" And over a few years now of observing the difference between my ego and my wiser self (Mind V. Gut) I have come to trust that it is likely these passages will be my sharpest and wisest offering. Nonetheless I will write on and see what I unearth. My intention is a flowing exploration of the terrain related to what we're calling engaged spirituality. My expectation is that this paper will raise questions in many corners of the territory and touch briefly on texture, color, and climate.

As I begin to write, though, I am starkly aware of how poorly I have done with the language around this work. From contemplative practice, to engaged spirituality, to unlimited love I find myself using the words offered here and there in our fledgling movement but feeling aligned with none of them. In my office, we refer to personal mastery and compassionate leadership. And, I still find myself deeply unsatisfied.[2] Today, I am humbled by how transformative this work is and how empty my language is. Though, as I ponder it maybe I shouldn't be so surprised. In my tradition we are clear that the G-d that can be named is not G-d. Just as the Taoists say the same of the Path that is named and the Buddhists of the Buddha that is named. Fittingly then, naming the work – let alone doing the work – of *cultivating authentic spiritual practice that it might infuse public struggle for the purpose of systemic transformation is an elusive and humbling endeavor.*

So let's bracket the word game. Let's leave it side, knowing that it is one topic that deserves thoughtful and engaged exploration on the ground, and turn to the work itself..

It has been my experience that "engaged spirituality" and the sustenance nurtured in love and compassion show up in remarkably diverse places – some might contend divergent and contradictory ones.

I stood between a line of police and line of anarchist activists at a global justice demonstration to diffuse the distraction. I sat for 7 days at a Jewish meditation retreat, found solace in the silence and glimpsed a face of equanimity. I cultivated a set of organizational contemplative practices that enable social and economic justice organizations to sustain their employees' alignment with, and efficacy in pursuing, the organization's noble purpose.

These have been among my "Thorong-La" or peak work experiences of the last few years. On the surface, diverse, self-reflective, and publicly engaged – not a bad gold, silver and bronze. But the victory stops just about there. In fact, the breadth of these experiences is in tense relationship with context I – and I believe we - currently work in and has meant non-integration to the detriment of the work. While I have been clearing a wholistic transformative path through experiences like these, the sectors in which these experience are defined – economic justice, Jewish and spiritual - at times lack a sense of themselves as coherent sectors and at other times see themselves as hostile to each other. So the questions emerge from the spiritualist, the Jew and the economic justice organizer:

2 Maybe we could focus group some organizer types and test words (maybe even concepts and practices) to see where there is resonance

- What is so spiritual about cops vs. protesters?
- Where is the Jewish in global justice?
- How do you tell a movement it's time has come and gone too soon?
- How can any organizer work effectively without a deep personal practice?
- How is meditation Jewish?
- How is Jewish meditation economic justice?
- Aren't you just dressing up OD work retain young organizers as spiritual?
- How can you be such a movement progressive when activists are so quick to condemn "Apartheid" in Israel?
- Can't I just work for justice instead of doing all the touchy-feely woo-woo stuff?

Despite the questions and the lack of answers, I have been committed for some years now to integrating my Jewish life, my spiritual practice and my work for economic justice. Committed in a deep, called upon way. An integration that doesn't privilege any of the three sectors (Judaism, spirituality, and economic justice). An integration that holds them to a mutually defined and equitably rigorous set of standards of efficiency and effectiveness. Integration that counters the nasty history of elite spiritualities' flirtation with fascism, democratizes the models, undermines the hate & fear mongers and leaves the world a better place.

I am humbled and rendered wide open by the observation that by and large the fighting for progressive change over the post-World War II period has proven virtually incapable of yielding sustainable structural change and the contemporary American phenomenon of personal growth and inner exploration have proven to be equally futile vehicles for societal change. I fear these flaws are built into the structures of both routes and may well render them detours not short-cuts. So what's the landscape?

The Dalai Lama is a spiritual light to many but remains out of power and in exile. Lula's government is caving (says the left) and out of touch (says the right). The top 50 leaders of the Central Committee of Poland's Communist Party in 1989 dominated the ranks of Poland's richest businessman less than 5 years later. Mandela's South Africa can't compute the scale of the AIDS epidemic and so buries its head in the post-Apartheid sand. Are you tired yet?

Back at home, the Right tells people to pick themselves up by their bootstraps. The Left blames the system for its structural barriers to classes of people succeeding. Our tendency is a knee jerk siding with the Left, but what if we question the American experience for answers. We turn then to experience as the arbiter of this dispute. And the American experience is inconsistent on this front. Wealth has been amassed by new comers to our shores at a pace and on a scale hardly imaginable and certainly incontrovertible. Yet side by side with this experience is the story of our highest office held only by White Protestant men (with one exception) and there is a compelling on-the-face-of-it case against our exclusive development model that has littered the terrain with whole cities, classes and nations cast aside like debris. So without a simple answer, in our experience, to the propositions of the Left and Right poles, I turn to my ideology for explanations -- and this "engaged spiritual activist" comes out a bit lost.

My political ideology is grounded in a structural critique of an inconsistent and reckless free-market system[3] that condones and even fosters axes of oppressions along lines of difference and power imbalance. So my politics tell me to blame the system. Yet my spiritual practice of yoga, meditation and Jewish ritual has cultivated a deep knowing inside me that we all have limitless choice in every situation to live life to the fullest. An irreconcilable difference? No! A call for a new ideology? Yes?

It seems to me that we sure need a new model. And I believe my small contribution to the model resides in my practice at the intersection. Why? Because the scales of justice have been swung so far out of sync that it is nearly impossible to see what justice – pure, simple and without excuses – for the majority of the world's population would look like.

Because I have been organizing long enough to learn that often even when we win they still win. And no number of victories insures that the meanness and the anger don't seep into the soul and give them the ultimate victory.

Because the Jewish community too often entertains the needs of its Republican donors rather than staking out a bold counter-cultural position that says our tradition stands against the hoarders and the multipliers who loot and pillage with ever newer technologies.

Because the President-select is leading an horrific crusade that dehumanizes millions of innocent people and puts our country squarely in the cross-hairs not just of fanatics but of any one who is paying attention and on the short end of our mighty stick.

Because I lost my Mom in 2002 and a day doesn't go by that I'm not gutted by the loss as well as sense the clarity and wisdom that she left with me.

Because non-profit and mediocrity have become synonymous for too many people. And, if I have one impact that outlives me please let it be that "compassionate leadership that is uncompromising on results" becomes the touchstone of a united progressive movement that achieves systemic change.

And because I have lived moments where these intolerable conditions are challenged in revolutionary ways that transformed systems and souls. I have experienced a model of change work that eliminates the illusions of stress and drag, embodies less is more and achieves impeccable results. I have seen instinct cultivated and braided with strategy. I have seen the potency of leaders leading from the deepest places in service purely of love and tied only to the truth of the moment. From my lived experience I discern that at the three way intersection of my Jewish lineage, spiritual practice and economic justice organizing there is a model being born. Yet the intersection and the experi-

---

3   While I will refrain from a diatribe about the free-market system it is at least worth noting that part of the quandary for us is that the largest corporations on the planet operate in an insulated and closed state driven system that is a far cry from a free market and so a useful critique of the market must include true seeing about what are market limitations and what is the impact of the dishonesty about what is free-market.

ences are not the norm.

The obstacles to developing this new model and the integrated, faith-filled ideology that serves it are complex and multi-faceted. Obstacles that have the tips of their roots in the depths of our culture and the ends of their branches wrapped all around us. And so our limited answers come most frequently in the form of compartmentalized move-ings. Movings (not movements) that offer glimpses of hope yet quickly find themselves perilously close to reinforcing some deep-seated counter revolutionary cornerstone of the current order.

For example, a thriving yoga studio that underpays its teachers, avoids politics and functions as a highly successful capitalist venture. Or, a labor movement that doesn't know it lacks soul, spirit and values, thinks John Kerry will save it and can't imagine how many old burdensome models it holds on to for dear live as their sheer weight plunges it to the depths of the sea.

And so the reflective change agent must ponder when can I work within the system to glean what is true and capable of clearing another yard on the path and when am I merely replicating an old model in increasingly insidious ways and so must move to new and unexplored forms. Is it a question of *Kavanah* (intention) or is the answer in the outcome or is it not ours to know?

Then sometimes you just glimpse it. When the rant has gotten to be a bit too much and you think to give up. There is a kernel of wisdom. A quiet, nearly silent, insight. You feel the gentle warmth of the flame that flickers constantly in the pit of your stomach. The flame that is your timeless "I am" as well as the eternal "we are". And this is the purpose of the spiritual path. It is our source. Some years ago as I grappled with the same systemic injustice, and the wobbily movement that claims to challenge it, but without the spiritual grounding I daily failed to glimpse it. Not because it wasn't there, but because I wasn't.. I hadn't felt Abraham Joshua Heschel's words resonate inside me, "Awe precedes faith."

Now I am much more clear. This elusive notion of spiritual path is the open space, the well spring, the sweet spot, from which the old models are made new and the tired are made fresh. As singer and song write Jon Fromer writes, "My feet are tired but my soul is rested."

Maybe that awareness, that settling in, is brought forward by a note of music, the smell of a season, the touch of a loved one, the thrill of victory, the agony of defeat, or a piece of writing. And when you feel it you know there is a power available there that can be harnessed for truly transformative and revolutionary purposes. A power that when accessed is inexhaustible. A new way of being that won't be engulfed in the system's inconceivably elastic, resilient and pliable matrix. It is from this place only that the most true work of transforming the world can be started.

So let's collaborate:
1. Interview key cross-over "spiritual" spokespeople on the topic of collective ac-

tion and structural change;

2. Team teach an integrated curriculum on spirituality and social justice (pardon the language)

3. Develop the body of knowledge about applied transformative practices for the high performing organization (study the adaptation of personal transformation practices to organizational practices that have the organizational benefit that the personal practices have on individuals);

4. Academic and practitioner writing projects and speaking opportunities to legitimate the field;

5. Generate PR for this work;

6. Create a hybrid academic/practitioner Center for study, training and practice;

7. Take each other frightfully seriously and lightheartedly, as the moment requires just that.

11
JESSE MACEO VEGA-FREY

Jesse Maceo Vega-Frey is an artist, meditator, and activist from and living in Holyoke, Massachusetts. He currently works with STONE circles, an organization dedicated to helping activists integrate spiritual practices into their lives and work.

Jess likes to sit on my stoop and hang out with the kids on my block.

He helps out at an organic farm [a CSA], where he is a member.

He spends time with friends and family.

Over the past few years, the conversations about "spirituality and social change" that I have been a part of have revolved largely around the integration of spiritual practice into activism and social justice work. The resulting lines of inquiry are vital to our understanding of how sustainable change happens, and should be pursued to their fullest ends. Yet I also believe that the way in which we've defined the discussion has pushed some important aspects of the conversation to the margins that are in some ways the essence of what is really radical about committing to a spiritual activist path.

I have begun to feel more confident in the notion that considering the role of love in social justice work or activism is actually secondary to an understanding of the relationship between love and a revolutionary way of being. A revolutionary way of being should certainly include activism as a fundamental pillar. But it also seems important to offer the possibility that activism as a way in itself actually avoids challenging some of the fundamental unhealthy assumptions that underlie the prevailing order we are trying to change. In fact, spirituality's gift to activism is to provide an understanding that it is within the realm of love that we may most clearly evolve our understanding of what functional and radical ways of being in the world can really look and feel like.

Both the word "activism" and the phrase "social justice work" point directly towards an underlying assumption that change comes about through a whole lot of doing. In Buddhism, which is the spiritual practice I am most familiar with, the degree to which a fundamental aspect of the path of transformation is deeply rooted in a whole lot of "non-doing" cannot be overstated.

Progressives are quick to point out and criticize the frightening patterns of over-consumption we are engaged in as a culture, but rarely address the corollary—i.e., the idea that we are in fact an overproductive society that is simply unable to question the blind belief in the value of productivity. We are unable to acknowledge even the possibility that our lack of synchronicity with nature, more humane ways of being in the world, and happiness are a direct result of our obsession with productivity and action, as much as they are of our addiction to consumption. So if we can step back from activism as the core component of our understanding of spirituality and social change and open our awareness to a broader consideration of "revolutionary ways of being," I think we can truly explore the relevance of love to personal and social transformation.

I am not trying to say that if we stop trying to make peace happen it will just happen on its own. It's more that I think we could have a more liberated approach to what "work for change" actually looks like. Does it need to look like a 60 hour work week with no benefits and a garbage diet? Or is the refusal to work, be productive, and consume, and the insistence on being a human, being in community, hanging out with friends and family, eating, playing, worshiping actually more revolutionary?

As humans and as communities, we need to do less for peace at this point in history. Reclaiming our humanity is the truly revolutionary act. While surely the traditional activist cringes at the thought [and even my own internal skeptic raises its eyebrows], I believe that a truly healthy community requires us to be doing a lot less than we are currently doing.

I have two heroes on the path of a revolutionary way of being guided by a deep sense of love and justice: Wally and Juanita Nelson. When Wally passed away a few years ago at 93, he was still working on the organic farm that he and Juanita have cultivated for over 25 years. At 84, Juanita continues to work the land to provide the majority of her sustenance. For over 50 years, they refused to pay their income taxes because an unacceptable portion of them are directed toward military spending. Wally participated in the first racially integrated bus ride into Jim Crow states, and the two of them have dedicated themselves to living peacefully and radically on this planet in ways that continue to inspire me. He said once:

> Nonviolence is the constant awareness of the dignity and humanity of oneself and others; it renounces violence both in method and in attitude; it is a courageous acceptance of active love and goodwill as the instrument with which to overcome evil and transform both oneself and others. It is the willingness to undergo suffering rather than inflict it. It excludes retaliation and flight.

The first insight Wally had into overcoming violence came when he was only about nine years old. The son of sharecroppers in Arkansas, one day he was made responsible for getting the mule to till the soil. Because he was inexperienced in controlling the animal, the mule was quickly agitated and began to run around the field, out of Wally's control. Wally remembers being dragged around the field, flailing, terrified, and screaming when a neighboring farmer in the distance saw his distress and began to yell instructions at him. "Let loose the line! Let loose the line!" Unfortunately, Wally couldn't understand the words of the neighbor and kept pulling harder and harder on the mule to get him to slow down. Finally, he and the mule passed close enough to the neighbor's field to hear him yell at the top of his lungs "LET LOOSE THE LINE, FOOL, AND YOU'LL BE FREE!!" Wally quickly released the harness and came tumbling to a stop. The mule trotted on a little further but also slowed down and stopped once it had been released.

When Wally told me this story, it was the first time that I understood the possibility of withdrawal as an act of resistance. I understood that every part of the tax-resisting lifestyle that they had chosen –from growing nearly all of their own food, to pulling their water from a well, to living without the use of electricity—was exactly this kind of aikido maneuver of 'letting loose the line,' at once liberating themselves from a relationship of violence and providing a powerful opportunity for the violence to desist. Juanita still says to me about many modern activists, "These people can protest the war all they want but as long as they're paying for it, it will never stop."

This kind of radical withdrawal means sacrifice and is an attempt at profound renunciation akin to monastic practices in many of the world's spiritual traditions. It requires conviction and love, will and selflessness, strength and surrender. It requires a complete reexamination of livelihood and community. And, to be clear, it is not a simple withdrawal from society that Wally and Juanita have been engaged in all these years. It is a withholding from society the means, methods, and attitudes of propagating violence and hatred. It is being engaged with society in a way that attempts to only offer the peaceful, the liberatory, and the wise. This is the essence of what I understand to be a revolutionary way of being. It is radical non-doing par excellence. It is simple, calm, difficult, and just. And the explicit foundation, method, and outcome of this way is love.

Love, the absolute surrender of "self" and "other," allows us to rest in void, groundlessness, fluctuation, and insecurity. It is the engine of faith. Growing comfort in these places of unknowable change provides for and develops the capacity to engage in true risk, to offer our own comfort and security for the benefit of others. It is the thing that allows us to sit at a lunch counter when we hear the sirens getting closer, to refuse to fight in territories we know should be left unoccupied, to withhold taxes from a Caesar who has lost its perspective of humanity and goodness. In some ways, I think the capacity to engage in socially-oriented risk is the outcome of love that has the greatest potential to manifest lasting social transformation.

It may be just because we are in such dark times that in some ways I have come to feel that to engage in the traditional forms of activism and political change is more or less like playing different games at the casino. You may get ahead over here and at that table over there, but in the end the house always wins. They designed these games we play and they make up the rules as the game goes along. We who care to change things often seem to be caught eternally scrambling to negotiate the specifics of these new rules, rather than confronting the fact that the whole game is set up for certain people to win and others to get left behind.

Of all of the ways to think about who the house is, who is controlling the game, and who is designing the rules, I have been most grounded by the sense recently that it is in fact the forces of greed, hatred, and delusion that are running the show. These are called the three poisons in the Buddhist framework, and are considered to be the root causes for all of our suffering. Rather than exhaust ourselves and be manipulated into hatred by our engagement with these systems, forms, and venues that are seeded in, cultivated in, and now bear the fruit of the three poisons, I think it is worth looking at efforts to create our own systems: formal and informal, activist and effortless, underneath, around, and in between these prickly vines that point toward real freedom because they are based in love, compassion, wisdom, and justice.

We need to create and pursue alternative economic, health care, communication, and community models that can truly allow people to be in the radical ways we need to be in order to really function as breaking mechanisms to the violent stampeding cattle that form this society. Activists need access to health care for ourselves and our families. We need to have support systems for the retaliation that the state enacts upon those who withhold their taxes, refuse to fight, or engage in civil disobedience—i.e., those who do less for peace. We need theories and thought on what a variety of healthy economies can look like, and how GDP and consumer spending cannot be the be-all and end-all gauges of economic success.

And again, I'd like to hold on to the possibility that new strategies and models for change may require less doing, take less work, be less exhausting, less alienating, and less dehumanizing because they flow naturally from a revolutionary way of being that finds its primary driving force in love, community, and in the possibility for liberation in our lifetime.

12
SHARON SALZBERG

Sharon Salzberg is a leading spiritual teacher and writer. Her latest book is <u>Faith: Trusting Your Own Deepest Experience</u> (Riverhead Books, 2002). She is also the author of <u>Lovingkindess: The Revolutionary Art of Happiness</u> and <u>A Heart as Wide as the World: Living with Mindfulness, Wisdom, and Compassion</u> (both Shambhala Publications), co-author with Joseph Goldstein of <u>Insight Meditation: A Step-by-Step Course on How to Meditate</u> (Sounds True), and editor of <u>Voices of Insight</u> (Shambhala).

Sharon's work is non-sectarian, though based on the ancient Buddhist practices of mindfulness and metta (lovingkindness), the aim of which is to cultivate love and compassion for ourselves and for others. "This," she explains, "is the heart of spiritual teaching: in each of us is a genuine capacity for love, forgiveness, wisdom and compassion, and by practicing meditation these qualities are brought to life. Any of us can discover for ourselves the unique happiness that is our birthright."

After she first became interested in meditation, Sharon spent several years engaged in intensive practice and study with respected meditation teachers from India, Burma, and Tibet. In 1976, she, Joseph Goldstein, and Jack Kornfield established the Insight Meditation Society (IMS) in Barre, Massachusetts -- now one of the most prominent and active meditation centers in the Western world. IMS offers retreats of varying lengths that provide intensive training in meditative skills and contemplative practices throughout the year. They are attended by people of many diverse religious backgrounds and interests.

Sharon also teaches internationally, and has spoken or taught at such prestigious events as the State of the World Forum, the Peacemakers Conference (sharing a plenary panel with Nobel Laureates His Holiness the Dalai Lama and Jose Ramos Horta), and Jerry Brown's inauguration as mayor of Oakland. She has delivered keynotes at Tricycle's Buddhism in America event, Yoga Journal and Omega conferences, the Gethsemani encounter (a Buddhist-Christian dialogue including His Holiness the Dalai Lama and various Christian dignitaries,) and the Mind-Life Institute, addressing scientists involved in meditation research. In November, 2002, she was the Resident Teacher at the Sacred Circles women's interfaith conference at the Washington National Cathedral, and will be taking that role again in February of 2005. **AGAIN in 2005?**

I believe all authentic spirituality is engaged spirituality. I would describe spirituality as the transformation of our usual self-preoccupation into an inclusive, open, connected awareness. We can easily go from morning until night engrossed in thinking, "What do they think of me? Does he like me? Do they consider me inferior? Am I winning? How do I look to her?" This habitual state of disconnection, from both genuine contact with others and more fundamental aspects of our own experience, leaves us feeling uncertain, afraid, imprisoned by a sense of separateness, and exhausted. Spiritual practices of ethics, meditation, generosity, service, and lovingkindness turn this tendency around toward actual engagement; they also become the manifestation of a free mind.

In many ways activism, which fosters concern with others more than with ourselves, is a natural form of spiritual endeavor. In addition to the way it changes a community or society, there is a question as to how activism can be most liberating for the person practicing it. Another question is if, and how, contemplative disciplines such as meditation might enhance the spirit of activism, enabling it to be sustained through obstacles over the long haul most projects require, and to sustain the activist in the face of frustration, disappointment, or despair.

Meditation releases us from the grasp of the habitual tendencies that distort our perception (e.g., holding on to what we like as though we could control change, and pushing away what we don't like as though our rejection could make it disappear), and allows us to see life more clearly. Clear seeing reveals a world in which no one and no thing stands apart. The realization of interconnectedness becomes the basis for how we act, both in a personal way, such as within our families, and in a more global way, as we participate in social justice efforts.

Ordinarily, we are prodded by many different motivations when facing suffering and attempting remedial action. As human beings, we often use outrage to escape from helplessness and despair. The sheer energy of anger can be very important in that way. It is as though our life force is asserting itself. We are drawing boundaries, declaring certain behavior unacceptable, and definitely (maybe at long last) refusing to be mistreated or to allow someone else to be mistreated. But once we get lost in the anger, saying in effect, "This is who I really am, this defines me," we are vulnerable to perpetuating cycles of violence, lashing out reflexively instead of acting consciously, or thoughtlessly giving up.

If we are motivated by a vision of interconnectedness, then love and compassion, which are every bit as powerful as anger without its destructive force, will keep us going in our efforts. Interconnectedness isn't an abstract, fanciful notion; it is a direct seeing of a deeper reality. Consider for a moment something like a tree. We think of it as a distinctly defined object, standing there by itself. But on another level of perception, it's not so completely separate. It's also the consequence, the manifestation, or the function of an extremely subtle net of relationships. The tree is affected by the rain that falls upon it, and the wind that moves through and around it. It's affected by the soil that nourishes and sustains it. It's affected by the weather, the sunlight, the moonlight, and the quality of the air. So many conditions help to make the tree what it is. It is the same for a homeless person, a survivor of domestic violence, or an adversary.

In the Mahayana Buddhist teaching, there's a very famous image that tries to convey this sense. It's "Indra's Net," in which the universe is depicted as an enormous net. In one place, where you can imagine the strings of the net meeting right at the nexus, there's a jewel—a very polished multi-faceted jewel such as a diamond or a piece of crystal. Now, imagine that there's another jewel, just like that original one, at every place where there is a joining in this infinite net. In each of these places there's a jewel that is reflecting every other jewel all at the same time. If you look at one thing, you see all things.

In day-to-day life, this translates into a much more realistic perception of the larger patterns and confluences of which we are all a part. It is said that there was a monk in the Buddha's time who came from an extremely wealthy aristocratic family—which he gave up to become a monk. His life had been limited by his very sheltered existence. One day some of the other monks were teasing him, and they asked him, "Where does rice come from, brother?" And he said, "It comes from a golden bowl." They asked him, "Where does milk come from?" He replied, "It comes from a silver bowl." And he really thought that was true. The only times he had seen rice in his entire life had been at home, when it was presented to him in a golden bowl. He thought that was how it grew. There are times any of us can be like that monk. But we can take the time to have an under-standing of the layers of conditions coming together for our meal: the people growing our food, the animals giving up their milk, the planet nurturing us all. We have a different sense of the interdependence in which we live, and the fallacy of a rigid sense of separa-tion, self, and other. This clarity of perception is the root of understanding. It's also the root of compassion and the root of social action born of love.

The understanding of interconnectedness also reminds us that we can never know how our actions will ripple out and affect others. Through force of habit, we may disparage ourselves, considering an action to be inadequate, or resign ourselves to its seeming mediocrity. But we can't possibly know the ultimate result of anything we do. The poet T.S. Eliot wrote, "For us there is only the trying. The rest is not our business." This larger vision of life is what sustains activism beyond immediate success and failure.

When we assess the value of our actions, we commonly do so in terms of whether or not they will produce a certain result—doing the good we envisioned, in the time frame we anticipated. If it doesn't work out that way, we may lose confidence in what we do, and grow dispirited. Unless we can guarantee the result we want, we might even decide not to take certain actions at all. Such attachment to achieving results can lead to relentless expectation, burnout, and the desolating habit of feeling we can never do enough.

In Buddhist teaching, however, the immediate result of an action, and how others respond to it, is only a small part of its value. There are two other significant aspects: the intention giving rise to an action, and the skillfulness with which we perform it. The intention is our basic motivation, or the inner urge that sparks the action. As His Holiness the Dalai Lama said, "Motivation is very important, and thus my simple religion is love, respect for others, honesty: teachings that cover not only religion but also the fields of politics, economics, business, science, law, medicine-everywhere. With proper motivation these can help humanity..."

The skillfulness with which we act involves carrying out the intention with sensitivity to and awareness of what might be appropriate in any given situation. While the skillfulness of an action has a great deal to do with the result, it is the intention behind an action that is critically important. We can't control the results of an action. We can do our best to act skillfully. But it is at the level of intention where we make a crucial choice. An action can be motivated by love – or by hatred and revenge. Self-interest can be the source of what we do – or generosity can. If our intention is wholesome, we can have trust in the workings of interconnectedness to continuously unfold our action in positive ways, no matter how small or big it may be. So, first knowing and then refining our intentions, the place from which we act, becomes a large area of inner work.

Aung San Suu Kyi, leader of the pro-democracy movement in Burma, is an exemplar of this. She was placed under house arrest in 1989 for her political activities. While still confined, she received the Nobel Peace Prize in 1991. Suu's sons were 16 and 12 when she was arrested, and she was not able to see them again for years. It was over two years before she saw her husband again. Describing her imprisonment, Suu writes, "I refused to accept anything from the military. Sometimes I didn't even have enough money to eat. I became so weak from malnourishment that my hair fell out, and I couldn't get out of bed." Despite the depth of her suffering, Suu later said, "When I compared notes with my colleagues in the democracy movement in Burma who have suffered long terms of imprisonment, we found that an enhanced appreciation of metta (lovingkindness) was a common experience. We had known and felt both the effects of metta and the unwholesomeness of natures lacking in metta."

This commitment to love as the motivation fueling our efforts for change and our response to injustice is the essence of enlightened social action. By turning away from causing suffering, we turn toward the compassionate urge to bring about happiness and well-being. In the formal meditative practice of metta, we declare, "Just as I want to be free from pain and suffering, may all beings be free from pain and suffering. Just as I wish to be happy, may all beings be happy." Imprisoned in her own house for years, Aung San Suu Kyi lived daily with the contrast between "the effects of metta"(the development of greater love for all) and the effects of "natures lacking in metta" (the dehumanization of herself and her colleagues). While lack of metta gave rise to suffering, the power of metta, both within her own mind and within the minds of others, gave rise to a wholly different place from which to work for change.

Qualities like love and compassion will lift our efforts beyond dualistic struggles between "us" and "them." Having a sense of a bigger picture of life will imbue our efforts with patience, encouraging us to keep trying beyond the initial, perhaps flawed, result we see in front of us. Realizing and then remembering that tomorrow doesn't have to look like today forms the basis of our aspirations, hope, and diligence. These can all be summed up as having faith underlie our work towards social justice. By "faith," I don't mean the conventional sense of belonging to a religious tradition and accepting its tenets; I mean the power to open our hearts, without dogma but with intelligence and discernment, to that which is bigger than our immediate circumstance. This reference to faith isn't at all about adherence to a belief system, blind surrender, unthinking devotion, or a lack of questioning. Instead, it refers to affirming and then relying on those spiritual values, such as love, that lift our actions out of time, rigid duality, and expectation. Even in periods of immense suffering, these values help us relate to the present moment in such a way that we can go on with wisdom, instead of becoming lost in resignation or despair, or choosing anger as the only means to move forward.

We can nurture a new sense of our actions in many ways. In meditation, we can practice viewing the world more clearly and with increased wisdom, which inclines the mind towards faith. If we see, for example, how much everything and everyone is constantly changing, we realize that in the midst of change we are not trapped and that there can always be a sense of possibility; this realization dissolves hopelessness. In times of suffering, if we can still recognize the ties we have to others—i.e., that all are vulnerable to pain and loss, and that we are still held by the flow of life itself, even in our unhappiness, then in truth we are not cut off and alone; this power of connection awakens our love. In many ways, a spiritual path is essentially about connection – a deep connection to our own inherent capacity for wisdom and love no matter what, a connection to a bigger picture of life no matter what.

Over the last few years, even when despair has been growing in the world, I've heard many people speak about finding something inside them that they didn't know they had. Perhaps they remember to stay more connected to their deepest values, or to the immediacy of love, or to the need to live a meaningful life. One must draw on one's own deepest resources in order to move forward in times of great difficulty. Therefore, tools of spiritual development, such as meditation, are of inestimable value in bringing us in touch with the depths of wisdom and love within each of us. We can choose to pursue these for our own sakes, as well as for the benefit of all we may seek to help.

13
LISA RUSS

Lisa is currently the Associate Director of the Movement Strategy Center (www.movementstrategy.org), a movement-building intermediary dedicated to creating and delivering tools that support sustainable alliances to plan, thrive, and succeed together. We do this through the support of individuals, organizations, and alliances.

Lisa worked for 5 years as an outdoor experiential educator, working with groups of high school and middle school students on weeklong programs throughout California. In 1996, Lisa founded a program at Global Exchange called Exploring California, which integrates experience-based learning with human rights issues by providing multi-day trips throughout California that are focused on immigration, trade, and labor. These programs created and fostered partnerships with grassroots groups around the state, and engaged hundreds of students, teachers, journalists, activists, and others every year in deepening their understanding of the complex impacts of these policies.

Since 1999, Lisa has worked intensively with organizations as a consultant, mentor, coach, board member, and interim executive director, with the goal of building capacities of constituents to lead the organizations. Much of her work was focused on San Francisco's low-income neighborhoods during the intense period of gentrification in the Bay Area.

As MSC's Associate Director, Lisa provides direct support to groups (mostly through strategic planning), leads a consultant learning group, facilitates and supports emerging alliances, and nurtures MSC's internal development.

Lisa thrives in fresh air.

The question I am working with these days is how can my social change work, and the work of those I am engaged with, be more rooted in our best selves. Put very simply, much organizing work is based on the idea of identifying "targets," the people who can give us what we want (a landlord who controls the fate of a building, a policy maker with the power to pass legislation funding head start, a CEO we want to agree to outside monitoring of her factories). The basic plan is to create enough energy or pressure from multiple directions to convince the target to agree to do things our way. We build this energy or pressure by educating and mobilizing "our people" into pushing the target to move.

It doesn't usually feel good to be part of these efforts, which are soaked in opposition and anger. The culture of this kind of interaction is rooted in many of the organizations and coalitions that strive to make change, which makes it difficult to engage and sustain participation over time and beyond a small group of people.

At Movement Strategy Center, we are looking at ways to shift the culture of opposition into a more sustainable approach to social change. This is very difficult, of course, as often these campaigns are born from a feeling of powerlessness and desperation, and after much abuse has been absorbed by those in the position of having less power.

We are approaching this in several ways. We understand this work to be culture shifting, which requires reaching many people over a long period of time in order to take root. One way we are doing this is through our Spirit in Motion program, which provides support to individuals and organizations through individual sessions and large and small group work. The following assumptions underlie this work:

- Many of us come to social change work with significant pain from our life experiences, many of which are rooted in our powerlessness (including economic hardship, domestic violence, poor education, etc);
- The power imbalances we are fighting are real (not just perceived) and have been constructed over time, in some ways very intentionally (systems of race, class, and gender oppression), and their deconstruction will need to be just as intentional and powerful;
- Healing ourselves is the first step toward creating positive change;
- Much of the "movement culture" reinforces ways of distancing ourselves from our own healing; we must create space and permission to take time to even notice how we are feeling and then to address it. The pressure to work "fast and furiously" is often driven by/reinforced by our own pain, and our clinging to this work style is both a cause and effect of our continued numbness or pain;
- We don't have the answers to HOW we do this work, but are committed to engaging with the question and reflecting on our own experiences as a way of learning;
- While we do not believe necessarily that "the enemy will be disarmed by love," we do believe that to build effective, sustainable movements that engage people and can win, we need to be rooted in a powerful foundation of love.

We strive to bring individuals and organizations permission and tools for becoming awake to our own experience, and bringing that reality into our social change work.

We hope that over time, this leads to:

- A change in workstyle, toward a pace that is more sustainable over time, that allows activists and organizers to tend to their own physical, social, psychological, and financial needs, rather than placing them in opposition;
- A heart-felt recognition that those who are fighting for justice are worthy of benefiting, and that suffering as activists brings change about more slowly, not more quickly. If we allow ourselves to have healthy lives, resilient and powerful relationships, and thriving families, we are in fact creating the change we want to see more quickly;
- The ability to engage and maintain more allies! Folks that have been turned off by our combative style and our insistence on purity (and suffering) will be drawn to our healthy relationships, the fun we have at parties, and the success we each have in our own lives and goals (if I can't dance, I don't want to be part of your revolution!!).

MSC is also developing a model that looks at the relationship between organizing, racial justice, spirituality, and organization development. The idea is that the way each of these is practiced currently is often in direct conflict with the other areas. We are working with a group of OD practitioners to explore ways to create and use a framework that brings what is most alive in each of these areas into alignment with the other areas. This will be used as a way to help groups assess their work, and see whether and how to shift areas of their work to encourage dynamic interplay rather than destructive tension.

How are Love and Compassion Integral to the Success of Social Justice Work?

By holding love and compassion as central, it is possible to create the change we want to see. When I am compassionate for myself, for the ways in which I am selfish or small, I can be compassionate toward the person who I perceive as preventing us from having what we want. Rather than creating polarized "us/them" struggles, we can unite on what we share (e.g., wanting the best for our children).

It is a lifetime of work to develop compassion for those I perceive as enemies, but every time I do it, even for a second, I am more free. It is also a lifetime of work to consistently do my work from a place of love. Every time I do it though, I am creating more love in the world. In order to do this, I need space to examine my purpose and my drive, to heal the places in me that are not loved and that are afraid. When I am able to do this, I am able to see beyond the oppositional and into the united.

Social justice is most powerful when creating alternatives, rather than fighting what exists. This takes immense energy to begin and to sustain. Love and compassion for self and others is required when staking out this terrain in order to create a vision that does not collapse into ego, personal gain, or fear.

What Beliefs and Practices Successfully Give Rise to or Sustain Activism?

The practice of reflection seems like the key to effective activism: reflecting on what drives us and what feeds us, reflecting on how our actions impact others.

The other practice we are striving to instill in our work is long-term visioning and planning. Part of what leads to frustration and burnout is our tendency to fight campaigns reactively, and to plan only 1-3 years into the future. When we are able to think 30-50 years ahead, we have the opportunity to envision and plan for real change.

In order to conceive and plan for change on a large scale, we need to be able to work effectively in coalitions, networks, and alliances—i.e., groups and individuals who sign up for a long-term change are larger than any individual or distinct goal. We are striving to develop tools for supporting groups to do this kind of work together.

Research should be focused on identifying effective examples of efforts that were led by a positive vision of what is possible, and pulling out what made them work. This involves sharing information in accessible formats and creating places (virtual and physical) where information is located and easily accessed.

14
ANDRE CAROTHERS

Andre Carothers is Executive Director of the non-profit Rockwood Leadership Program and is a life-long agitator, including a 13-year stint on the staff and Board of Directors of Greenpeace.

Andre is currently on the Board of Directors of the Rainforest Action Network and the Center for Environmental Health. In the past, he has served on the board of the California Institute of Integral Studies and the Solar Living Institute. He regularly trains and consults for non-profit leaders, their organizations, coalitions, and networks. He holds a Master's Degree from the Energy and Resources Group at the University Of California in Berkeley.

> *The improvement of society does not call for any essential change in human nature, but, chiefly, for a larger and higher application of its familiar impulses.*
> *—Charles Horton Cooley*

For those of us engaged in full-time advocacy and its allied support functions (in our case, training non-profit leaders), the perennial question is: how can we further develop our ability to successfully achieve our social change goals? The mission of the Rockwood Leadership Program is to strengthen the movement for progressive social change by delivering training and consultation to established non-profit and civic leaders, organizations, coalitions and networks.

In this paper I will:
- Describe the Rockwood Leadership Program's training curriculum and orientation;
- Review survey data that discuss the reported value received by clients of the program;
- Discuss the relevance of Rockwood to the links between helping behavior, spiritual insight, and political effectiveness;
- Offer tentative conclusions about further study and effort.

BACKGROUND

In 2000, Rockwood assembled a team to develop, deliver, and assess a standardized and carefully scripted curriculum for a short (three-day, 27-30 hours) intensive workshop billed as the "Inner Arts of Effective Leadership." The goal of the training was to link a "spiritual" approach to social change work with specific skills relevant to the workplace, and to the orientation of people who have committed their lives to social change.

The development team was chosen for:

- Experience developing and leading workshops based in training modalities associated with inner development and self-awareness;
- Experience with private sector leadership training and management consulting, including whole-system and culture change inside large companies;
- Familiarity and experience working on environmental, economic, and social justice issues;
- Experience inside the senior leadership of large and medium-sized progressive non-profit organizations, coalitions and networks.

This team developed Rockwood's *Art of Leadership* training, as well as additional trainings and offerings, such as the *Art of Collaborative Leadership* and the Year-Long Intensive, that have emerged as a result of the high demand for our services.

The training has proven very popular (see data and discussion below) for individual leaders, as well as for networks or coalitions that assert the wish to forge a stronger value- and skill-based foundation for deeper collaboration, more effective implementation, and more ambitious and visionary outcomes.

Since its start in 2000, the Rockwood Leadership Program has trained more than 1,000 paid employees of non-profit advocacy organizations. The target population is overwhelmingly focused on environmental protection, social and economic justice, human rights, and, to a lesser degree, direct aid. It is notably skewed toward groups and individuals with an interest in progressive values and policy outcomes —the "Democratic wing of the Democratic party" and beyond.

CURRICULUM

The central guiding tenet of all Rockwood trainings, made explicit on Day One, is that in order to be successful and fulfilled in the long term, we must align inner and outer forces, and "be the change we wish to see in the world." In addition to providing communication, conflict resolution, presentation, and other essential leadership skills, the Art of Leadership and its offspring explicitly focus on the development of a "spiritual" posture regarding life, defined as:

- Searching for and adopting a strong and self-transcending purpose and mission in life—to serve a cause greater than one's self;

- The desire to achieve a deep level of inner self-awareness;
- Self-transcendence: the awareness of the limits and subjectivity of individual perceptions of reality;
- The desire to be compassionate toward others, and to serve the well-being, both inner and outer, of others;
- Gratitude and acceptance of "life as it is."

The training is built and framed around seven practices of leadership—Purpose; Vision; Partnership; Emotional Intelligence; Performance; Authenticity; Personal Ecology. The curriculum employs framing, exercises, and perspectives drawn from personal growth training workshops, corporate leadership training programs, communication and conflict resolution skills training, the perennial wisdom(s), contemplative disciplines, and emotional intelligence work. Examples and stories used include lessons from the most successful organizations, the lives of prominent social change leaders, and exemplars of spiritually-based social change leadership, such as Gandhi and Martin Luther King.

We consider it a "transformative" experience, in that we fully intend for participants to examine deeply their "current state" as leaders, their capacity to see and choose their mission and purpose in life, the level of and nature of their commitment to social change, and their willingness to step outside their psychological frames and perspectives toward both a "witness stand" to their own lives and toward intimacy and empathy with the experience of others.

Outcomes

A considerable majority of participants in the *Art of Leadership* and the other Rockwood offerings describe the training as an important milestone in their development as social change leaders. The comments found in the many feedback surveys we solicit illustrate, generally speaking, three types of outcomes:

1) Utilitarian: The development of a specific skill related to a desirable characteristic of successful leadership. For example:

"I learned to give feedback that is more authentic and accurate, and now I am much more effective in producing results I need from my team."

"I think it's fair to say that all of the 30-plus participants—all non-profit or foundation leaders—found this a powerful experience. I don't think there's a person in the group who is not now working for social change more efficiently and more effectively."

"The survey of my colleagues' assessment of my strengths and weaknesses was most helpful. It helped me identify some weaknesses that had been in my "blind spots." It also taught me the value

of finding ways of providing feedback to colleagues on an ongoing basis."

2) Personal/Transformative: An insight linked to the curriculum that is deeper than day-to-day work, and that can serve in some instances as an impetus for deeper inquiry into who I am, and who I am becoming. For example:

"I learned that I have an impact on people just by being there, and that I need to understand the other person first, and be aligned with them, regardless of how I am feeling."

"I saw how my emotions can take over and make me smaller than I really am. I am learning how to be calm and centered in each interaction."

"What I thought was being smart and strategic was in many ways actually being selfish and afraid. This work is making me so much more courageous and visionary, and relaxed and accepting at the same time."

3) Transpersonal/Transcendent: An assertion of an insight that resulted from the training that can be credibly linked to current definitions of "spiritual" insight. For example:

"The Art of Leadership is invaluable to keeping the energy, the passion and the spirit flowing in this work. This workshop helped me to identify personal issues and patterns that limit my ability to be the most effective team leader that I could be. I leave with passion pulsing from my fingertips once again, ready to continue on the path for social change with my heart and eyes wide open."

"This gathering has fostered courage on the part of all of us to address conflicts in our community such as sexism, racism, and competitiveness. The openness here has allowed us to acknowledge our need to treat each other, even those who oppose us, with respect and compassion. I think we have matured through this experience—we are now committed to merging the guiding principles of compassion and justice, as taught by Gandhi, Buddha and Jesus, with our day-to-day work. I am sure the causes we work for are served by a more open and compassionate corps of activists deeply rooted in the meaning of their work."

"The Art of Leadership training taught me concrete management skills that I can apply immediately. But more importantly, I am able to link management and leadership with the more elusive questions of self, soul and spirit. It's like someone pulled back the curtain and revealed to me the twelve other levels on which the work is taking place."

All three categories of learning are consistently found in the survey data generated after the trainings. They also are regularly found in one person's responses—that is, there is no evidence that one type of reported insight precludes another.

DISCUSSION

> *Education is…the knowledge of how the soul can most easily and*
> *most effectively be turned around—Plato*

Despite the lack of a consensual definition, most authors' definitions of spirituality include elements such as transcendence of personal concerns, connectedness to others, finding meaning and purpose in life, and a sense of inner peace. Spirituality is variously described as a way of being, an "energizing force that propels individuals to reach their optimal potential," and "a sense of spiritual, psychological, physical health and well-being."

While relatively few of our graduates subscribe to a conventional ("God-based") view of their spirituality, the vast majority ascribes considerable meaning and purpose to their social change work, maintaining that it is "more than a job"—that the work is central to their sense of themselves. Many also describe their work as frustrating, draining, "too much." And, they are, generally speaking, not particularly patient with appropriations of their time and energy that are not perceived as germane to their work. They can be a "tough audience" for training of any kind.

It is perhaps safe to say, generally speaking and with exceptions, that our community reports that the pressures associated with the choice to devote their lives to systematic social change in the context of an organization or "movement struggle" is thought of as a sacrifice to be tolerated in pursuit of a professional goal—rather than a life process capable of offering avenues of self-development and moments of joy, grace, peace, and fulfillment.

The range of frustrations reported parallels the range of reported outcomes described above. Social change professionals desire greater facility and skill in their jobs, a greater sense of personal well-being and grace in their interactions, and a stronger connection to their stated purpose in life and to the larger "arc of history" as it pertains to their pursuit of social, economic, and environmental justice.

Drawing on a not untypical, if generous, definition of spiritual growth— "spiritual transformation is evidenced when one embraces a new and broadened perspective in life and transcends beyond difficulties" (Benjamin & Looby, 1988), it is apparent that the Rockwood training more than achieves this goal for the vast majority of participants. And, very importantly for us, the insights gained from the training are very clearly linked to political results.

The survey data, and our reasonable extrapolation of it, suggest that this can be attributed to:

- Careful choices regarding wording, framing, and examples, all of which are designed to be familiar to people who have chosen to devote their lives to progressive social change;
  o For example, the training curriculum deliberately eschews much of the lan-

guage associated with spirituality, concentrating instead on framing the curriculum as centered on issues of mission and purpose, leadership, collaboration, vision, self-aware-ness, communication, authenticity, emotional intelligence, and self-care. (If, as often happens, a participant comments that he/she "had no idea that the training would be so spiritual," we tend to, like the Pentagon, neither confirm nor deny the accusation.)

- Our choice to position the training, by careful choice of language, framing, and the selection and discussion of exercises, as central to their success as non-profit leaders—that "how we are on the inside" is inextricably and intimately linked to our ability to achieve our social change goals;
- A careful selection of curriculum and trainers.

Needless to say, these results beg for further analysis to create a more refined picture of the causes and effects of the training. It is probably safe to infer, though, that other-regarding behavior and the other characteristics that we are interested in introduc-ing to life-long non-profit leaders can be taught fairly cheaply and easily, and that there is a clear link between a spiritual perspective on life and tangible political results.

I welcome inquires from all disciplines into how we can analyze further the dynamics of this phenomenon, in order that we may "help the helpers" more effectively, graciously, and comprehensively.

References

1) Benjamin, P. & Looby, J. (1988). Defining the nature of spirituality in the context of Maslow's and Roger's theories. *Counseling & Values* 42:92-100.

15
BETTY ROGERS

Betty A. Rogers is a writer, audio producer, and media consultant with extensive field experience in Africa, South Asia, Europe, and Latin America. She has enjoyed a 23-year association with non-commercial radio production (National Public Radio), UN Radio, and Public Radio International. Her work has alternated between radio documentary and consulting on development of effective media strategies. Her last decade of work was spent exploring issues around violence against women, sex trafficking of young girls into prostitution, and integrating women into the political process. Her spiritual practice is rooted in the Methodist faith tradition of her birth and a practice of Tibetan Buddhism.

> *"The common eye sees only the outside of things, and judges by that, but the seeing eye pierces through and reads the heart and soul, finding there capacities which the outside didn't indicate or promise, and which the common could not detect."*
>
> Mark Twain.

My aspiration for engaged spirituality is to live an ever more seamless life that steadily dissolves distinctions between the personal and the professional, and between outer and inner experiences. My own tendencies to reduce or increase suffering around me seem in proportion to how bound I am by labels or expectations. My level of inner resistance to work, people, or obstacles is a rather reliable measure of my potential for disengagement.

One memorable experience of transformative seamlessness occurred at the 1993 UN Human Rights Conference in Vienna. I arrived steeped in the familiar rhetoric of U.N. conferences: Rich vs. Poor Nations; Male vs. Female; North vs. South; Activists vs. Researchers vs. Politicians. The Bosnian war and its atrocities were at a high pitch only a few hundred miles away.

The Tribunal on Violence against Women, which I covered for NPR, shifted that viewpoint. Women survivors of violence from every continent transcended fear and shame to speak aloud their stories: a Pakistani bride set on fire by her husband; a young

American woman sexually abused by her university professor father; a Muslim woman raped in Serbian ethnic cleansing. Activists and researchers framed the personal with far-ranging studies and statistics.

The tribunal soon demonstrated that whether rich, poor, educated, uneducated, black, or white, all women stood at risk for violence in a documented global war on women. Mid-morning, I left the sound recording booth to readjust a speaker's microphone that had been knocked out of position. As I opened the theatre doors, a wave engulfed me that I could even sense across the surface of my skin---not of anger, but of a profound and attentive silence. My tiptoes to the stage seemed to echo like gunshots in the packed audience. This shared transcendence generated a sanctuary for confronting a very dark side of human nature. By the closing remarks, its safety had transformed us all.

Yes, we heard horrifying stories. Bok Dong Kim testified as a Korean "comfort woman" imprisoned as a sex slave for conquering Japanese soldiers in WWII. The Japanese authorities calculated that one female could sexually satisfy twenty-nine men a day. The men waited their turn in long lines outside Bok Dong Kim's workplace: a bed in a crude building partitioned by dirty blankets, filled with captive women at work without adequate food or sleep. Many suffered venereal diseases, tuberculosis, and other chronic conditions; many died in their beds. As the Allies approached, soldiers chained the women to beds and siphoned off their blood for their own wounded.

Yet this elderly woman later spoke of new hope after finally naming aloud the indignities her own husband had never heard. Many of us left inspired and focused even as the UN conference itself collapsed into factions (mired in its own contradiction that U.N. delegates represent the world's governments; governments commit or sanction all human rights violations). This forum launched my decade-long activism on trafficking. I continue to wonder how we might sustain this "seamless" transcendence of suffering and also our commitment when it appears absent.

Engagement often strengthens when we grasp that many of the social ills and conditions we fight to change are not new phenomena. Researchers and archivists can cultivate this "long view" approach. For example, sex trafficking was once carried out by horse and carriage; today's world trade first evolved with the global shipping routes that appeared near the beginning of the last century. It is the magnitude of the current exploitation and profit that is unprecedented and overwhelming, not the dynamics.

The data and case stories within this magnitude can sometimes paralyze us. The current sex trade relies on airplanes, automobiles, fax, e-mail, cellular phones, and even satellite communication to generate a steady supply of females for a thriving and expanding sex market. Post-war economics and international lending policies are increasing the pool of young women uprooted from their communities through unemployment, low wages, environmental degradation, or modern agriculture. Natural disasters, war, civil conflict, and the population boom of the last decades force young women from their homes.

Even this short, simple checklist can bring concerned persons to their knees. I have repeatedly wrestled with my own despair and anger. Sex trafficking and many other social justice issues are urgent and immediate; the perspective is global, national, and yet intimately personal. Spiritual engagement encourages us to commit to practices of inner development of comparable magnitude. Creating a larger community of concern can also reduce the stress of paying close attention.

Engaged spirituality affirms that vibrant life forces exist in the midst of the worst suffering. In recognizing these slender threads of resilience, we gain new starting points. I have witnessed them everywhere. In the midst of the Sudan famine, each morning a ridge of odd bumps on the horizon materialized as the newest wave of starving refugees by nightfall. Weakened by days of trudging through desert heat, the malnourished survivors doggedly set up tents. By the next morning, they would renew their practice of prayers and ancient coffee rituals surrounded by their sick and dying---even as the next distant wave of destitution appeared.

At nighttime in the Kapenguria Hospital pediatric ward in western Kenya, critically ill children sleep encircled in their small beds with a pile of caring parents and siblings who had braved a first trip away from their remote rural village. In the brothels of Burma, young girls trafficked in from China and Cambodia comb each other's hair and massage foreheads before the evening work begins. Engaged spirituality can condition us to trust in, look for, and recognize these tender signs as entry points that invite new possibilities and counter the fallout of burnout and despair.

Activists and researchers share a fundamental goal to transform suffering. Our conference honors our common need to expand our potential to transform----and reconnects me to an insight gained years ago in doing interviews or visiting project sites: No matter the country or culture, with or without translators, in a refugee camp or five-star hotel, when I am fully present and listen attentively, my work transforms both me and the others. When I am distracted or unprepared, we depart little-changed or out of balance. I welcome this chance to hear what others have discovered.

HOW ARE LOVE AND COMPASSION INTEGRAL TO THE SUCCESS OF SOCIAL JUSTICE WORK?

> *"True compassion is not just an emotional response, but a firm commitment founded on reason. Therefore a truly compassionate attitude toward others does not change, even if they behave negatively. Through universal altruism, you develop a feeling of responsibility for others: the wish to help them actively overcome their problems."*
>
> *The Dalai Lama of Tibet*

I am grateful (and relieved) to work at this time when compassion, love, and other invisible dimensions of our minds are gaining a new respect and value. We are no longer reduced to only what we can see or quantify. Many are drawn to the Dalai Lama and the Tibetan Buddhism tradition because Tibetan practitioners invested their energy and resources into conquering the inner mind and the cause of suffering-- while the West made gigantic strides in the material external world. We are privileged to participate in this early fusion of material and mental expertise.

Compassion and love are among our strongest states of being. A stable experience and practice also requires that we first learn to be compassionate and loving to ourselves, and then gradually extend this capacity outward to others. This approach is much harder that it might appear, and is often neglected in goal-oriented projects. "If it's true that how we treat ourselves eventually expresses itself in how we treat others," psychologist Lorne Ladner observes, "then any tendency toward harming yourself works directly against compassion."

WHAT BELIEFS AND PRACTICES SUCCESSFULLY GIVE RISE TO OR SUSTAIN ACTIVISM?

"Injustice anywhere is a threat to justice everywhere. We are caught in an inescapable network of mutuality, tied in a single garment of destiny. Whatever affects one directly, affects all indirectly."

Dr. Martin Luther King

The often challenging practices of meditation, conscious breathing, listening, and laughter can be good antidotes for staying engaged. The all-purpose belief in the interconnectedness of all beings and things is often valuable.

Another useful touchstone is that, in any given moment, we have the choice to mindfully consider ways to live with genuine purpose, energy, and joy, or to risk the possibility that life can pass us by. Any time we are aware and awake in any given moment, whether in solitude or in the midst of great injustice, we have the capacity to make that moment extraordinary.

A root practice is to develop a personalized approach to observing and transforming our own afflictive emotions as a contribution to the success of social justice activism. Any practice that trains and attunes our minds and bodies can only help--- from yoga to meditation to anger management to self-hypnosis practices. Has there ever been such widespread access to so many innovative possibilities for self transformation?

WHERE SHOULD RESEARCH IN THIS FIELD BE DIRECTED AND FOCUSED?

"When we want to understand something, we cannot just stand outside and observe it. We have to enter deeply into it and be one with it in order to understand."

Thich Nhat Hanh

I would always be interested in research on what enhances or blocks our capacity to generate compassion. A training manual for those working in arenas of suffering could be developed, tested in focus groups, and revised for effective implementation.

Perhaps a review of the ways sports training programs have appropriated meditation and mental techniques for enhanced athletic performance might suggest new approaches.

A N.Y. Times cover story on sex trafficking of young women from the former Soviet Union into Israel reported: "Economic hopelessness in the Slavic world has opened what experts call the most lucrative market of all to criminal gangs . . . white women with little to sustain them but their dreams." The article led me to question social workers as to whether this intangible "dream" could also serve as an intervention point for preventing trafficking. I did eventually discover a program in the Netherlands that created "action strategies" based on reconstruction of original "dreams" for young women suffering the psychological lethargy common among trafficking survivors. It would be helpful to better understand what mental states make people more vulnerable to victimization, poverty, or suffering, and, conversely, which mental states enhance prevention and survival.

HOW CAN RESEARCHERS HELP ACTIVISTS IN THEIR WORK, AND HOW CAN ACTIVISTS HELP RESEARCHERS?

"We are already one. But we imagine that we are not. And what we have to recover is our original unity. What we have to be is what we are." Thomas Merton

Each might help the other to use their talents and resources to create and cultivate visions of unity. I recently read a paper by Jim Tucek, a student at Washington University, on how quantum physics differs from traditional physics: *"The model of an atom that you were taught in high-school is wrong. The electrons don't orbit like planets; they form blurred clouds of probabilities around the nucleus."* That language makes me wonder whether researchers might work to distinguish between "traditional" and "quantum" models for social action, where the "blurred clouds of probabilities" of compassion and love contribute. Perhaps generating new models and frameworks would make an activist's program goals more compelling to funders open to pioneering approaches.

Activists might guide researchers to frame the collection of data and its analysis in a more dynamic flow that invites fluid approaches to prevention and solution. They might work together to learn how to cultivate and maintain positive mindsets in the face of social justice issues that exist on a global scale.

Research is always welcome on the challenging issues surrounding cross-cultural communication, conflict resolution, and the careful listening required for effective action. A mutual respect for both hard data and anecdotal insights might further cooperation.

16
MIRABAI BUSH

Mirabai Bush is Director of the Center on Contemplative Mind in Society, a nonprofit organization whose mission is to encourage contemplative awareness in American life in order to create a more just, compassionate, and reflective society. Established in 1995, the Center works to create cultural climates that value contemplative practice as a significant aspect of a vibrant, diverse, democratic society. The Center has coordinated a series of contemplative retreats for corporations, conducted a survey of contemplative practice, and established a Contemplative Practice Fellowship awards program with the American Council of Learned Societies to explore such practices in academic courses. The Contemplative Law Program engages law students, law faculty, and attorneys in an exploration of the role of contemplative practice in legal education and the practice of law. The Center also sponsors a program on contemplative training for youth leaders, and an initiative to bring contemplative practices into social justice organizations.

*Mirabai formerly directed the **Seva Foundation Guatemala Project,** which supports sustainable agriculture and integrated community development. She co-developed Sustaining Compassion, Sustaining the Earth, a series of retreats and events for grassroots environmental activists on the interconnection of spirit and action. Several of these retreats are described in Nourishing the Roots of Social Activism and Reclaiming Our Common Strength for the Common Good, prepared for Cummings and New World Foundations. She is co-author, with Ram Dass, of Compassion in Action: Setting Out on the Path of Service.*

How is engaged spirituality, which is rooted in generosity and love, practiced and sustained in social justice work? What are the links between spirituality, love for a common humanity, justice, and active efforts to solve social problems?

At the Center for Contemplative Mind in Society, encouraging contemplative practice in secular life seemed at first to be an unlikely strategy for social change, but it is proving to have extremely positive and practical potential for the creation of a more just and compassionate society. The contribution of contemplative practices to stress reduction and enhanced well-being is widely documented. But we are now also seeing that contemplative awareness can enhance wise, compassionate citizenship, activism, and leadership in every sector of American life. We are not, of course, saying that contemplative awareness alone will lead to a fully just and sustainable society, but that it can make a critical contribution when combined with education, analysis, and resources. We also recognize that the practices must be taught with skill and integrity in order to have positive impact. The programs we have begun are not easy, and they do not always produce short-term improvement; they are seeds of change for a long-term sustainable cultural shift in our individual and social lives.

The goal is liberation, of each of us and of all of us. Inner (or spiritual) liberation reveals states such as compassion, wisdom, loving kindness, sympathetic joy, and equanimity; outer (or social) liberation means a life on earth that includes not only basic human needs of food, shelter, and clothing, but less tangible needs such as good work, respect, sense of belonging, security, rootedness, and freedom. The goal of liberation is the work of many kinds of people on the planet—rich and poor, formally and naturally educated, of every race, age, and spiritual tradition. So when we talk about offering contemplative practices to activists, the potential constituency is very large. It includes grassroots activists, foundation staff and donors, politicians, and members of all kinds of organizations in society committed to social change.

These practices are a set of tools for overcoming fundamental obstacles to leading effective, creative, and compassionate lives. They address the causes of burnout: stress; psychic exhaustion; anger; fear; frustration; loss of motivation. They awaken insight, wisdom, and compassion. They link people's inner and outer lives. Although religious and spiritual institutions and some psychological programs have traditionally performed this function, the Center and other secular organizations are now offering diverse contemplative opportunities in secular settings that are designed to be appropriate for particular sectors of society. The Center has hosted contemplative retreats for a wide range of activists and leaders in environment, law, media, philanthropy, youth leadership, and other sectors of American life. Participants report renewed energy and motivation for themselves, improved interpersonal skills with others, and a deeper sense of interconnection with others in their field and with the planet as a whole.

These practices also awaken a wide range of questions at the heart of activism: If I give up my anger, will I still be motivated to work for change? Can I have compassion for an adversary and still be a zealous advocate? Can I accept things as they are in the moment and still work whole-heartedly for change in the future? How can I do a practice of silence when throughout my life I have been silenced by others? These questions are usually best addressed through a combination of experiencing practice and discussion with others who have common concerns.

A study funded by Ford Foundation and others found that religious belief and participation emerged as key indicators of civic involvement, though Robert Putnam (author of Bowling Alone) also cautions that "people with strong religious views and connections also tended to rate lower than average in tolerance for people with ideas different from their own." On the other hand, we have heard repeatedly from participants in our retreats that meditation, walking the labyrinth, contemplative arts, and other contemplative practices learned outside a religious setting increased their tolerance, compassion, and ability to see the positions of others and work creatively with them. At a meeting on philanthropy and the inner life, Leah Wise of the Southeast Network for Economic Justice, who works with ethnically and racially diverse groups toward a common goal, said, "The real work is developing ways to address our differences and build community together.... Building a community of inclusiveness requires the spiritual practices of ritual and celebration." Pat Harbour, Director of Healing the Heart of Diversity at Fetzer, includes meditation, contemplative music, and altar building in all their training sessions. Awakening the wise heart outside any parochial form is proving to be powerfully healing in socially diverse settings. (This is not to make a "new age" distinction of spirituality vs. religion—we just note that sometimes religious affiliation can reinforce a sense of "us" and "them," and that does not seem to be a factor in the secular settings in which we have worked.)

During the first stage of the Center, we interviewed 40 well-respected teachers of contemplative practice from diverse religious, spiritual, and secular traditions. One of many questions we asked them was this: What is the connection between contemplation and social change? Most of these teachers stated that meditation not only does not lead to antisocial ("navel-gazing") behavior, but that there is a causal connection between contemplative practice and social action.

Many people experience a deepening sense of the interconnection of all life in the process of quieting and cultivating awareness; greater compassion flows out of this sense of interconnection. "It seems to me," Rabbi Meir Sendor explained, "that there are certain ethical postures or stances that you come to appreciate, to be understood more deeply as you meditate. A sense of equanimity that meditation helps generate also gives you a deeper sense of equality that spreads to your relationship to others, as you can diminish your own ego obsession and get a greater sense of reciprocity and mutuality. These are all the great principles of every moral tradition. It seems that, in a certain sense, meditation or contemplation, helps bring these principles alive. You get to understand them in a much deeper way. It's not just on the surface. It's not just weighing one thing against another. You really feel your sense of oneness with others, your connectedness with others, with all beings in the universe."

The relationship between contemplation and social action is deep, one balancing the other. Ram Dass points out that, "One shouldn't see it as contemplation versus action. I think contemplation is a form of action. I think that one needs a contemplative mind in order not to get trapped in seeing things a single way, which can be the predicament of the activist."

Some teachers are concerned about the dangers. Rabbi Omer-Man cautioned that meditation could also be used as a way to avoid dealing with life. "My concern was that people - my students and other practitioners - were using meditation for a means to become too detached when there was a need to be attached." But Rabbi David Cooper reminds us that it is about balance: "In our day, you need both; you can't do one without the other. If you become a person of incredible social action and you're just out there, burning the candle at both ends, what happens is you burn out very quickly. You need a place where you can come back and regenerate yourself. On the other hand if you just go inside and become completely dedicated to practice and don't have social consciousness and social action in mind, what happens is you shrivel up and lose your juices." Father Thomas Keating also felt that "contemplation is the basis for social action, in the sense that without contemplation such action can be draining, while if one's activity is rooted in a spiritual center nourished by contemplative prayer, there is much greater chance of perseverance and effectiveness in one's service."

In 2002, The Center conducted a multi-phase qualitative research study aimed at revealing and supporting the use of contemplative practices in organizations and programs. Forty leaders in the field of integrating contemplative practices into social justice work were interviewed. Our key findings were:

- For the great majority of interviewees, social justice work and contemplative practice are inseparably linked;
- Contemplative awareness helps to provide a balance to some of the inherent challenges of social justice work and contributes greatly to the effectiveness and sustainability of this work;
- While the benefits of contemplative practices for individuals have been well-documented, this study revealed a multitude of ways that practice in a group and organizational context has transformed the way people work and function as a group;
- The Contemplative Organization is emerging as a distinct entity that uses contemplative practices as both a technique and an organizing principle;
- Interviewees faced the challenge of offering contemplative practices in a secular setting in innovative ways, and place a premium on finding language and teaching approaches that make practices accessible to a wide audience;
- Research participants generally feel that they are part of a broader movement, but identified a need for this movement to be better defined and more inclusive.

WHAT ARE THE PRACTICES THAT SUCCESSFULLY GIVE RISE TO OR SUSTAIN ACTIVISM?

When we asked people in the study to tell us about the kinds of contemplative practices they use in their work, they described an amazing number of practices. Certainly, contemplative practice can take the form of a lone meditator sitting on a cushion in an empty, quiet room. But it can also manifest as a group of high-energy environmentalists slicing tomatoes in preparation for a dinner together, or a group of social activists listening and speaking to each other in an intense, yet focused conversation. Father Thomas Keating noted that, "Contemplative practices are quite varied and they emphasize different parts of the psyche."

Intention is a critical factor. Many activities not included here (gardening, practicing a musical instrument, taking a bath) could be considered contemplative when done with the intent of cultivating awareness, attentiveness, sensitivity, and a stronger connection to God/Spirit and/or one's inner wisdom. And a practice can be included in more than one category, depending on the context. For example, chanting can be either a Generative or a Creative Process practice (or both).

Stillness Practices: Practices that cultivate stillness, with the intention of quieting the mind, increasing awareness, and/or creating space for God/wisdom to come forward—e.g., insight meditation.

Movement Practices: Practices that emphasize movement of the body as a path to awareness and connection—e.g., yoga, tai chi.

Creation Process Practices: Practices that emphasize artistic creative process rather than product—e.g., calligraphy, brushwork, sand mandala.

Relational Practices: Practices that involve communicating either with others or oneself in a reflective process—e.g., deep listening.

Generative Practices: "Generative: the ability to give birth, to bring into being, or to evoke." Practices done with the intention of generating devotion to God/Spirit/the Divine, or evoking compassion, love, etc.—e.g., lectio divina.

Ritual/Cyclical Practices: Practices done either alone or in community to mark passages of time or milestones in a person's life, to acknowledge and/or catalyze change—e.g., Sabbath rituals.

Activist Practice: Work/activism as practice; "Compassionate action, if done in the right frame of mind and heart, is contemplative practice" (Joan Halifax).

There are also contemplative practices in every spiritual tradition that focus specifically on love. These are especially helpful for engaged spiritual activists. They must, like all practices, be done with right intention and moral/ethical guidance, or they can lead the way to fundamentalism. When done with the intention to increase awareness and deepen community, they are powerful methods for change. Here are some examples:

Christianity: A deeper faithfulness to the spirit of the gospel of love
- The Prayer of St. Francis of Assisi: "Lord, make me an instrument of your peace. Where there is hatred, let me sow love...."
- Pilgrimage: "The ultimate aim of the quest, if one is to return,
- must be neither release nor ecstasy for oneself, but the wisdom and the power to serve others. –Joseph Campbell

Buddhism:
- Lovingkindness ("metta") Meditation: Cultivation of unconditional, inclusive love, a love with wisdom. It has no conditions; it does not depend on whether one "deserves" it or not. It is not restricted to just friends and family, but extends out to include all living beings.
- Chanting the Heart Sutra: "The One is none other than the All, and the All none

other than the One. Take your stand on this, and the rest will follow of its own accord….."

Hinduism:
- Karma Yoga (the path of service): "Do all that you do for others without attachment to the fruits of your labors."

Islam:
- Wasifah (repetition of the names of Allah): "There is a means of polishing all things whereby rust may be removed. That which polishes the heart is the invocation of Allah."

Judaism:
- Singing: "For breath is the conduit to God, and song the sound of breath in love." --Rabbi Rami Shapiro

For more information, see www.contemplativemind.org for the Tree of Practices and the reports, "Inviting the World to Transform" and "Creating the Contemplative Organization: Lessons from the Field."

17
KENNETH BAILEY

For the past decade, Kenneth Bailey has worked within the fields of Youth Development, Community Building, and Organizational Development. Before starting his fellowship at MIT's Center for Reflective Community Practice, Bailey was an internal consultant at Third Sector New England (TSNE), assisting it in developing its organizational learning infrastructure and practices. While at Third Sector New England, he assisted in developing annual conferences, co-edited a Nonprofit Quarterly with Najma Nazy'at, Youth: Take A New Look, and developed an approach to organizational conflicts that culminated in the article "On Organizational Resolution" (published winter 2003). Outside of his responsibilities at TSNE, he trained several residents in community assets mapping and taught a course on community building at Cambridge College.

Bailey was recently a board member for Resource Generation, the Interaction Institute of Social Change's Community Building Curriculum, and the Nia Project. His prior work experience includes program development for Boston Freedom Summer, and capacity building at campuses nationwide with Campus Outreach Opportunity League.

With Project Communitas, Bailey is interested in figuring out how to bring many of the lessons he's learned as a practitioner to addressing "ordinary injustice," the ways that injustice and power play out in real interactions—in front of ordinary people's stoops, their bedrooms, corners, and backyards. Ordinary injustice never merits a protest or an action, but "hums along" and functions as the adhesive to larger more apparent forms of injustice. He's interested in figuring out ways to work within three particular scenes of struggle in order to reveal the normalized ordinary injustice in which they operate: communities struggling over public spaces as sites of contestation; communities dealing with their own atrocities; organizations dealing with noxious conflicts. The potential for profound social transformation is the common thread he sees within these kinds of scenes.

As I indicated in my bio sketch, some of my work background is in both organizational development and a field of neighborhood development called community building. I want to highlight a contribution I made to both of those areas as a preface to my questions for this conference.

A contribution I made to organizational development was an article asking leaders of organizations to rethink how they intervene in their organization's internal conflicts. In this article, I ask leaders to avoid their urge to go for obvious solutions to big and/or old organizational conflicts, as the consequences of these solutions could be detrimental to their organizations in the long run. I also ask leaders to seek the perspectives of others internal to their organization, yet external to the actual conflict, because they often have a pretty good sense of what's really going on with the conflict.

For the field of community building, I developed a workshop where community leaders and residents consider their neighbors as assets within their communities. Before starting the workshop, community leaders and residents often believe that they already consider all of their fellow neighbors as assets to their neighborhoods. Once they get into the meat of the workshop, however, leaders and residents tend to struggle with the idea that all of their neighbors are assets in an honest and practical way.

I give these two examples to say that one aspect of my work is about supplying practitioners with techniques to be better practitioners. And I believe these techniques are expressions of ideals.

A leader has to go against one's sense of the obvious solution to a problem and include the perspective of others; this is a technique of justice—i.e., it helps a leader do justice in a concrete situation. I also think that the work a community leader or a resident has to do to see all of their fellow residents as assets to their neighborhood is a technique of justice; it asks community leaders to develop a stance to difference in their neighborhoods in a practical and often difficult way.

An assertion about justice and other abstract ideals such as love and compassion is implicit in my work; it's one thing to speak it and another thing to apply it when it counts. I'm also asserting that general practitioners don't necessarily know how to practice the ideal they espouse when the rubber hits the road. This leads me to my question for our conference: How do I deal with disagreement about what it means to practice such abstract ideals?

For example, a friend of mine went to hear noted cultural critic and author Bell Hooks on a tour about one of her recent books on love. She told me that a few of the African-American women in the audience disagreed with Bell's critiques of black male-female amorous or love relationships. If I remember correctly, the argument focused on trying to get Bell to say whether she was asserting that black men aren't doing a good job of loving black women. The statement that stuck out for my friend, and for me as she told this story, was that one of the women said to Bell, "Don't tell me that I'm not being loved!"

Don't tell me that I'm not being loved!
Don't tell me that I'm not being just!
Don't tell me how to be just!
Don't tell me!

Those women might have been able to tell Bell Hooks that about their private relationships, but I don't know if the same applies to the public sphere – and I'm of many minds about my thinking here. I do want a kind of expression of love and respect for my niece and nephews in their school and after-school program. And I know that the kind of expression I want is thoroughly informed by East coast, owning class, intellectual exposure and the ideology that comes with it. So, where does teaching how to be just and loving end and cultural imperialism begin?

18
DIANE BIRAY GREGORIA

Diane is a Ph.D. Candidate studying sociology, social psychology, and organizational behavior at Harvard University. She is interested in the social consequences of compassion for organizations and social movements. As part of her dissertation project, she is working with the "Cultivating Emotional Balance Project," an initiative based at the University of California San Francisco Medical School. The project emerged from meetings organized by the Mind and Life Institute between His Holiness the Dalai Lama and the scientific community. The project is currently conducting a randomized clinical trial to test the efficacy of an 8-week training program that integrates Western psychology and secularized Buddhist meditations regarding the reduction of destructive emotions and the promotion of positive emotions. Diane's research specifically focuses on the social consequences of compassion as a strategy for regulating negative emotions in others. In terms of her study of social movements, she will also focus on the emotional dimensions of activist work as it relates to effective tactics and strategies for organizing.

Prior to graduate school, Diane worked for five years at Oxfam, an international development organization that supports anti-poverty and human rights projects in over 100 countries worldwide. There, she focused on programmatic issues related to gender, human rights, and microfinance, and was a staff-elected board member. She also conducted research and lobbying targeted at changing the World Bank's policies to be more supportive of and less harmful to the poor, the majority of whom are women and children.

Since 1994, she has been a student of Theravada and Tibetan Buddhism in the lineages of Thai master Ven. Ajahn Chah, His Holiness the Dalai Lama, and Lama Zopa Rinpoche. In terms of supporting the work of organizations promoting engaged spirituality, she is currently a board member of Stone Circles and Buddhist Peace Fellowship.

At the individual level, I see engaged spirituality as a self-reinforcing, ascendant, and virtuous cycle—a dance between service and awakening. The more we practice our spiritual path, the more we desire to be of service. The more we are of service, the more we are aware of the suffering that exists in the world, and the more fuel we have for spiritual inquiry. In turn, the more we engage in spiritual practice, the more wisdom, compassion, and energy we have to offer in service. In a sense, both elements of this dynamic are driven by the same questions: Why is there so much suffering in the world, and in myself? What, if anything, can we do about it?

The collective level of engaged spirituality is naturally contingent upon the processes of individual transformation. All the manifest forms of our society, including the people and institutions that perpetuate injustice, merely reflect the overall state of the human heart and mind. Until we transform the greed, hatred, and delusion within the human heart and mind, we are destined to perpetuate injustice despite our social, economic, and political struggles. Engaged spirituality at the collective level means finding ways to link the processes of individual transformation to the mainstream currents of society—while preserving the integrity of those processes and avoiding the degeneration of the wisdom traditions from which they spring. Emerging from this collective effort is the possibility of a "culture of awakening" that transcends and includes the plurality of traditions.

Given this daunting task, we must deepen our spiritual practice and build strength within our own spiritual communities. But we must move beyond our like-minded circle. We must engage with the mainstream in order to find skillful secular means of providing those who will never step into a monastery, church, or temple an opportunity to connect to that which is transcendent and transformative in themselves, and to link this with broader social transformation. I am fascinated by the potential languages we can use to bridge those worlds—whether it is psychology, sociology, integral philosophy, or human rights. At the same time, the effective translation of those languages can only be accomplished if we are grounded in our own practices, our own transformation, our own connection to the truth. Activism takes many forms, from avant-garde innovating from the edges to the tempered radicals making change from within the belly of the mainstream beast. In reality, we need both.

How are Love and Compassion Integral to the Success of Social Justice Work?

Love and compassion are absolutely essential to the success of social justice work because they help us to redefine what it means to have success, identify the "enemy," and determine the effective means for overcoming that enemy.

My thoughts about the role of love and compassion are fundamentally grounded in the Buddhist perspective on karma, or the law of cause and effect. It is taught that the fruits of an action rest on the state of our hearts and minds in the moment when that action is taken. Therefore, actions motivated by delusion, greed, and hatred will result in similarly unbeneficial effects. Often the problem for activists (for all of us, for that matter) is one of expectations and timeframe. Within a karmic context, we can control our mind state and our motivation in the moment of taking action. Due to the infinitely complex set of causes and conditions also at play in any given moment, we cannot control the ultimate fruits of that action. Based on our own direct experience, we rely instead on the sure-fire law of cause and effect: In the long run, virtuous mind states and activities inevitably lead to happiness, and non-virtuous mind states and activities inevitably lead to suffering. The workings of karma are said to be one of the Four Imponderables (others include the mind of a Buddha); therefore, it is basically impossible to comprehend the infinite threads of cause and effect at play in any given situation and when that karmic fruit will ripen.

That's nice, you might think, but let's get practical. The way that we get people to show up at rallies and engage in collective action is to create an "enemy," demonize them, and get people angry. I reply with two questions: 1) Is anger a sustainable source of energy for activism? 2) If we are clouded by greed, hatred, and delusion, can we see really see clearly how to cut through the Gordian knot of highly complex social problems?

Many times, I have heard concerns (even within my own mind) that practicing meditation may increase an activists' inner peace, but will cause us to "lose our edge." The assumption here is that anger, or a sense of righteous indignation, fuels our relentless efforts for change. On the contrary, I would argue that anger is a very limited source of energy for our social justice work. The experience of anger is often one of energetic constriction. In fact, many scientific studies have shown the detrimental physiological and psychological effects of sustained anger. While anger may be useful in the momentary fight-or-flight situation, it is just plain exhausting to maintain. By contrast, love and compassion are experiences of energetic expansion and spaciousness, with many positive physical and psychological effects. I am not referring to rosy and romantic ideas of love and compassion. Within the Buddhist tradition, genuine compassion is fundamentally infused with a sharp and discriminating wisdom that cuts through appearances to the ultimate nature of reality. To paraphrase a quote by His Holiness the Dalai Lama that I recently read, compassion energizes and gives us energy to take action to alleviate suffering. If our compassionate activities exhaust us, then it is a sure indication that our compassion is not sufficiently tempered with wisdom. Joseph Goldstein, another Buddhist teacher, once remarked that the only thing large enough to contain the vastness of suffering is the wisdom that realizes the ultimate truth. From this perspective, then, compassion and love are inherently more spacious and boundless sources of energy—not to mention psychologically and physiologically sustainable—than anger will ever be.

Secondly, to cut through the Gordian knot of our most intractable social problems, we need to call upon a clarity of mind and heart that is qualitatively different from the dynamic of suffering and confusion that caused these social problems in the first place. If attachment, anger, and confusion lie at the root of our social ills, does it follow that the solution to them lies in their perpetuation? From the Buddhist perspective, these destructive emotions are not only harmful in terms of their karmic consequences; they fundamentally distort our perception of reality so that we are less, not more, in touch with the way things really are. Thus, love and compassion are necessary to social justice work because they enhance our ability to understand the true nature of reality; they provide us with a clarity of heart and mind that begins to reverse the negative spirals that cause our social ills. Based on this more accurate view of the way things truly are, we are far more likely to be able to discern the most skillful way to act that will be of most benefit to the most sentient beings—i.e., to cut through this Gordian knot.

It is not possible to move beyond the dualism of "us vs. them" with a mind that is constricted by hatred and indifference. Therefore, love and compassion are also necessary to activist work because they enable us to break through this dichotomy to redefine our true "enemy." I am reminded of some concepts from the radical Christian theories of Liberation Theology; consistent with Buddhist perspectives, they argue that it is not possible to achieve social justice without attending as much to the liberation of the oppressor as well as the liberation of the people. In this light, the true enemy is an internal one. If the true enemy is internal, then this realization redefines the means through which we subdue that enemy. In all spiritual traditions, love and compassion are essential tools for subduing the enemies of ignorance, hatred, and greed. The question of how to translate this insight into practical activist strategies for social change is not a simple one, and must be driven by the specifics of a particular situation.

WHAT BELIEFS AND PRACTICES SUCCESSFULLY GIVE RISE TO OR SUSTAIN ACTIVISM?

I can only answer this question in terms of my own life. It is my experience that Mahayana Buddhism, specifically the Tibetan tradition of which I am a student, offers a truly vast array of beliefs and practices that successfully give rise to and sustain activism. A central spiritual ideal within this tradition is the bodhisattva. A bodhisattva is a being whose purpose in life is spiritual awakening, not just for herself, but to be of service to others by helping them to become free of unenlightened existence and realize their ultimate spiritual potential. In this teaching, I find a beautiful and profound integration of a life of service and social justice with a path of spiritual practice and awakening.

The practices of a bodhisattva are all aimed at the cultivation of bodhichitta, or the mind that aspires to realize full enlightenment for the benefit of all sentient beings. Bodhichitta is, in fact, a profound unity of compassionate methods and the wisdom that realizes the ultimate nature of reality. It is argued that it is not enough to to reach full enlightenment to develop extensive compassion; this compassion must be infused with a wisdom that understands how things really are. Likewise, it is not possible to realize the most subtle understanding of ultimate truth without the positive potentials created by compassion. In this light, bodhisattvas have a different definition of success and the means to that success. Bodhisattvas are, of course, in the business of alleviating suffering. However, there is the acknowledgement that until we have completely uprooted our own attachment, anger, and confusion, and fulfilled our ultimate spiritual potential (in other words, we have become buddhas), our efforts to help sentient beings in the most profound ways will always remain imperfect and incomplete. In a sense, this is a relief because it releases us from getting caught up in having particular results. By the same token, it does not let us off the hook—as part and parcel of our spiritual commitments, we must do everything we can to alleviate others' suffering. Perhaps the most important task of all is to deepen our spiritual practice.

To cultivate these mind states, it is said that the Buddha taught 80,000 means. Although Buddhism certainly has an extensive philosophical system, it also encompasses a very practical science of the mind, complete with very concrete meditation techniques for cultivating compassion and wisdom. In fact, there are currently many efforts to translate these techniques into non-religious contexts, including the project on which I am currently working called "Cultivating Emotional Balance." This project integrates Western psychology and secularized forms of Tibetan Buddhist practices for reducing destructive emotions and cultivating positive emotions (see biosketch).

I argue that being an effective activist is really not that different from becoming a fully integrated human being devoted both to processes of internal growth and engagement with the world. The fundamental point is to engage in the external transformation of society from the foundation of that internal transformation—using whatever means is effective for that particular mind, whether or not it is overtly spiritual.

WHERE SHOULD RESEARCH IN THIS FIELD BE DIRECTED AND FOCUSED?

Putting aside for the moment the thorny matter of whether we know what this "field" is, research should balance basic and applied approaches. In terms of basic research, at least from the perspective of my own disciplines of sociology and social psychology, there is much work to be done to understand the fundamentals of the positive processes involved in human flourishing and the cultivation of human strengths. For example, in emotions research, an area in which I am currently engaged, conducting basic research regarding the psychological and physiological concomitants of compassion and other positive emotions will be extremely valuable. Although activists may be uncomfortable with the longer time frames and not immediately useful findings involved in basic research, it is nonetheless important for deepening our understanding in the long run.

I am also an organizational behavior researcher, and consequently have a strong inclination towards applied research. I believe that organizations are one of the crucial locations in our society where people spend much of their time; therefore, they offer a promising site for catalyzing the links between inner transformation and societal change. Applied research in this area will be successful to the extent that findings translate into concrete practices and processes that are linked to improved outcomes and performance. While we may value these practices and processes in and of themselves, our performance-oriented culture will only pay attention if we attend to variables that are linked to improved outcomes. From the perspective of social movements research, f or example, there are many interesting questions about the link between the emotional dimensions of social organizing and effective strategies and tactics.

If these efforts are to last longer than the latest fad, they must be grounded in solid empirical research, as well as the foundation of whatever wisdom and compassion we have cultivated thus far. Since rigorous research will also require the involvement of colleagues who are not particularly of a spiritual bent, it is crucial to find a secular language to establish our common aspirations for happiness and the reduction of suffering. Continuing with a theme I sounded above, I believe that this type of research needs to be engaged with the mainstream—whether mainstream academia or mainstream social movements—in order to make the findings as accessible to as many people as possible. At the same time, innovative basic research must also be given space and resources. Of course, as in any emerging field, the work of junior as well as senior scholars should be supported.

In sum, I believe that reaching the pinnacle of human potential involves the channeling of the keenest intelligences into genuinely compassionate aims. In this light, researchers should attend to the development of their intellects as well as to the internal development of compassion and wisdom that are fundamentally non-conceptual and non-dualistic. In the final analysis, accumulation of intellectual knowledge alone is not the source of lasting happiness.

How Can Researchers Help Activists in Their Work, and How Can Activists Help Researchers?

Building alliances between researchers and activists is undoubtedly valuable when done effectively. However, we need to consider the conditions under which this type of alliance can succeed. Some thoughts:

- Researchers and activists need to understand the differing institutional pressures and incentive systems under which each group operates. In academia, for example, the coins of the realm are peer-reviewed publications whose incubation periods are often quite long. In activist circles, the emphasis is often on immediate short-term results, in no small part due to the institutional pressures of securing funding to continue the work. While these contradictory orientations can, in the worst case, sabotage any collaboration, they can also be a source of fruitful creative tension. In order to realize the latter, both sides must make a serious and sincere effort to understand and work within the other's reality.
- To make a blatant, frequently inaccurate, and trite generalization, researchers can help activists be more rigorous while activists can help researchers be more practical. This statement is made in the spirit of building stronger links between basic and applied research.
- We need to support and invest in those people who have the capacity to bridge these worlds. By definition, these bridgers are both "of" and "not of" these spheres. This role is inherently isolating. Therefore, those engaged in these activities may benefit from finding like-minded individuals and receiving support for their work.

19
MARK C. JOHNSON, Ph.D.

Mark C. Johnson is the former director of national executive initiatives for the YMCA of the USA, a position created in 2003 to bring the energy and work of the YMCA of the USA and the YMCA around the world to the attention of philanthropists and the public sector in new ways. His primary responsibilities are for the support of the Jerusalem International YMCA, needs of the National Association, and resources for leadership development and training in the Movement at large.

Most recently, Johnson served as the executive director of the Silver Bay Association for Christian Conferences and Training, the YMCA's oldest continuing conference and training facility. Silver Bay, an independent association, celebrated its 100th anniversary in 2002. Located in the Adirondack Park on Lake George, the jewel of America's lakes, Silver Bay is a place of unparalleled beauty that serves to renew spirit, mind and body for all. Accomplishments there included a successful $11+ million capital campaign for the anniversary, award-winning architectural work, and a multi-faceted year-round rural community development program with a service area of more than 100 square miles.

Mark is in his 34th year with the YMCA, a career that has included service in Beirut, Lebanon, New York City with International Student Services, and the University YMCA at the University of Illinois in Champaign/Urbana—all in addtion to 18 years at Silver Bay. In addition to service on the National Task Force on the Environment in the 1990s, Mark chaired World Camp '98 and the Young Adult Leadership Summit prior to the 150th Anniversary Celebrations of the YMCA of the USA in New Orleans in 2000.

He served eight years as the President of the Lake George Land Conservancy, a Trustee of the Adirondack Nature Conservancy, and Chair of the Lake George Park Commission, following his appointment by the Governor of New York State in 1999. Mark is married and has three daughters. He has a Master's Degree and a Ph.D. in sociology from Columbia University in the City of New York, a B.A. from the College of Wooster, and has also studied at the American University of Beirut in Lebanon. An Elder in the Presbyterian Church, his current extracurricular activities include serving a Chicago Chapter of the Fellowship of Reconciliation, perhaps the oldest interfaith, non-violence peace organization in the world. Mark loves to ask for help for good causes.

What Does Engaged Spirituality Mean to You?

I understand it to be a form of witness – a living out of a set of examined values and beliefs, as well as following the leading of the spirit from unexamined interiorities, on inspired and transformational paths. It is an absence or resistance to conforming to societal expectations and conventions, and a living out of the intersection of mind (intellect and reason), body (heart and gut), and spirit (intuition, subconscious, wisdom). It means doing what one is called to do, sometimes kicking and screaming, but in the end with a sense of satisfaction that only the still small voice of the spirit affirming can instill. It can also mean that organizations or institutions have been constructed or transformed to permit their members to offer their gifts of the spirit, as well as their intellects, their labor, and their capital, to the work of the corporate collectivity.

How are Love and Compassion Integral to the Success of Social Justice Work?

Justice is a right and value that is grounded in both philosophical frameworks and historical trajectories. Successful social justice work integrates the abstract and the concrete, belief and action; it results in an alignment, a congruence, of beliefs with behaviors. Justice is the result of access to equality and liberty, and respect for the sanctity of human life, without regard to distinguishing attributes of individual or collective identity (gender, age, race, ethnicity, citizenship, etc.). Motivations for the practices that result in justice and the creation, cultivation, and engagement of communities of such practices are, in my mind, based on love and compassion, the relationship of self to other, the I to the Thou. Perhaps the placing of service to the relationship above the interests of the self is critical (servant leadership). There is a necessary, if not sufficient, relationship between the internalization and inculcation of love and compassion and the successful work of social justice, an external, other-focused act.

What Beliefs and Practices Successfully Give Rise to or Sustain Activism?

Beliefs in equality, liberty, sanctity, perseverance, longanimity and practices of dialogue, respect, openness, tolerance, reflection, asceticism and love give rise to awareness of injustice, responsibility for change, and commitment to hope and transformation. Conditions sustaining activism are (ironically) injustice, sin, and evil. Discipline sustains activism (conscious, examined, practiced habits). The affirmations of those who lead (saints, heroes, champions) sustain activism.

Where Should Research in this Field be Directed and Focused?

It should first focus on the vocabulary (language, definitions) and the creation of classes and categories that will permit the identification of exemplars (models worthy of emulation), both of individuals and communities of practice that can be captured descriptively and anecdotally as narratives and stories. How do we know it when we see it?

It should then focus on the development of explanatory hypotheses, positing what works to transform individuals and communities into instruments of social justice. What works and why?

And then it should focus on what allocation of resources serves to effect desired outcomes (as determined by parallel paths of practices of axiology and public policy). What needs to be invested (people, practices, wealth) and where in order to make a difference?

How Can Researchers Help Activists? How Can Activists Help Researchers?

This may be the point where I should acknowledge the facet of engagement that brings me to this conversation, which is the work of the YMCA. While my affiliation is with the national offices of the federated, distributed community of associations found in the United States, the conversation makes more sense, historically and prospectively, if the focus is expanded to include the varieties of work done under the rubric of the YMCA in 135 countries globally.

For me, the question is: How do I infuse the choice and condition of membership in the YMCA with the experience and benefits of love? Restated as an affirmation: The choice, freely made, and the condition, celebrated in and as membership in the YMCA, are experienced as a transforming love grounded in my relationship with others.

My lifelong career as member and staff of the YMCA has been rather consistently focused on young adults (conference center staff, university YMCA work, international programming). Even as I finish and e-mail this draft statement, I have just left a group of 12 Israeli young adults (Christian, Moslem, and Jew) on a month-long program of peaceful coexistence and conflict resolution studies in Charlotte, North Carolina, to fly to Jerusalem to further expand the program as a service of the Jerusalem International YMCA in Israel (with impact and intention in Palestine as well, if not yet fully present there).

This one program fits into a larger national initiative that has many facets, but one common underlying recognition: We need to more fully capture and employ our original and generative insights about the necessity of energizing the whole person (spirit, mind and body) if we are going to successfully achieve personal goals, and we must embed the whole person in relationships of membership to reinforce and sustain learnings and intentions successfully. Two questions have particular richness for me here: (1) what can we learn from our past to inform our present efforts? (2) How can our learnings shape our future design and delivery of programs to positively impact individuals and communities?

Among our current efforts to focus our approach to such questions is a recently released report titled "Hardwired to Connect." A summary is attached as background material.

Research can be used to help answer the question of what works and why. It will enable us to posit hypotheses in a rigorous testable fashion.

Activists, which is to say practitioners, can help researchers by providing access to communities of practice for purposes of investigation, and by serving as expert informants sharing in the articulation of hypotheses for investigation.

20
WILL KEEPIN, PH.D.

Will Keepin, PhD, is President of the Satyana Institute, a non-profit organization founded in 1996 to integrate spiritual wisdom into social change leadership. Will's passion is to bridge the inner mystical journey with an outer life of service. Originally trained as a physicist, his advocacy work on sustainable energy influenced environmental policy in several countries. He later founded training programs for social activists, including Leading with Spirit and Gender Reconciliation. Will is widely published, and is Adjunct Faculty at the Calfornia Institute of Integral Studies. He leads retreats on interfaith mysticism in India, and raises funds for an interfaith project for battered women in India. Will was profiled in "The Cultural Creatives,"written by Paul Ray and Sherry Anderson (Harmony Books, 2000).

By love has appeared everything that exists. By love, that which does not exist, appears as existing. —Shebastari

Guidelines for Engaged Spirituality

In facilitating inner work with social change leaders in Satyana Institute's programs over the years, a set of guidelines or principles has emerged that support the practice of engaged spirituality. These guidelines were developed for professionals and activists working in the trenches who wanted to bring greater love and wisdom into their daily professional lives. Taken together, these guidelines address the first four substantive questions that Stephen asked us to reflect on in this paper. So I have articulated these guidelines below, with added commentary and reflections. Attempting to formulate such guidelines for general applicability is, of course, fraught with peril, so these are certainly not offered as definitive or authoritative. They simply comprise a summary of learnings that we found helpful to socially engaged activists as they grappled with how to integrate their "inner" spiritual values into their "outer" practical work.

Transformation of Motivation from Anger/ Fear/ Despair to Compassion/ Love/ Purpose

This is a vital challenge for today's social change leaders, particularly those of you confronting injustice in its various forms. This is not to deny the noble emotions of appropriate anger or outrage in the face of social injustice. Rather, it entails a crucial shift from fighting against evil to working for love; the long-term results are very different, even if the outer activities appear virtually identical. Action follows Being, as the Sufi saying goes. Thus "a positive future cannot emerge from the mind of anger and despair" (Dalai Lama).

Martin Luther King emphasized that we must purify our intentions before moving into direct action for social change. Otherwise the results of our work may actually undermine our noble purpose, in the name of advancing it. As Thomas Merton cautioned, "If we attempt to act and do things for others or for the world without deepening our own self-understanding, our own freedom, integrity and capacity to love, we will not have anything to give to others. We will communicate nothing but the contagion of our own obsessions, our aggressiveness, our ego-centered ambitions."

NON-ATTACHMENT TO OUTCOME

This is difficult to put into practice, yet to the extent that you are attached to the results of your work, you tend to rise and fall with your successes and failures—a sure path to burnout. Hold a clear intention, and let go of the outcome—recognizing that a larger wisdom is always operating. As Gandhi stressed, "the victory is in the doing," not the results. Also, remain flexible in the face of changing circumstances: "Planning is invaluable, but plans are useless." (Churchill)

In our trainings, several social change leaders have reacted strongly to this principle. As one environmental lawyer stammered, "How can I possibly go into court and not be attached to the outcome? You bet I care who wins and who loses! If I am not attached to the outcome, I'll just get bulldozed! And when I lose, the Earth loses!" His exasperation underscores the poignant challenge of implementing these principles in the real world of political and social conflicts. Yet he kept coming back to our retreats, actively looking for ways to love his adversaries. He came to see that non-attachment to outcome does not mean passive indifference to outcome. He also acknowledged that although it was difficult to love some of his adversaries, he could do it by loving them for creating the opportunity for him to become a passionate voice for truth and protection of the natural environment.

INTEGRITY IS YOUR PROTECTION

If your work has integrity, it will tend to protect you from negative energy and circumstances. You can often sidestep negative energy from others by becoming "transparent" to it, allowing it to pass through you with no adverse effect upon you. This is a consciousness practice that might be called "psychic aikido."

Integrity in means cultivates integrity in the fruit of your work. A noble goal cannot be achieved utilizing ignoble means. Some participants in our trainings engaged regularly in political debates, testimony, and hearings. We suggested they apply the Tibetan tonglen practice for transmuting negative energy into compassion and love—right there in the hearing room. The few that actually experimented with this reported that it was indeed helpful in defusing charged psychological situations, and reducing tension in heated debates.

DON'T DEMONIZE YOUR ADVERSARIES

It makes them more defensive and less receptive to your views. People respond to arrogance with their own arrogance, creating rigid polarization. Be a perpetual learner, and constantly challenge your own views.

The ideal is to constantly entertain alternative points of view so that we move from arrogance to inquiry. This is sometimes hard to do, as we often feel very certain about what we think we know, and the injustices we see. As John Stewart Mill observed, "In all forms of debate, both sides tend to be correct in what they affirm, and wrong in what they deny." Entering into an adversarial situation, we are acutely aware of the rightness of our own affirmations, but there is usually a kernel of truth in what is being affirmed by our opponents—however small it may be. We need to be especially mindful about what we deny, because this is where our blind spots often lie.

YOU ARE UNIQUE

Find and fulfill your true calling. "It is better to tread your own path, however humbly, than that of another, however successfully." (Bhagavad Gita) Each one of us has a unique song to sing in the symphony of life. Discover yours, and sing out with confidence, joy, and abandon—the harmony parts will take care of themselves.

LOVE THY ENEMY

Or at least have compassion for him. This is a vital challenge for our times. This does not mean indulging falsehood or corruption. It means moving from "us/them" thinking to "we" consciousness, from separation to cooperation, recognizing that we human beings are ultimately far more alike than we are different. This is challenging in situations with people whose views are radically opposed to yours. Be hard on the issues, soft on the people.

The practice of loving our adversaries is obviously challenging in situations with people whose views and methods are radically opposed to ours, but that is where the real growth occurs. As we discover that the problems of humanity are also found in our own hearts and lives, we realize that the "them" we often speak of is also us. We are not exempt and we are not different.

SELFLESS SERVICE IS A MUST

Your work is for the world, not for you. In doing service work, you are sowing seeds for the benefit of others. The full harvest of your work may not take place in your lifetime, yet your efforts now are making possible a better life for future generations. Let your fulfillment come in gratitude for the privilege of being able to render this service, and from doing so with as much compassion, authenticity, fortitude, and forgiveness as you can muster. This is the traditional understanding of selfless service, and yet its opposite is also true:

Selfless Service is a Myth

In serving others, we serve our true selves. "It is in giving that we receive." We are sustained by those we serve, just as we are blessed when we forgive others. As Gandhi says, the practice of satyagraha ("clinging to truth") confers a "matchless and universal power" upon those who practice it. Service work is enlightened self-interest, and it cultivates an expanded sense of self that includes all others. So although we are not here to serve ourselves, nothing serves us more than serving others.

Do Not Insulate Yourself From the Pain of the World

Shielding yourself from heartbreak prevents transformation. Let your heart break open, and learn to move in the world with a broken heart. As Gibran says, "Your pain is the medicine by which the physician within heals thyself." When we open ourselves to the pain of the world, we become the medicine that heals the world. If we block the pain, we are actually preventing our own participation in the world's attempt to heal itself. This is what Gandhi understood so deeply in his principles of ahimsa and satyagraha. A broken heart is an open heart, through which love flows and genuine transformation begins.

What You Attend To, You Become

Your essence is pliable, and ultimately you become that which you most deeply focus your attention upon. You reap what you sow, so choose your actions carefully. If you constantly engage in battles, you become embattled yourself. If you constantly give love, you become love itself.

Rely on Faith, and Let Go of Having to Figure it all Out

There are larger "divine" forces at work that you can trust completely without knowing their precise workings or agendas. Faith means trusting the unknown, and offering yourself as a vehicle for the intrinsic wisdom and benevolence of the cosmos to do its work. "The first step to wisdom is silence. The second is listening." If you genuinely ask inwardly and listen for guidance, and then follow it carefully—you are working in accord with these larger forces, and you become the instrument for their music.

This is not Pollyannaish fantasy or naïve idealism, as some "realists" might interpret it. Rather, it entails an instinctive trust in the mystery and wonder of life itself, invoking something real yet hidden that goes quite beyond traditional scientific principles. Faith is not blind adherence to any set of beliefs, but a knowing from experience and intuition about universal forces and energies beyond our direct observation. We can draw upon and engage these hidden forces, firstly by knowing they are there; secondly, by asking or yearning for them to support us—or more precisely, asking them to allow us to serve on their behalf. This realization actually brings great relief. We see it is not up to us to figure out all the steps to change the world because we are just participants in a much larger cosmic will.

LOVE CREATES THE FORM

Not the other way around. The heart crosses the abyss that the mind creates, and operates at depths unknown to the mind. Don't get trapped by "pessimism concerning human nature that is not balanced by an optimism concerning divine nature, or you will overlook the cure of grace." (Martin Luther King). Let your heart's love infuse your work and you cannot fail, though your dreams may manifest in ways different from what you imagine.

As engaged spiritual activists at the dawn of the third millennium, it has been said that we are called to serve in two distinct capacities: as hospice workers to a dying culture, and as midwives to an emerging culture. Both tasks are required simultaneously; they call upon us to move through the world with an open heart—present to the grief and decay of a waning civilization—while at the same time maintaining a heartful optimism as we experiment with new visions and forms for the future.

In closing, the last point from Martin Luther King is fundamental, and is something the rational mind cannot fathom. Yet the "cure of grace" is no less real for being hidden and ineffable to the senses. It is the power of love in action, and love is the greatest power in the universe. On this point, King strikingly refuted even the most compelling socio-political pessimists (e.g., Reinhold Niebuhr's *Moral Man, Immoral Society*). To overlook the cure of grace is to overlook the very source and foundation of all life.

Can any of this be proven? Perhaps not in the concrete terms demanded by the rationalist and the skeptic. But engaged spiritual activists do not live by their proofs; they prove by their living. As the mystic poet Rumi put it, "If you are in love, that love is all the proof you need. If you are *not* in love, what good are all your proofs?"

SECTION TWO:
PERSPECTIVES FROM RESEARCHERS

21
JAMES YOUNISS, Ph.D.

James Youniss is the Wylma R. & James R. Curtin Professor of Psychology at the Catholic University of America in Washington, DC, from which he received his Ph.D. in 1962. His career has been devoted to research on various aspects of children's and adolescents' development. His early work was focused on children's cognitive development within the framework of Piaget's theory. He then extended Piaget's epistemology to the study of social development, as exemplified in books published by the University of Chicago Press: <u>Parents and Peers in Social Development,</u> 1980; <u>Adolescent Relations with Mothers, Fathers, and Friends,</u> coauthored with Jacqueline Smollar,1985. In the past decade, he has adapted this model to political-moral development, focusing on community service as a means for promoting the formation of civic identity. This work is illustrated in the books: <u>Community Service and Social Responsibility in Youth,</u> co-authored with Miranda Yates,1997, University of Chicago Press; <u>Roots of Civic Identity: International Perspectives on Community Service and Activism in Youth,</u> 1999, co-edited with Miranda Yates, Cambridge University Press.

His research has been funded by the National Institute of Child Health and Human Development, the William T. Grant Foundation, the Fetzer Institute, and the Carnegie Corporation of New York, among others. In 1992-93, he received a life-time achievement award from the Alexander von Humboldt Foundation; in 1996,he received a senior fellowship from the Japanese Society for the Promotion of Science; in 2001-02, he was a Fellow at the Radcliffe Institute for Advanced Study at Harvard University; in 2002, he received the alumnus award for "outstanding achievement in research and scholarship" from the Catholic University of America. He has served as Chairperson of the Psychology Department (1988) and as Director of the Life Cycle Institute (1989- 2000). He enjoyed teaching developmental psychology to undergraduates for over 40 years, and takes special pleasure in having helped to train Ph.D. students who have carried on the teaching and research tradition with distinction at various academic institutions and government laboratories.

FORMING A POLITICAL-MORAL IDENTITY

I will address the questions posed for our meeting from a developmental perspective that asks how individuals come to have compassion for other people and become engaged in long-term justice work. This essay has three parts. The first provides an example of how young people can become engaged in social justice work through a school-based community service program that is religiously grounded. The second reviews studies that report longitudinal connections between activism during the youth era and sustained engagement through adulthood. Part three presents data on adults who have led exceptional lives of moral or political activism. Their self-reports support the findings from the prior two sections, suggesting that understanding one's common humanity with others, within a moral-political identity, can lead to activism on behalf of social justice.

Part 1. Our first research venture into connections between spirituality and social justice occurred in a study of 160 African-American high school juniors in a required religion class on Social Justice that involved quarterly stints at a soup kitchen in Washington, DC. The teacher, a committed Christian activist who had taught this class for 17 years, challenged the students by stating he was going to teach them how they could make a better world. Students read essays by and about models of social justice—e.g., Franklin Delano Roosevelt, Martin Luther King, Jr., John F. Kennedy, Dorothy Day, et al. The syllabus covered just war theory, the death penalty, welfare policy, environmental protection, and other similar topics. The teacher's ideology was signified by the large poster over his desk that read: "It's a sin to vote Republican," and by his gesture of genuflecting whenever FDR was mentioned.

To determine whether students benefitted from this class, we had them write an essay after each visit to the kitchen. We also ran small groups in which students discussed their experiences that week at the kitchen. By tracking individuals over the year, we found that this class stimulated change in at least one-half of the students.

1. Many of the students began the year thinking of homeless people as "lazy," "dirty," "mean," "crazy," out," etc. Over the course of the year, they came to see them "just as people," as "normal human beings" whose lives had run downward because of drug abuse, unemployment, mental illness, or other unfortunate circumstances. Beneath the surface, students found "human beings just like me or you;" "like my dad who wants a shave, a warm shower, and hot coffee in the morning."

2. Although the students were not themselves well off financially, they came to see their own lives as relatively fortunate. They had food to eat, safe homes to go to every night, and loving parents who cared for them. In contrast, the homeless had to "sleep on the hard concrete, worrying about their physical safety"; "wait another 24 hours for their next meal of terrible food"; "not knowing if they would wake up the next morning or be assaulted during the night."

3. As the year progressed, students connected their observations with the class content by reflecting on the political and moral aspects of homelessness. They moved behind the visible details of homelessness to ask why legislators would rather purchase more bombers than house and feed the 12,000 homeless people in DC. They asked about policies regarding mental health services, drug rehabilitation programs, job training,

prison reform, and other issues implicated in homelessness. In addition, several students imagined themselves in the future as government officials or influential citizens who would address the root causes of homelessness in our nation.

These results have direct bearing on some of the questions posed for our meeting. The teacher hoped to cultivate engaged spirituality by having students incorporate it into their emerging identities. Knowing that students came to class steeped in doctrine, he wanted them to learn how to put principles of Christian social justice into actual and intended actions. He did this by giving students opportunities to connect their service at the soup kitchen with the tradition of Christian social action. Abstractions about love and compassion were turned into palpable issues about the provision of health services, quality education, affordable housing, and other matters that this tradition considered important. During this class, students were encouraged to picture themselves as participants within this tradition, as actors who could help to bring about a more just world.

Because these students were in adolescence, it is reasonable to view their experiencing of this tradition as a resource for the formation of political-moral identity. Participation in social justice traditions allows young people to step into and partake in history, as each tradition comes with respected accomplishments—for example, the role of Southern Black churches during the civil rights struggle. Each also provides an intellectual structure that gives present actions transcendent meaning—e.g., when the students saw their work at the kitchen as a continuation of their parents' role in lifting Blacks out of poverty. Each also offers hope for the future in that, were the principles to be enacted, a more just world would result. Hence, service within such traditions is an opportunity for the construction of engaged identities that have the potential to be sustained through a collective effort that transcends time, place, and individual preferences.

Part 2. Sustained activism. A question follows from these results: Do the identities we saw in the making last or simply wither as young people confront the realities of further education, gaining employment, and starting families? There is empirical evidence that favors the former alternative; many youths who perform service and partake in activist causes become adults who remain engaged in the political and civic life of their communities. The data come from studies that compare individuals who had or had not been involved in service or activism during their youth on indicators of adult involvement—for example, self-reported voting or membership in voluntary organizations. Some of the data project forward from youth to adulthood, whereas others complement these results with adults' retrospective recall of their more and less active youth.

Examples of the former type of study include adults who, in their youth, were involved in civil rights or anti-war activities during the 1950s, 60s, and 70s. For example, McAdam (1988) interviewed adults who had been selected to participate in Freedom Summer 1964, when Northern college students went to Mississippi to register Black voters and teach unschooled Black children. Twenty-some years later, there were clear differences between participants and "no shows" in rates of voting, membership in voluntary associations, and participation in social movements. Fendrich (1993) found virtually the same differences for white students from Florida State University who did or did not participate in the 1960s civil rights sit-ins in Tallahassee, FL. He found less of a difference among Black students from Florida A & M University, as both activists and non-activists had become "ideal citizens" through the collective rise in mobility of educated Blacks following the civil rights era. Jennings (2002) started with a sample of Midwest high school seniors in 1965. Of the seniors who went on to college, some actively participated in anti-war protests, whereas others did not participate. In grade 12, individuals in the two groups did not differ in their political outlooks; in 1973 and still in 1997, however, they differed in their rates of voting and membership in voluntary associations—with the activists being decidedly more engaged.

Retrospective accounts of youth from more and less active adults reinforce these findings. For example, Stewart, et al. (1999) found current rates of civic participation in adult females to be directly related to whether they had been active participants, sympathetic observers, or non-participants in anti-war, civil rights, or feminist causes as college students. Ladewig and Thomas (1987), Verba, et al., and Stolle and Hooghe (2001), et al., found that adults' membership and leadership in various types of voluntary associations were directly related to their affiliations in youth organizations during adolescence.

Two recent studies added to this picture with forward projections from community service during high school to civic participation 4 and 8 years later. Zaff, et al. (2003) and Hart, et al. (2004) found that adults who had done community service during high school (1990-1992), were significantly more likely to vote and to volunteer in 1996 and 2000 than were their counterparts who had not done service during high school.

These studies form a coherent picture in which service-activism during youth (e.g., 16- to 24-years) predicts long-term involvement in political-moral activism. Three interpretations seem notable. (a) Activism during the youth era leads to the construction of an activist identity, which stays with individuals as they advance through the life cycle. (b) Early activism introduces youth to networks of other activists. Members of these networks stimulate one another to remain active over time in a succession of causes. (c) Early activism connects young people to organizations that promote certain political, religious, etc. traditions that persist over time. Affiliation with them enables individual involvement to be sustained. Obviously, these interpretations are not exclusive, but are compatible with one another.

Part 3. I live my tradition with others. This part of the essay seeks to address the bases of "love" and "compassion" and their role in social justice work. It is based on studies of individuals who have led morally and civically exemplary lives. Colby and Damon (1991) and Teske (1998) interviewed adults who devoted their lives to justice activism, such as union organizing, racial integration, and environmental conservation. Both studies found that these unusual adults did not perceive themselves as unusual, but understood their activism to be unremarkable because it was simply an expression of "who they are." This result is supported by Hart's (1996) finding that youth who did exceptional service were forming a self in which activism was integral. In sum, sustained service-activism shapes one's identify as a self that lives within a justice tradition. Consequently, when an individual takes action, it is considered an expression of who that individual is and what that individual does as a matter of course.

Complementary results come from recent studies that have looked at aging Europeans who rescued and protected Jews from the Nazis during WWII (e.g., Oliner & Oliner, 1988; Monroe & Epperson, 1994). The strongest theme that connects all of the interviews is that rescuers saw their behavior as something "anyone" in their situation would have done. "When someone comes to your door desperate in the middle of the night, what are you supposed to tell them − `Sorry, we are full already?' When someone comes and says, `I escaped from camp,' what is the alternative? One alternative is to push him out and close the door − the other is to pull him in and say, `Sit down, relax, wash up. You'll be as hungry as we are because we have only this bread" (Oliner & Oliner, 1988, p. 197). This theme recurred in Monroe and Epperson's (1994) interviews; for example, "When you save your fellow man, you save yourself, too ... You should always be aware that every other person is basically you. You should treat people as though it is you ... Always see yourself in those people, for good or for evil both" (p. 212).

These results resemble the statements given by our high school students as they came to view the homeless people they served as "human beings" ... "just like you or me," or "like my mother who would cry too if she hadn't seen her daughter in 10 years." This sharing of common humanity may be considered as the core of love or compassion that leads to social justice. Because these terms have come to evoke notions of individual, trait-like characteristics, they tend to make love and compassion a matter of individual preference. It may be more productive, however, to view them as expressions of collective participation in political-moral traditions that allow one to recognize others as essentially like the self. When people act to help others within the framework of these traditions, it is the principles of these traditions that form the basis for a shared humanity and compel social justice action.

This point is illustrated in another aspect of the interviews with rescuers. Gross (1997) studied rescuers from a French Huguenot community and a Dutch Calvinist community in the Netherlands, when the entire village participated in rescuing Jews. Whereas these religiously-based communities could easily have designated Jewish families as outsiders, they felt obliged to accord Jews equal rights as fellow citizens. Some individuals noted that, had they not done so, they would have betrayed their Christian and democratic principles. Separating themselves from their Jewish neighbors would have been to deny their shared humanity and undermine the principles that formed the basis of their communities.

Kurek-Lesik (1992) gives another example from a religious community of Catholic nuns in Poland. Their convent, which was located across the street from an SS headquarters, operated as a soup kitchen for the needy. One evening at prayer, the Superior read to her nuns St. John's gospel calling us to love one another. She interpreted these passages to imply that the convent should become a shelter for persecuted non-Christians. Without responding overtly, the nuns went to their rooms feeling elated, but knowing that their new duty would be the "sheltering of these hunted people," a duty that "flowed from the most important Christian commandment, from the commandment of love" (p. 331)

CONCLUSION

Insofar as individuals construct their identities within certain political-moral traditions of justice, they define themselves as collaborating actors with past, present, and future others who share those traditions. For young people, identity may hinge on the opportunity to experience oneself as an actor within these traditions. In this regard, service within a tradition allows youth to step into history and become virtual participants with past and future others. "By acting and participating in politics [and I add, a religious or moral tradition], you implicate yourself in a historical story and the unfolding of a political community (Teske, p. 138). Or as one of the civil rights activists said: "When I go near a voting registrar in Mississippi, I feel I'm dueling with the whole history of my race and the white race. It gets to you just like that, in your bones. You're doing something for the books; for history too" (Coles & Brenner, 1965, p. 910).

22
PAUL WINK, Ph.D.

Paul Wink received his Ph.D. in Psychology from the University of California at Berkeley. He is currently Professor in the Psychology Department at Wellesley College, and was visiting faculty at the Department of Psychology at the University of Michigan, Ann Arbor. Wink has published extensively in the areas of religiousness and spirituality, adult development, generativity, and narcissism. Since 1997, he has directed a follow-up study of participants in the Berkeley Guidance and Oakland Growth Studies in late adulthood. Wink's research has been supported by grants from the Open Society Institute, the Lilly Foundation, the Fetzer Institute in collaboration with the Institute for Research on Unlimited Love, and the Templeton Foundation. He is a reviewer for numerous journals including Psychology and Aging, Journal of Personality and Social Psychology, and Journal for the Sociology of Religion.

RELIGIOUS DWELLING AND SPIRITUAL SEEKING AS TWO MODES OF SOCIAL ENGAGEMENT

Stephen Post challenges us to understand three types of spiritually engaged individuals: those who are involved in face-to-face charity (FFC); those who confront social, political, and economic structures (SPES); those who combine these two types of activism. This is clearly a complex task that requires a consideration of cultural, social, biological, and personal forces that influence human behavior at any given time in history. Taking a psychological perspective, I will argue that in order to understand the FFC-SPES relation it is helpful to consider two overlapping but different approaches to religion: religiousness—denoting commitment to institutionalized religious beliefs and practices; spirituality—denoting commitment to more individualized and de-institutionalized religious beliefs and practices. My collaborator, Michele Dillon, a sociologist at the University of New Hampshire, and I study the social and personal implications of religiousness and spirituality using data from the Institute of Human Development longitudinal study, established at the University of California at Berkeley in the 1920s.

These data are particularly useful for an in-depth investigation of the relationship between religion and altruism because the IHD participants were born just before the Great Depression and reached retirement age in the 1990s. Thus, they have witnessed the important social and cultural shifts that have spanned twentieth-century American society, including the rise of a therapeutic culture and globalization, and the allegedly progressive decline in social bonds. Because the IHD study uses extensive open-ended interviews, this allows us to preserve the complexity of human lives in our research. In my presentation, I will discuss the relationship between religiousness and spirituality, describe the characteristics of the IHD sample, and present evidence on the relationship between religiousness and spirituality and psychosocial functioning in late adulthood, with a special emphasis on generativity (the concern for the welfare of future generations that is closely related to altruism). I will argue that religiousness is more characteristic of FFC, spirituality of SPES, and the combination of the two in individual lives leads to the blending of FFC and SPES.

RELIGIOUSNESS AND SPIRITUALITY

The tendency to conceive of religiousness and spirituality as different ways of relating to the sacred dates back only to the 1970s, a time when increasing numbers of Americans abandoned traditional religious structures and chose instead to seek a more individuated way of connecting with the divine. Although religion in America has a long history of emphasis on individuality and establishing a personal relation with God, unmitigated by church structures (e.g., Emerson and the Transcendentalists – see Fuller [2001]), the changing religious landscape since the 1960s helps us discern more clearly that religious beliefs and practices include both a dwelling and a seeking component. "Religious dwellers" tend to accept traditional forms of religious authority; they inhabit a space created for them by established religious institutions and relate to the sacred through prayer and public communal worship. In contrast, "spiritual seekers" regard individual autonomy as taking precedence over external authority and the hold of tradition-centered religious doctrines (Wuthnow, 1998). They are explorers who create their own space by typically borrowing elements from various religious and mythical traditions. They frequently blend participation in institutionalized Western religion with Eastern practices. Unlike religious dwellers, spiritual seekers place a greater emphasis on self-growth, emotional self-fulfillment, and the sacredness of ordinary objects and experiences, and typically construe religious belief as connectedness with a sacred Other (e.g., God, Higher Power, nature, other individuals) (Underwood, 1999).

For the purpose of understanding socially engaged spirituality, it is important to note that the cultural shift ushered in by the 1960s has elicited a very different response from cultural critics and psychologists. As early as the mid 1960s, Philip Rieff (1966) prophesized the rise of a "spiritual man" desirous to "preserve inherited morality freed from its hard external crust of institutional discipline (p. 2)." Since then, a number of cultural critics (e.g., Bellah, Madsen, Sullivan, Swidler and Tipton 1985; Lasch 1979) have echoed Rieff's concern that a therapeutic, self-centered, and narcissistic individualism is displacing the socially responsible individualism that historically characterized American culture. Bellah and co-authors (1985) contrast the communal ties and responsibilities fostered by traditional forms of religion, such as church attendance, with the self-serving (narcissistic) quest promoted by a deinstitutionalized spirituality.

For humanistic psychologists, by contrast, the newfound focus on the self signified a positive personal and social development. Scholars such as Fromm, Maslow, and Rogers argued that the established social order, tradition, and conventional religion alienate individuals from their fundamental purpose in life—that is, from personal growth and self-realization. In their view, altruism/generativity and a mature individuated spirituality can flourish only when individuals reclaim their personal freedom (Fromm 1941/1965) and self-actualize (Maslow 1964); they typically say little about how the transformation of self-interest into social concern is to be achieved.

Our research recognizes the overlap between religiousness and spirituality but, for analytical purposes, we have operationalized them as independent constructs. We define religiousness in terms of the importance of institutionalized religious beliefs and practices in the life of the individual; it combines frequency of church attendance and prayer and the salience of religious belief. We define spirituality in terms of the importance of de-institutionalized religious beliefs and practices (Wink and Dillon 2003) in the life of the individual (e.g., emphasis on sacred connectedness with God or nature; blending of diverse religious and mythical traditions). This operationalization captures an important aspect of the distinction between religiousness and spirituality as it is used in public culture (e.g., Marty, 1993), while simultaneously recognizing the overlap between the two constructs (the two measures are moderately correlated). The seriousness of effort to incorporate the sacred in their lives is not what differentiates individuals high in religiousness from those high in spirituality; rather, it is their relationship to religious authority and tradition.

CHARACTERISTICS OF THE SAMPLE

Our data come from the Intergenerational Studies established by the Institute of Human Development (IHD) at the University of California, Berkeley in the 1920s. The original sample was a representative sample of newborn babies in Berkeley (California) in 1928/29 (the Berkeley Guidance Study), and of pre-adolescents (ages 10-12) selected from elementary schools in Oakland (California) in 1931 (who were born in 1920/21 and included in the Oakland Growth Study). Both samples were combined into a single study in the 1960s. The participants were studied intensively in childhood and adolescence and interviewed in-depth four times in adulthood: early adulthood (age 30s; interview conducted in 1958); middle adulthood (age 40s; 1970); late middle adulthood (age 50s/ early 60s; 1982); late adulthood, when the participants were in their late 60s or mid 70s (1997-2000). At each interview phase, the participants also completed self-administered questionnaires. Three hundred individuals took part in at least one of the three assessments conducted between early and late middle adulthood. In late adulthood, I interviewed 90% (N = 184) of the available IHD participants.

In late adulthood, the sample was divided equally between men and women; a third were born in the early 1920s and two-thirds were born in the late 1920s. All but 6 of the participants are White, reflecting the racial composition of the Bay Area in the 1920s. Just under 50% are college graduates, a figure that is substantially higher than for same-age Americans nationwide, (approx. 20%), but slightly more typical of educational levels in California. When interviewed in late adulthood, the study participants resided primarily in Northern (69%) or Southern (12%) California, and the Western or Southwestern states (12%).

The majority of the sample (73%) grew up in Protestant families; 16% grew up Catholic. In late adulthood, 58% of the study participants were Protestant (of these, 78% were members of mainline denominations, primarily Presbyterian, Episcopalian, and Methodist); 16% were Catholic, 2% were Jewish, and 24% were not church members. Forty-five percent reported weekly church attendance, and 81% said that religion was important in their lives. These figures closely parallel national polls; 52% of Americans in the 65-74 age category attend church weekly, and 90% say that religion is important in their lives. Forty-nine percent of the participants self-identified as Republican, 30% as Democrat, and 21% as independent; this distribution closely approximates political affiliation data for mainline Protestants in the Pacific region (Wink, et al., in press).

RELIGIOUSNESS, SPIRITUALITY AND PSYCHOSOCIAL FUNCTIONING IN LATE ADULTHOOD

For the IHD sample, we found that both religiousness and spirituality were related to observer-based ratings of generativity in older adulthood. In other words, both highly religious and highly spiritual individuals were likely to show a deep and genuine concern for the welfare of future generations. We also found that both religiousness and spirituality were positively related with involvement in a variety of everyday activities and pastimes, such as socializing with family and friends or doing arts, crafts, and carpentry (Wink & Dillon, 2003). These patterns of psychosocial functioning in late adulthood could be predicted with religiousness scores in early adulthood, a time interval of close to 40 years, and spirituality in late middle adulthood, a time interval of 15 years.

Although generative and purposeful everyday activities were common to both religious and spiritual individuals, the nature of their emphases differed. Religious individuals were more likely than spiritual individuals to express their generativity in a communal way by caring for family members or friends and, in general, through interpersonal relations (Dillon, Wink, & Fay, 2003). They tended to be described by observers – who read their interview transcripts – as giving, sympathetic, protective of others, and warm. Similarly, the everyday routines characteristic of highly religious individuals showed a stronger involvement in spending time on social activities (e.g., visiting or entertaining family members and friends) and in community service done with a group. In terms of political activism (petitions, contributing money, attending meetings), religiousness was associated positively with concern for alleviating local crime and homelessness, but correlated negatively with an emancipatory social agenda (e.g., support for gays, immigrants, racial minorities, feminism).

In contrast, the generativity of spiritual individuals was more likely to be expressed through involvement in creative projects and in social activities that would make an impact beyond the domain of family and friends, and that might leave a legacy that would "outlive the self" (Kotre, 1984). The generative concerns associated with spirituality tended to show a broad societal perspective and incisiveness into the human condition, rather than an emphasis on interpersonal relations. In terms of everyday pastimes, highly spiritual individuals were more likely to work on creative and knowledge- or skills-building projects than to socialize with friends or family. The political activism of spiritual individuals was focused on such global issues as AIDS, the peace movement, civil rights, and the environment, but also included child-care and homelessness. Spirituality was related to awareness of issues of power and social injustice.

The different, more self-expanding focus of individuals who were spiritual was not, however, excessively narcissistic. In fact, we found no relationship between spirituality and pathological narcissism. Instead, spirituality in late adulthood was positively related to a healthy form of self-investment (narcissism) in early adulthood that is characterized by independence of judgment, creativity, introspection, and skepticism of the existing status quo. Importantly, then, when spirituality is linked to systematic practices (as our measure is), it does not have the negative features that cultural analysts (e.g., Bellah, et al., 1985) are concerned about (Wink, Dillon, & Fay, 2004).

In conclusion, our findings support the presence of a connection between religiousness and FFC and spirituality and SPES. The fact that religiousness and spirituality are associated with different types of social engagement does not mean that one is better than the other. The social engagement of religious dwellers derives its strength from membership in an organized community of believers that offers members well-established, exemplary narratives of charity and practical ways of helping others. These strong communal traditions and bonds, however, may pose the danger of magnifying in-group/out-group distinctions that may result in social exclusivity and intolerance. The social engagement of spiritual seekers finds its strength in openness to experience, personal autonomy, and the ability to pierce through the veil of Maya. The emphasis on self-exploration, however, poses the risk of self-absorption and selfishness masquerading as charity (see Albert Camus, The Fall). Spiritual seekers may also find it hard to find the social outlets for expressing their altruism, especially when it comes to action at the local level. Although a balance between religious dwelling and spiritual seeking may seem to offer the ideal solution for the promotion of engaged activism (I will present illustrative cases of individuals who are high on both religiousness and spirituality at our meeting), a full integration of the two modes of being religious is not easy because it requires the fusion of two psychological functions (agency and communion; Bakan 1966) that tend to pull individuals in opposite directions. Perhaps it is not accidental that Mahatma Gandhi was a much better parent to India as a whole than to his own children, and that Mother Theresa was not involved in social structural activism. After all, the attainment of psychological wholeness is rarely a completed journey.

REFERENCES

Bakan, D. (1966). The duality of human experience.

Bellah, R., Madsen, R., Sullivan, W., Swidler, A., & Tipton, S. (1985). *Habits of the heart: Individualism and commitment in American life*. Berkeley: University of California Press.

Camus, A. (1965). *The fall*. Harmondsworth, England: Penguin Books. (Originally published in 1956).

Dillon, M., Wink, P., & Fay, K. (2003). Is spirituality detrimental to generativity? *Journal for the Scientific Study of Religion*, 42, 427-442.

Fromm, E. 1965. *Escape from freedom*. New York: Avon Books. (Originally published 1941.)

Fuller, R. C. 2001. *Spiritual, but not religious*. New York: Oxford University Press.

Kotre, John. (1996). *Outliving the self* (2nd ed.). New York: Norton.

Marty, M. (1993). Where the energies go. *The Annals of the American Academy of Political and Social Science*, 553, 11-26.

Maslow, A. 1964. *Religions, values, and peak-experiences*. Columbus, OH: Ohio State University Press.

Rieff, P. 1966. *The triumph of the therapeutic: Uses of faith after Freud*. New York: Harper & Row.

Underwood, L. (1999). *Daily spiritual experiences. In Multidimensional measurement of religiousness/spirituality for use in health research: A report of the Fetzer Institute/ National Institute on Aging working group* (pp. 11-17). Kalamazoo, MI: John E. Fetzer Institute.

Wink, P., & Dillon, M. (2003). Religiousness, spirituality, and psychosocial functioning in late adulthood: Findings from a longitudinal study. *Psychology and Aging*, 18, 1-9.

Wink, P. Dillon, M. & Fay, K. (2004). Spirituality, psychotherapy, and narcissism: *How are they related?* Manuscript under review.

Wink, P., Dillon, M., & Larson, B. (in press). Religion as Moderator of the Depression - Health Connection: Findings from a Longitudinal Study. *Research on Aging*.

Wuthnow, R. 1998. *After heaven: Spirituality in America since the 1950s*. Berkeley: University of California Press.

23
LYNN G. UNDERWOOD, Ph.D.

Lynn G. Underwood received her Ph.D. in Epidemiology from Queens University School of Medicine in the United Kingdom, following medical studies at the University of Iowa School of Medicine. She spent ten years in cancer epidemiology, designing and implementing a public and professional education program that resulted in decreasing the death rate from malignant melanoma in Northern Ireland, and subsequently taught and worked in the area of research methods. In addition to journal publications and chapter contributions, she has co-edited two methodology textbooks, "Measuring Stress" and "Social Support Measurement and Intervention," both published by Oxford University Press. She has led the development and co-sponsorship of various research agenda development workshops with the National Institutes of Health (NIH), including one on the bio-behavioral aspects of pain with 10 NIH Institutes, one on spirituality and aging with the National Institute on Aging, and two on end-of-life issues. She developed a joint request for applications for research funding on the role of spirituality in preventing and treating alcoholism with the National Institute on Alcoholism. She led a cross-cultural study of the role of spirituality and religiousness in quality of life with the World Health Organization, and an initiative on scientific research on altruistic and compassionate love, which has funded over 25 projects in this area to date. She co-edited and contributed chapters to the text: "Altruism and Altruistic Love, Science Religion and Philosophy in Dialog." Current research interests include various aspects of spirituality, including compassionate love, and study of the interface of art, science and spirituality. She has served on a number of advisory boards, including that of the National Center for Medical Rehabilitation Research within the NIH. Formerly vice president for research for a the Fetzer Institute, she is currently president of a research organization that works with private foundations and the federal government on collaborative and interdisciplinary initiatives. She also continues to teach and write.

GIVING OF SELF FOR THE GOOD OF THE OTHER:
SCIENCE RESEARCH ON COMPASSIONATE

LOVE AND SPIRITUALITY

One of the advantages of science research is that it can expand an individual's horizon beyond "what I believe" and "what I've experienced" to a wider world of the beliefs, motives, and experiences of others, which might be quite different from one's own. One of the ways researchers can help us in our actions is to illuminate where other people may be coming from, what beliefs and attitudes they may have. Research can sometimes also help to illuminate our own motives, which are often a mixed bag, and sometimes out of our easy reach.

Before being able to do worthy scientific research on love and on spirituality, scientists needed to clarify the definitions. Not everyone will agree about these definitions, but they can provide a starting point for future discussions and additional research. The definition of *compassionate love*, as used in the many research projects funded by the Fetzer Institute under their science research initiative in 2002, was a "love that centers on the good of the other, self-giving love." This definition was designed to distinguish this compassionate love from hormonally-driven romantic drive, the natural bonding with offspring, the tit-for-tatness of the business world, practical support given out of obligation, and the platitudes of love and forgiveness trotted out by both the religious and non-religious. The names for the concept varied and overlapped with other concepts and names. "Agape," "altruistic love," "compassionate love," "unconditional love," "compassion," and "unlimited love" have all been used.

Work carried out both qualitatively, using in-depth interviews, and in the context of a cross-cultural World Health Organization project encouraged use of the words "compassionate love" to describe this concept. In a series of structured, in-depth interviews with Trappist (Cistercian) monks, Underwood explored the meaning and nuances of compassionate love (Underwood, 2005). These monks have worked for years to develop discernment into their motives and behavior, particularly as it involves loving actions towards others. The interviews resulted in both a clearer, deeper understanding of the concept and in useful hypotheses for future scientific investigation. Key qualities of the concept include: 1) some element of free choice; 2) some degree of cognitive understanding of the situation; 3) some understanding of self and motives; 4) fundamentally valuing the other; 5) openness and receptivity; 6) response of the heart. (Underwood, 2002).

In each act of compassionate love, a person begins with an individual substrate: cultural differences; social and historical setting; physical; intellectual; emotional strengths and limitations; environmental constraints. Within that setting, a decision is made—to act or not act, and an intention is formulated. Discernment operates: mercy and justice are balanced and the various benefits and drawbacks, to oneself and other, are weighed. Following this, an attitude is expressed, and/or an action is taken. In the midst of all of this, spirituality is engaged: in the situation and environment, in our beliefs and cognitions, in our emotions, in grace in the midst of attitudes and decisions, and in the facilitation of the work of love in action.

All motives are mixed. We want to express a love that nourishes, that encourages ourselves and those we care for to flourish. Some attitudes that can get in the way are: a need for reciprocal love and affection; a need to be accepted and belong; a desire to avoid confrontation; seeing the other as an extension of oneself; pleasure in looking well in the eyes of others; control of the other through their indebtedness; desire to exercise power over another by feeling superior (Underwood 2002). These other attitudes can drain us, and leave us burned out. Having our love fueled by a grounded spirituality can help direct our motives and be energizing. This can be called "engaged spirituality."

We also need to define spirituality clearly in order to do scientific research in this area. For many people, features of spirituality are grounded in a faith tradition, whether they articulate it as such or not. This has been shown in research done in a worldwide setting and survey research done in the U.S. One way to formulate this is to use the construct of Spirituality/Religiousness as overlapping circles, made up of many factors, with a relatively small number of people in the areas outside of the overlap. Factors included in the construct used to construct a multidimensional measure designed for health research included: 1) Daily Spiritual Experiences; 2) Private Religious Practices; 3) Religious and Spiritual Coping (positive and negative); 4) Religious Social Support; 5) Religious/Spiritual History; 6) Forgiveness of self, other, and being forgiven; 7) Commitment to the translation of beliefs into action; 8) Organizational Religious Practice; 9) Affiliation; 10) Meaning, Values, and Beliefs (Fetzer/NIA 1998/2003). Most people, both in the U.S. culture and worldwide, as demonstrated in a World Health Organization study, are comfortable describing their spirituality in a way that includes some form of relationship to the divine (Saxena, et al, 2002).

Studies can also help us to understand the feelings and desires that motivate actions and attitudes. The Daily Spiritual Experience Scale (DSES) (Underwood and Teresi, 2002) is composed of sixteen items measuring various aspects of spiritual experience, the kinds of mundane inner experiences that can help to fuel the daily spiritual life. They are scored on a scale of "many times a day" to "never or almost never," and the introductory remarks allow for substitution for the word "God" with another word that "indicates the divine or holy for you." In the U.S., on the General Social Survey (GSS) from 1998, in response to the question from the DSES, "I feel God's presence," 88% of the population reported experiencing this anywhere from once in a while to many times a day (Idler, et al, 2003). In addition to items that have a theistic element, the DSES includes items that address the beliefs of those who are not theistic. It also uses overall language that is easily understood, and demonstrates how Spirituality/Religiousness might function as an integrated construct.

The DSES items are as follows:

1. I feel God's presence.
2. I experience a connection to all of life.
3. During worship, or at other times when connecting with God, I feel intense joy which lifts me out of my daily concerns.
4. I find strength in my religion or spirituality.
5. I find comfort in my religion or spirituality.
6. I feel deep inner peace or harmony.

7. I ask for God's help in the midst of daily activities.

8. I feel guided by God in the midst of daily activities.

9. I feel God's love for me directly.

10. I feel God's love for me through others.

11. I am spiritually touched by the beauty of creation.

12. I feel thankful for my blessings.

13. I feel a selfless caring for others.

14. I accept others even when they do things I think are wrong.

15. I desire to be closer to God or in union with the divine.

16. How close do you feel to God or the divine? (scored from as close as possible to not at all close)

Compassionate love items are nested within the sixteen-item DSES scale of spirituality, which "hangs together" well psychometrically, demonstrating that a loving attitude can form a part of the larger notion of spirituality. In the 2002 General Social Survey data, two items from the Daily Spiritual Experience Scale (DSES) were added to this random survey of the US population. In response to the selfless caring item, 25% of the population state that they feel a selfless caring for others every day or many times a day, 20.3% most days, 46.3% some days or once in a while, and 10.4% never or almost never. The other item from the DSES that taps the notion of mercy – accepting the other person— was "I accept others even when they do things I think are wrong": 24.9% reported experiencing this many times a day or every day, 32.4% most days, 37.8% some days or once in a while, and 4.9% never or almost never (Underwood. 2005). These two items have been added again to the 2004 GSS, along with the entire DSES and additional questions addressing altruism and love. It will be illuminating to examine these results in the future.

Specific examples of engaged spirituality are found in other recent research in the area. A study of helping behaviors by members of Alcoholics Anonymous (AA) showed that helping could be fueled by both self-transcendent spirituality and a more theistically articulated approach, and that spirituality increased helping behaviors (Zemore and Kaskutus, 2004). In a study of volunteering, Alan Omoto interviewed members of two retirement communities, including one whose members were retired Christian leaders. The transcripts indicated that the religious participants found volunteering to be a significant part of their lives. They saw it as part of "God's purpose" and as "an expression of Christian faith." They found volunteering to be "something that nourishes." On the other hand, those from the other retirement community who did not have extensive church service, often viewed volunteering as something to "keep busy" or "make me feel better." In a separate set of interviews, those with higher degrees of religious affiliation showed higher participation in volunteer organizations (rs> .24) (Omoto, Conference Presentation, Washington, D.C., May 2004). These studies give examples of how different kinds of spirituality can be linked to altruistic actions and what kinds of motivations might be involved.

Other survey data can give us useful information about people's attitudes and beliefs. In the GSS in 1998, a number of specific questions were asked, including: "I feel a deep sense of responsibility for reducing pain and suffering in the world." 62.4% of people agree with this statement. This should be encouraging to us in terms of the desire to help others that is present in the general population. It also points out the degree to which people consider the suffering of others their own responsibility. The Sorokin concerns of extensivity and intensivity apply here (Sorokin, 1954; 2002). Some people donate most of their energies within the communities they belong to or to their families. Some feel called and are able to give more time and resources to the wider world. Both of these count as love fully expressed and the balance of priorities is different for each person. Harm can happen when each of these arenas is neglected or inadequately attended to in the context of the world community.

One goal for science research in this area is to better understand when, how, and under what conditions behaviors and attitudes centered on the good of the other might be fostered, and to discover ways to appropriately encourage the expression of compassionate love in the world. By doing this, science can inform us as we seek to give of ourselves for the good of others.

REFERENCES

Idler, EL; Musick, MA; Ellison, CG, George, KL; Krause, N; Ory, MG; Pargament, KI; Powell, LH; Underwood LG; Williams, DR, "Measuring multiple dimensions of religion and spirituality or health research - Conceptual background and findings from the 1998 General Social Survey." *Research on Aging,* 2003, V25,(4)327-365.

General Social Survey, 1998, 2000, *NORC,* University of Chicago.

Multidimensional Measurement of Religiousness/Spirituality for use in Health Research: A Report of the Fetzer Insitute/ National Insitute on Aging Working Group. Ables R., Ellison C., George L., Idler E., Krause N., Levin J., Ory M., Pargament K., Powell L., Underwood L.G., Williams D., Fetzer Insitute, Kalamazoo, 1999/2003.

Saxena, S., O'Connell, K., Underwood L., "Cross-Cultural Quality of Life Assessment at the End of Life: A Commentary", *The Gerontologist,* Vol 42, Special Issue III, October 2002, pg 81-85.

Sorokin, P.A. *The Ways and Power of Love: Types, Factors, and Techniques of Moral Transformation.* Templeton Foundation Press. 2002 (originally published 1954).

Underwood, Lynn G. "Interviews with Trappist Monks as a Contribution to Research Methodology in the Investigation of Compassionate Love." Journal for the Theory of Social Behavior, 35:3 (September, 2005), in press.

Underwood, Lynn G., "The Human Experience of Compassionate Love: Conceptual Mapping and

Data from Selected Studies", in Post et al., *Altruism and Altruistic Love: Science, Philosophy, and Religion in Dialogue,* Oxford University Press, 2002.

Underwood, Lynn G., "Interviews with Trappist Monks as a Contribution to Research Methodology in the Investigation of Compassionate Love. Forthcoming, *Journal for the Theory of Social Behavior.*

Underwood, L. and Teresi, "The Daily Spiritual Experience Scale: Development, Theoretical Description, Reliability, Exploratory Factor Analysis, and Preliminary Construct Validity Using Health Related Data," J., *Annals of Behavioral Medicine* 2002,24 (1):22-33.

Zemore SE, Kaskutas LA. Helping, spirituality and Alcoholics Anonymous in recovery. *J Stud Alcohol.* 2004 May;65(3):383-91.

"Compassionate Love Research Conference," May 2004.
http://www.researchintegration.org/documents/LoveResearchConf.pdf

24
DON S. BROWNING, Ph.D.

Don Browning is Alexander Campbell Professor of Religious Ethics and the Social Sciences, Emeritus, Divinity School, University of Chicago. He has worked primarily on the borderline between Christian ethics and the social sciences. In recent years, he has been the director of the Lilly Endowment-funded Religion, Culture, and Family project, which produced over 20 scholarly books on various aspects of family life viewed from the perspective of a critical retrieval of the Christian faith. Among his various books are <u>Generative Man</u> (1973, 1975), <u>Religious Thought and the Modern Psychologies</u> (1987, 2004), <u>A Fundamental Practical Theology</u> (1991),and <u>Marriage and Modernization</u> (2003). Most recently (2001-2003), he has been Woodruff Professor of Religion and Interdisciplinary Studies in the School of Law, Emory University.

It would be dishonest to claim that I have lived a life of social activism, although I have had my political and religious commitments and supported causes of various kinds. But I have been primarily an academic committed to research and writing.

Most of my study has been in the field of practical moral action. In recent years, I have tried to bring together a fruitful dialogue between the discipline of practical theology and the discipline of Christian ethics by creating a somewhat new inquiry that I have dubbed "practical theological ethics." In my view of this enterprise, the social sciences play an important role in describing situations.

But what do I study? Primarily I study a rather wide range of practical action in the areas of Christian ministry, church life, the witness and action of religious people in public affairs, family life, and therapeutic and practical service in both religious and secular contexts. Hence, in one way or another, I reflect on the subject of our conference— i.e., the love that also does justice.

For a period of ten years, I became involved in a new specialty called "congregational studies." This inquiry was stimulated by the Division of Religion of the Lilly Endowment, Inc., and brought together historians, sociologists, anthropologists, and theologians to study one of the most understudied aspects of American life – religious congregations. We studied their worship and preaching, their religious education and spirituality, their social action or the lack of it. We asked what they really do, and how their beliefs, rituals, teachings, and actionsinterrelate and inform their lives and the public realm beyond their walls.

Some sociologists tell us that religious congregations are the largest single source of philanthropy and social service in American life. Hence, congregations are worth studying.

Allow me to make a few abstract generalizations that summarize the fruits of my studies. I will then illustrate these points by briefly describing a Black Pentecostal church that I studied for several months. I will state my findings as a list of propositions. Studying this church and others has led me to believe the following:

1. Ethical action (following Paul Ricoeur, I make a distinction between ethics and morality) first springs from our efforts to attain the goods of life – food, housing, human association and friendship, employment, reasonable wealth, family life, and children.

2. But the evaluation of the goods of life is never simply a felt bodily experience; it chiefly comes from acquiring traditions of discernment about the practices of life that truly lead to the goods of life. The love that does justice first comes from being socialized into a tradition of tested practices – practices that have a history of meeting individual needs and leading to the fundamental goods of life.

3. Acknowledging one's basic needs and experiencing enduring practices that satisfy them constitute the grounds for developing empathy for the needs of others and some sense of what will address these needs. Empathy springs from gratitude.

4. Communities of tradition that convey such enduring practices are surrounded by rituals and reinforcing narratives about the meaning of life. These rituals and narratives give significance to these practices. These classic practices (in the sense of truly satisfying practices) deal with such issues as family life, marriage, work, child rearing, help for the sick, service to the poor, and support for the aging.

5. But the pursuit of the goods of life, even through tested practices, never completely avoids conflict between goods and between people pursuing these goods. This is where morality, in contrast to ethics, comes into the picture. Morality tries to resolve the conflict of goods and does so through some theory of justice. It may be the Golden Rule, the principle of neighbor love, or something like Immanuel Kant's categorical imperative (which tells us to treat the humanity in self and others always as an end and never as a means only). But justice, to have substance, depends on a theory of the goods of life.

6. This leads to a definition of love. Love tries to actualize good in other and self, but does so with justice, even in the face of conflict. Furthermore, love seeks justice with sensitivity to the uniqueness of conflicting goods in specific situations.

The church I studied illustrates these generalizations. It was the Apostolic Church of God on Chicago's south side. This church rose to strength and prominence during the period when most of the southern portions of Chicago fell into poverty and disorganization. It has grown from 130 members in the 1960s to over 15,000 members at the present. The Apostolic Church takes seriously its people's aspirations for a better life – their desire for jobs, stable families, marriage, children, health, education, and decent housing. It works for these goods for its members and for its neighborhood. But it pursues these goods through the tested practices of the Christian tradition. A strong family life is a central practice. This also entails responsible fatherhood, marital faithfulness, care for and education of children, support for fatherless children, care for the sick, and attention to those struggling with addictions, joblessness, and loneliness. Each member of the congregation is supposed to have a ministry – a service within the total work of the church among its members and in the wider Chicago community.

In view of the 70 percent non-marital birth rate in the Black community and how this reality contributes to the exacerbation of poverty and child neglect, the emphasis on the goods of family life is not surprising. But families are not allowed to strive for their good at the expense of the good of other families. They are stimulated to find ways to reconcile conflicting goods between families, both within the church and in the schools, housing, businesses, and recreation of the wider south side community. The Apostolic Church, through The Woodlawn Organization and its coalition with the University of Chicago and the MacArthur Foundation, is one of the strongest social-action agencies in Woodlawn and adjacent neighborhoods.

In summary, the Apostolic Church is an *ethical* community helping its people to pursue these goods of life through tested and classic Christian practices. It is a *moral* community in that it helps its members and wider community reconcile conflicts between goods; it helps them seek justice. It is a *loving* community; it helps its members seek the good for self and other, but always within a framework of justice.

But it is also a religious community with a strong narrative about the meaning of life. Apostolic has a powerful theology about the goodness of creation. When members enter the doors of Apostolic Church, they greet each other with the words, "Praise the Lord." This is to overcome any sense of victimization; no matter how bad life seems, the members of Apostolic Church are taught that the blessings of life (the goods of life) outweigh its evils. *There is always much to be thankful for*. But even deeper, Apostolic's theology of creation leads its members to hold that basic human desires and wants are God-given and permissible to express and pursue, as long as they do this within accepted and just Christian practices. Hence, the desire for pleasure, love, sex, wealth, children, housing, education, relaxation are not evils to be denied but goods to be responsibly pursued. This is an important message for groups who have historically suffered discrimination and been denied their rightful access to these goods.

However, Apostolic Church also has a doctrine of sin and salvation. Although fundamental human desires are good and God-given in some pre-moral sense of the term, attaining these goods is not the measure of life. Grounding one's selfhood on God's abiding and justifying love is the foundation of the Christian life, and all human desires and attainments are finite, relative, and susceptible to loss and corruption. Hence, the goods of life, although acceptable to pursue, are not the standard against which life is finally to be judged.

For this reason, the members of Apostotlic Church are encouraged to risk, lose, and sacrifice to attain a wider good for community and progeny. Interestingly, the members of Apostolic Church are encouraged to live life to its fullest, even though the attainment of finite goods is not the final end of life. Hence, the capacity to risk for a greater good is part of the ethos of that church and illustrates how its more inclusive narratives surround and animate its ethical and moral teachings.

WHAT IS ENGAGED SPIRITUALITY?

Taking my clue from this church, engaged spirituality is work for the just actualization of the goods of life for self and other within a narrative that gives ontological affirmation to these goods and the persons pursuing them, even though it also projects a larger meaning that helps humans handle the loss of these goods.

HOW ARE LOVE AND COMPASSION INTEGRAL TO JUSTICE?

Justice is not simple mathematical equality. Justice entails a theory of the basic goods of life that justice should distribute. Love and compassion are about discerning and promoting these goods, as they also affirm as ends the people pursuing these goods.

WHAT BELIEFS AND PRACTICES GIVE RISE TO ACTIVISM?

I think activism is born out of a sense of the goods of life, the worth of persons, and the right of persons to pursue the goods of life. Narratives and rituals that realistically point to this goodness and also celebrate the ultimate worth of all individuals, promote activism – an activism that is first motivated by gratitude.

WHERE SHOULD RESEARCH GO?

More research needs to focus on describing and conceptualizing the conditions that make communities of compassion actually work. But this research will have more meaning if it is informed by the categories of moral philosophy and religious ethics. At the same time, studying these communities will broaden, enrich, and enliven moral philosophy and theology.

HOW CAN RESEARCHERS AND ACTIVISTS HELP EACH OTHER?

Researchers can help us identify the best practices of communities of compassion and share them with activists and the wider public. Furthermore, researchers can help activists understand how ideas and actions interact. For instance, if one assumes the dialectical relationship between ethics and morality (between the good and the just) set forth above, it follows that social action based on complete self-sacrifice on the part of either activists or recipients will soon become exhausted and ineffective. Self-sacrifice is a moment that extends the pursuit of the good, but it does not stand independently of these goods. At the same time, no activism can work for long unless there is an ideology that gives meaning to risk and the possibility of failure on the part of the activist. Researchers can help identify how these ideologies work.

25
RALPH HOOD, PH.D.

Ralph W. Hood, Jr. holds a joint doctorate in sociology and psychology. He has been in the psychology department of the University of Tennessee at Chattanooga for over thirty years. His major research interest continues to be the psychology of religion, with a focus upon religious experience in general and mysticism in particular. He is past president of the Division of Psychology of Religion of the American Psychological Association and recipient of its William James Award. He is a founder and former co-editor of the International Journal for the Psychology of Religion and a former editor of the Journal for the Scientific Study of Religion. He is a current co-editor of the Archiv für Religionspsychologie. He has published over 200 articles and book chapters. He has authored, co-authored, or edited nine books. His most recent book is Hood, R. W. Jr., Hill, P. & Williamson, W. P. (in press). "The Psychology of religious fundamentalism: An intratextual model." New York: Guilford.

Hood's interest in love and social justice stems from two related sources: He has long subscribed to non-violence as a political philosophy, beginning with his decision to obtain objector status during the Vietnam War years. Non-violence (especially in the works of Gandhi, Tolstoy, and Simon Weil) informed his professional interests, including his concern with the empirical study of mysticism. The notion that individuality is rooted in a deeper sense of transcendence in which all are one suggests that egoism and altruism are not antithetical. When the distinction between self and other is abolished, the realization of self is the realization of the divine other in all. In Gandhi's words, "God is love."

WHAT IS ENGAGED SPIRITUALITY?

A current debate within the psychology of religion is whether or not distinctions can or ought to be made between religion and spirituality. In American samples, it is clear that, from a purely empirical perspective, the majority of individuals identify themselves as both religious and spiritual. These are the persons for who religion is an effective expression of their spirituality. However, a minority of persons (about 1/3) identify themselves as spiritual but not religious. Quantitative and qualitative studies show that many of these are hostile to religion. Religion is perceived to be constraining, concerned with dead ritual, meaningless dogma, and leading to at best dubious moralities. These "spiritual but not religious" persons are engaged in an ever-changing search for a means of spiritual expression that is fluid, eclectic, and resistant to institutionalization.

The distinction is useful as it points to issues of "engaged spirituality." Many of the most engaged spiritual persons are committed to fundamentalist religions, where lives are led in closed communities bounded by religious beliefs. The various orders of the Amish are one example; Mormons are another. Each creates a community of love and justice defined by the parameters of their faith. The return to religious fundamentalism is one major (though controversial) means by which religious persons are expressing engaged spirituality. How these communities function and sustain their memberships needs more careful empirical investigation.

On the other hand, the non-religious who seek to engage their spirituality often seem to focus on more secular concerns. One example is the variety of ecological movements suggesting almost a new pantheism, but one informed by science and a concern for "nature."

Contextually, it appears that the notion of an engaged spirituality suggests motivational issues–ones that are intrinsic rather than extrinsic, interests that are finalized by an ultimate concern better felt than reasoned. Engaged spirituality existentially defines what it is good and true. It is also expressed in action directed by what ought to be pursued at all costs. It is a continual sense of an ultimate concern.

HOW ARE LOVE AND COMPASSION INTEGRAL TO THE SUCCESS OF SOCIAL JUSTICE WORK?

I am aware of the high praise many place on Sorokin's work. Upon re-reading this classic as part of a co-operative project with Margaret Poloma, it occurred to me that it is too abstract to handle the specific questions usually addressed in issues of social justice.

We tend to forget that, despite their individuality, most mystics worked in and through their faith traditions.

However, Sorokin's abstractness is very useful in one sense. Love is conceived by Sorokin to be a universal principle governing the universe. I think social justice must also be conceived as a universal and applied to the emerging globalization. That is, justice must be concerned with the entire world. Those seeking social justice cannot defend one nation over and above the others. This surely "politicalizes" the issue and requires consideration of the ways in which economic systems (such as capitalism) may inhibit as much as foster social justice. It seems important to me to not just feed the poor, but to eradicate the conditions that produce poverty. It may be that wealthy nations such as the US are as much tyrants in the world due to extreme consumerism as others are for their own reasons. It also seems to me that compassion is linked to mysticism. Insofar as we all are one, what we do to others, however indirectly, is done to our self. To love others, our self, and God is to demand to live in a world other than the one we have so far created. Social justice is an inherently radical enterprise. It is concerned with transforming what is into what ought to be. It is justice as opposed to law. From Jerry Falwell on the political right to the M. L. King on the left, justice often dictates that one defy secular laws in favor of transcendent principles that cannot be compromised. This I take to be part of Sorokin's claim that love must be "adequate."

WHAT BELIEFS AND PRACTICES SUCCESSFULLY GIVE RISE TO OR SUSTAIN ACTIVISM?

One of the most perplexing facts about the study of the social sciences is that beliefs are often very poor predictors of behavior. In the extreme, even the horrors of genocide committed in both religious and secular cultures indicate that we all are capable of great evil. In Arendt's famous phrase, we must acknowledge the "banality of evil." We know that the average person in genocidal contexts behaves as expected in terms of simple normative compliance. Neither a distinct personality nor authoritarian beliefs identify those who commit mass atrocities. The capacity for such behavior lies within us all.

In a similar fashion, laboratory studies by social psychologists are more likely to be about pro-social or helping behavior than altruism. Altruism implies a motivation that some think may even mask egotism. Pro-social behavior is simply that—desirable behavior that aids others. It is largely situationally or contextually determined, as is genocide.

The irony of the above is that it is the fanatic who believes and acts from passionate motivation, whether for good or evil. They are the motivated ones, seeking to realize a dream, or to actualize a faith tradition's practice. These persons, if they achieve some legitimating social recognition, produce social activism in others who are often unbelieving and surely not purely (intrinsically) motivated.   If this is correct, we must look to the encouragement of the fanatic for sustaining social activism. Here lie the Gandhis and the M. L. Kings who, during their lives, sustained activism by modeling their beliefs in a way others could share. Likewise, on the negative side, a Hitler or a Stalin reveals the darker side of a fanaticism that works as well as any other.

WHERE SHOULD RESEARCH IN THIS FIELD BE DIRECTED AND FOCUSED?

I have strong opinions here. Despite being an empirical social scientist who appreciates both experimental and quasi-experimental methods, I do not think much will be achieved by laboratory-based studies. It seems to me that focus should be upon historical struggles with communities and individuals whose engaged spirituality is within the "real world." Part of the focus should be based upon a concern with motivation, something studies of pro-social behavior have found less than useful. Pro-social behavior and altruism have been conceived as orthogonal to one another. It seems that if more stringent criteria are employed, one can once again bring motivational concerns to the front. It is clear that most of the major faith traditions are concerned with "purity of heart," whether for one's own realization or for the welfare of others.

I would focus upon two concerns that would allow for a unique division among groups often thought separate. First, a concern with non-violence. Here I return to Gandhi and look at those who refuse to do violence as they struggle to transform that which is unjust. Gandhi's notion that the means you use will be the end you achieve suggests that one could look at those who refuse to do violence (even in the name of "love"), yet also do not disengage from the struggle for social justice. A study of some of the dynamics of the historic peace churches would be helpful, as well as a look at those individuals who, even in the face of death, refuse to retaliate with violence. A second area I would focus upon is spiritual experience, particularly mysticism. It is a testable hypothesis that those who have mystical experiences where individual selves are "dissolved" or found to be united in some transcendent reality are those who can act non-violently, and by such means effectively engage and transform the world. Part of the transformation can be in accepting what perhaps is less in need of a change or "cure." A good example is Jean Vanier's Wit lecture delivered at Harvard on the L'Arche community movement. I would like to know what experiences lead one to accept and love the "other" rather than seek to cure them of a "disease."

HOW CAN RESEARCHERS HELP ACTIVISTS IN THEIR WORK, AND HOW CAN ACTIVISTS HELP RESEARCHERS?

I think this is one of the more important questions we can ask at this conference. Researchers and activists are not so different as we might think. Researchers are activists, even if only in supporting investigatory procedures and some claim to "knowledge." Social psychology is largely built upon a "lie" –or, more discreetly put, deceptions deemed appropriate for the knowledge they will yield. It is not clear what can be done in the laboratory if the motivation must entail "unconditional love." The fact that American psychology is largely built upon undergraduate psychology students as "volunteers" separates means from ends in a fashion Gandhi warned us about. Likewise, spiritual activists in the "real world" become independent variables, acting as causal forces to transform a world. We are long past the stage when disinterested, "objective" knowledge is even recognized as a possibility, much less something to be desired. It would seem to me that a truly engaged spirituality eschews "technique" for a more intuitive, transcendent, driven sense of knowing what to do. Here Jungian psychology needs to be reconsidered in terms of modern neurophysiology and how it is that myth [engaged spirituality either guided by tradition (religion) or struggling to create itself anew (spirituality)] is relevant. The spiritual activists I think of are those who engage the world as a necessary stage for action and whose transformations are directed at the realization of what Jungians identify as the imperatives of the "mythopoetic" imagination. No one dies for the ontological proof! Religious or spiritual insights seem essential to sustain an engaged spirituality. Research is desperately needed on how individuals recognize (or ignore) such insights.

26
GIACOMO BONO, Ph.D.

Giacomo Bono is a postdoctoral research fellow at the University of Miami. His research is broadly focused on interpersonal forgiveness and gratitude. He completed his Ph.D. in Applied Social Psychology at Claremont Graduate University in Jan 2003, where he previously completed his M.A. in psychology. His dissertation examined group and cultural factors relevant to common-place forgiveness, and involved an intergroup experiment in which a confederate's offense is staged (toward his own group vs. the other group) in the context of a competitive task between two groups. One study's findings revealed apology/appeasement factors related to forgiveness in group contexts. Another study demonstrated differences between Sicilians and Americans in terms of forgiving and apologizing for a hypothetical offense. He has taught a variety of psychology courses at different universities in Southern California. At the University of Miami, he is currently conducting research on intrapersonal and interpersonal processes, as well as mental and physical health outcomes associated with forgiveness and gratitude. This research has 2 components: (1) a longitudinal experiment that uses daily diary tracking methods to focus on everyday changes and conditions related to the unfolding or inhibition of the forgiveness process and the experience of gratitude; (2) an experimental comparison of the cardiovascular and immunological functioning of people who forgive or experience gratitude and those who do not. The aims of this research are to determine key predictors of forgiveness and gratitude and to explore how forgiveness and gratitude help improve physical, mental, and spiritual health. Future aims include conducting applied and cross-cultural investigations of gratitude and forgiveness and deriving practical applications as a result of this research. So far, this work has led to several publications in scholarly journals and books.

LOVE AND JUSTICE

Acts of love and acts of justice fundamentally require the ability to balance behavior in the service of egoistic needs, as well as behavior in the service of relationship-needs (broadly speaking). In fact, many scholars believe that when people align their own egoistic motives so as to better foster healthy commitments with their mates, family, friends, groups, communities, nations, and with humanity in general, they become more loving AND fair-minded. This may well be the essential characteristic of the person who

149

practices and spurs others to practice "love that does justice."

For most people, love and justice are often on separate paths; sacrificing or regulating one's behavior for important relationships is easier when it is done for the sake of love than when it is done for the sake of justice. In fact, it is common for people to demand or evoke notions of justice mainly when it serves them (i.e., after they, not others, have personally experienced an injustice). Moreover, people also commonly excuse themselves from obligations to extend love to others further out (e.g., volunteering for a good cause) because they are too busy. This more selfish form of justice lies at the opposite end of the spectrum from the form of justice that occurs as a function of love; though love for the greater good often gets trumped by more immediate demands in people's lives, it is important for practitioners of just love to keep such obstacles in mind so they are better able to relate to everyday people and effect change. Before directly answering the questions we have been asked to address for this conference, I want discuss how love and justice fit into my own research interests.

Though most of my professional experience has revolved around basic research related to the social psychology of gratitude and forgiveness, I hope to eventually work on developing practical applications. Gratitude and forgiveness are invaluable to the maintenance of stable and supportive relationships, which most psychologists agree are essential for human health and happiness, and which all people (even psychologists) have trouble attaining or keeping.

Psychologists suspect that the experience and expression of gratitude can help counteract materialistic goals and pursuits. Given the alarming rates of population growth and rapid shifts toward free-market economies across the globe, cultures of irresponsible consumption increasingly pose a challenge for the sustainability of the earth's resources. In addition to being a good way to counteract this global problem, gratitude may also help people strengthen their relationships, which can also assist humankind's survival. A recent longitudinal study that McCullough and I conducted revealed that when people felt more grateful than they normally did for the benefits they reaped in their daily lives (over the course of two weeks), they also tended to be less materialistic. When we looked at people's subjective well-being in relation to both of these variables, we found that greater materialism is linked to lower-than-typical moods, satisfaction with life, and perceptions of social support, as well as greater-than-typical socioemotional loneliness and negative social exchanges with others. The benefits of gratitude, however, tended to be twice as strong as the burdens of materialism! Thus, the experience of gratitude really seems to fix the harmful effects of materialism.

Forgiveness provides relationship benefits while counteracting conflicts between people and groups. I can assure you that increasing conflict is one thing we could expect in a world of rising population and limited resources. My dissertation research found no differences in terms of overt intergroup forgiveness, but I did find that ingroup biases affected how mitigating and helpful offenders' apologies were; I also found that collectivists and individualists had different reasons for feeling concern toward their offenders, and that people apologized for an offense in a manner that was consistent with how forgiving they would be for the same offense. These findings all suggested that people's forgiveness is tied to self-needs and justification processes—i.e., forgiveness tends to end where people start to differ from each other in terms of their views of the injustice in question.

My more recent forgiveness research adds more detail to this picture. People's forgiveness and views of injustice differ on the basis of how much an offense targets their sense of equality. Specifically, I found that people pardoned offenses and viewed justice as being served to the extent that the offense matched their Social Dominance Orientation (SDO, or how much equality a person thinks should characterize the social hierarchy). Thus, people who were low in SDO tended to be more lenient toward a low SDO-type offense (acting unethically for the sake of saving a community from potential harm by a nearby company's pollution); people who were high in SDO tended to be more lenient toward a high SDO-type offense (acting unethically for the sake of freeing a company from restrictive pollution-regulation standards). Moreover, we found that a greater overall dissimilarity between victim and offender (in terms of Big 5 personality traits and SDO) predicted less forgiveness, implying that people's forgiveness indeed tends to be reserved for relationship partners who are similar in personality, world views, or ideology.

The longitudinal research that McCullough and I have been conducting reveals more about the deterrents and facilitators of forgiveness. On days when people ruminated about the harm of an offense more than they usually did (over the course of 12 weeks), they also tended to be less forgiving than could be expected given the trajectories of their forgiveness over that same time period. Ruminating about the hurt one has experienced seems to re-elicit the initial reactions of anger that naturally occur just an offense has been committed. When people were more forgiving than they normally were, they also tended to have greater well-being (i.e., moods, satisfaction with life, and psychosomatic symptoms) than could be expected on the basis of their trajectories of well-being over that time period. Forgiving helped restore the closeness of an important relationship; in fact, the closer people were before the offense, the more they benefited as a result of forgiving. It is interesting, however, that above-average fluctuations in a person's revenge turned out to be positively related to satisfaction with life. This suggests, as recent PET research confirms, that revenge may help satisfy a person's needs to balance the scales of justice or safeguard what people consider important social norms.

Taken together, these findings on forgiveness indicate that the key to opening oneself up to forgiveness is the ability to rise above one's egoistic motivations and realize the value of the important interdependencies we have with others. My immediate research interests are geared toward determining how perceptions of injustice and changes in attitudes about experienced injustices and transgressors are related to people's decisions to forgive or seek revenge against their transgressors. Or, put differently, what reasons underlie people's decisions to mend or break a relationship in the wake of an offense? I am also planning to investigate forgiveness and revenge cross-culturally. My ultimate goal is to apply this knowledge toward first understanding and then challenging interpersonal and intergroup biases as a way of reducing (and hopefully preventing to some degree) interpersonal and inter-ethnic conflicts.

Therefore, the challenges in my research may be regarded as similar to those faced by practitioners of just love. The more we can identify the other within ourselves, the more effectively we can extend both love and justice to other people—people who are close to us as well as people who are further away from us. People who more strongly embrace egalitarian beliefs can better control their automatic reliance on stereotypes and overcome prejudice. Similarly, the better we can break down individuals' assumptions about people who are different from themselves the more we can open them up to realizing and caring about the commonalities in all people. This may be challenging in our culture of rugged independence and personal responsibility. It would require promoting alternative forms of freedom and liberty that involve the accumulation of material wealth as well as the pursuit of more simple pleasures that are more socially responsible and considerate of other people's freedoms and liberties.

What does "engaged spirituality" mean to me?

Because this question addresses "spirituality" and not "religiosity," I am inclined to think of "engaged spirituality" as similar to an important point expressed in Frost's poem, "The Road Not Taken." One must always make choices in life. Most people take the well-defined paths that bring expected or known returns for their efforts—e.g., their church may encourage "virtuous behaviors" that they directly put into effect. However, some people choose paths according an intrinsic motivation to do good in less traditional ways. This may be because they believe that adhering to traditional ways helps perpetuate presumptions or biases that may also be harmful for society in the end, or because they believe that alleviating the important social problems of our time requires means and transformations in social consciousness that traditional institutions do not or cannot encourage.

The person who takes the road less traveled is being driven by a set of beliefs about how to improve society. So when the person who is spiritually engaged confronts adversity or meets failure, he or she understands that difficult problems take time to mend; he or she might keep in mind that society often promotes behavior that is either hedonistic or fulfilling of the status quo, and that spreading benevolent attitudes and behavior seldom brings immediate satisfaction. Thus, engaged spirituality can be considered an altruistic condition that propels individuals to be leaders on fronts they consider important for society to address, but that are often overlooked or neglected. Individuals who are engaged spiritually try to heal injustices of the past and correct the injustices of today and tomorrow; their overall goal is to improve society to the benefit of all of humanity.

How are love and compassion integral to the success of social justice work?

Love and compassion are necessary characteristics of any person who works for causes of social justice. Social justice work is inherently prosocial because it involves helping the people who need help the most. It involves safeguarding fundamental opportunities and resources for all members of the human race (irrespective of their race, gender, age, or nationality) so that they can strive to achieve their potential. In human development, the seeds of prosocial behavior are planted once a child begins to experience social emotions (e.g., empathy and guilt). The ability to relate to other people's experiences enables people to regulate and control their own behavior. The inability to relate to other people's experiences, on the other hand, is what essentially underlies antisocial and aggressive behavior. Thus, advocates of social justice behave altruistically because they feel love and compassion for people whose fundamental human rights are threatened or violated by unfair practices; they also understand that failure to feel love and compassion indiscriminately for all people in society will have a cost downstream.

Unlike the love and compassion experienced in more intimate contexts, the love and compassion associated with social justice work are distinct in that they are emotional outcomes that can result from a mixture of emotions. The social justice advocate feels *empathy* for the many categories of people who are systematically underserved or even disenfranchised by a social order that predominantly serves those in power. He/she feels *distress* over the lack of fair representation made available to these people, *anger* for the unnecessary waste of human potential and the unnecessary public health costs that are incurred as a result, and persistent *hope* that society can some day be more effectively managed so that all its members are empowered and productive contributors to a stronger and more diverse society. Thus, the love and compassion of the social justice advocate is political in that it drives activist behavior primarily intended to effect immediate social change for the people who need it most and most urgently. The love and compassion of the social activist is what allows him/her to transcend egoistic motives and embrace a responsibility for another person.

WHAT BELIEFS AND PRACTICES GIVE RISE TO OR SUSTAIN ACTIVISM?

Activists believe that the whole system suffers if one person is discriminated against. Notions of karma inform the persistent activists because they regard their own efforts as functions of a greater cause—a cause that will, in turn, reward all who follow suit. They have a strong sense of political efficacy because they believe that one person can make a difference in the world, and that greater numbers of people can make even more of a difference. They believe that there are structural reasons for poverty, and are quicker than the average person to refute stereotypical beliefs that a person's unfortunate outcomes are personally controllable or deserved (e.g., that laziness is responsible for poverty or ignorance is responsible for underachievement). They believe that there should be accountability for institutions that are inequitable and unsupportive of freedom and liberty for all because such organizations maintain and reinforce prejudice and hostility between people and groups.

Unwavering activists always practice tolerance and indiscriminate respect for the inherent uniqueness of every individual. They practice patience because they acknowledge how difficult it is to break the habit of prejudice, and how long it takes to heal our social ills and the major problems of modern society. Perhaps most importantly, persistent activists believe in and practice Democracy on a daily basis. They are more deeply, more often, and more vocally disturbed by adulterations in democratic process.

WHERE SHOULD RESEARCH IN THIS FIELD BE DIRECTED AND FOCUSED?

Many people accept the Just-World Hypothesis to some degree—i.e., that you get what you deserve; they believe that giving extra consideration to other people prevents those people from trying to succeed on their own, thus creating dependence on the welfare-system. This poses a major obstacle for progress in social justice. How can we soften this culture of personal responsibility enough so that its strongest adherents can better consider the inequality of opportunity and circumstance realistically faced by many minorities in this country? The pursuit of self-interest is another major obstacle for advancing social justice causes in our society. Many people are naturally reluctant to compromise the quality of their own lives and those of their families in order to make our institutions more inclusive and beneficial for other people's quality of life. How can such fears be allayed? Research on applying effective negotiation strategies (e.g., integrative negotiation and win-win strategies) to activism would also be helpful.

It is important to understand how various people view acts of injustice in different ways, depending on their own political and ideological attitudes, and how people's attitudes can be changed so that they can dialectically move more toward the middle ground. This discrepancy is something that we all have experienced, and the ability to reconcile opposing viewpoints is also something we have all yearned for. Yet, social science can say little about such attitudinal differences and how to reconcile them.

Empirical research can also identify ways of instilling or encouraging social justice concerns in individuals. For example, I wonder if the experience of humility is an important way to invoke social justice concerns in people. Research is also needed on how psychologists and other social scientists can better influence and direct policy related to social justice. Finally, research that can speak to the potential benefits of reparations and the appropriateness of different forms of restitution is needed. This would enable the public to be more open to the possibility of overtly disavowing the commission of past injustices (e.g., American Indians, African American slaves) and restoring dignity to victims of these injustices for the sake of building peace in the future.

HOW CAN RESEARCHERS HELP ACTIVISTS IN THEIR WORK, AND HOW CAN ACTIVISTS HELP RESEARCHERS?

My first thought is that more applied research is needed so that researchers can better understand activism as it is actually practiced in the real world. For example, why do people persist at activist causes? How is activism qualitatively different across the different issue-domains? What characterizes effective or ineffective activism? When do activists become discouraged, and how can this be prevented? Answers to such applied research questions would be useful to activists. Perhaps such research can be modeled on the research on volunteerism. Research in some of these areas has no doubt already been done, so is there some way to make such findings more accessible to activists? There are many journals that seem to regularly include articles on activism from various perspectives (i.e., education, sociology, and communication). Perhaps a review journal that addresses activism AND the social scientific bottom line on best practices would make such research findings more accessible to the busy activist.

Similarly, activists can also communicate more with researchers. For example, they can work more with social scientists by personally informing them about some of the issues mentioned in the above paragraph. They can also help researchers develop more important or useful hypotheses related to activist behavior.

Finally, both social scientists and activists should assist education professionals with curriculum proposals and development. Courses could then focus on the importance of knowledge and activism for safeguarding the democratic process and quality of life for all members of society. Though diversity issues pervade many curricula, we need to learn how to actually cross-pollinate people from different groups and social networks so as to counter the self-confirmation biases, selective attention, and group polarization that threaten communication between groups and undermine democracy in our country.

27
THOMAS JAY OORD

Thomas Jay Oord, Ph.D., is Professor of Theology and Philosophy at Northwest Naza-
rene University, Nampa, Idaho. He serves as theologian for the Institute for Research on Unlimited
Love, as well as co-director of the institute's Altruistic Love and Science Course Competition. Oord
contributes frequently to Science and Theology News as its Academic Correspondent and Contrib-
uting Editor. Oord has written and edited a number of books, the most recent being "Science of
Love: The Wisdom of Well-Being" (Templeton) and "Relational Holiness" (with Michael Lodahl)
(Beacon Hill). His other books include "Thy Nature and Thy Name is Love" (Kingswood) and
"Philosophy of Religion: Essays" (Beacon Hill). His essays have appeared in dozens of journals
and books, and he is currently writing a volume that he titles, "The Love-and-Science Symbiosis."
Oord serves on the executive council of several scholarly societies, including the Open and Rela-
tional Theologies group (AAR), the Wesleyan Theological Society, and the Wesleyan Philosophical
Society. As well as being a professor, writer, and researcher, Oord serves his faith tradition as an
ordained minister.

A Vision of the Divine: Love that Does Justice With God

Countless individuals and groups working for justice believe that, in some way, they act as God's hands and feet. For them, God is not a figment of imagination, mere metaphor for life, or human projection. They believe that God is real, active, and living. Their belief in God provides meaning as they live lives of love that seek justice.
One need look no further than Martin Luther King, Jr. to find one whose belief in God inspired action for justice. King believed, however, that not just any vision of God is sufficient. Rejecting the idea that God acts all alone, King writes, "If God does everything. . . God becomes little more than a 'cosmic bellhop' who is summoned for every trivial need. . . . This view ends us with a God who is a despot and not a Father" (*Strength to Love*, 131 & 133). One's vision of God makes an enormous difference.

In this brief essay, I offer a vision of divinity. I believe that this vision incorporates key insights from contemporary theological scholarship and can empower us to love.

GOD DOES NOT SANCTION THE STATUS QUO

The theologies of Western civilization have time and again attributed to God the kind of power that implies, if not states outright, that God sanctions the status quo. These theologies do so by claiming that God either *could* or *does* entirely control any person, society, or situation. If God either could or does control others entirely, God must either cause or permit all evil and injustice.

Some who believe that humans have free will have balked, of course, at the claim that God causes evil. But they admit that God allows injustice to occur because God is self-limited. I reply, however, that the God with the potential to control others entirely is rightly said to endorse, at least indirectly, whatever happens. After all, if this God *really* wanted things to be different, the deity could unilaterally make things different. Nothing prevents this deity from unilaterally determining any event whatsoever. Consequently, those who worship a God who is or could be totally in control give allegiance to the God who either causes or allows all injustice.

By contrast, I suggest that God does not endorse persons, societies, or structures that cause injustice. God does not do so, because God is love. God's love is relentless, all-pervasive, and situation-specific. The vision I offer is of a deity who is not capable of controlling any person, society, or situation entirely. According to this alternative vision, God has neither caused nor allowed things to be the way that they are. Rather, the world is what it is in part because of the actions of nondivine creatures like you and me. And God's desire is for a new world order – one that is more just, beautiful, and loving.

GOD IS NOT CULPABLE FOR CAUSING, ALLOWING, OR FAILING TO PREVENT INJUSTICE

The problem of evil is a rock upon which many theological ships have crashed. The problem asks why a perfectly loving and omnipotent God fails to prevent genuine evil from occurring. If we believe that some events are unjust and also believe that God exists, we are left with three basic responses to the problem of evil and injustice.

One response to evil is to claim that God does not love relentlessly. Sometimes God takes a holiday from love or gets so pissed off that he goes about wreaking havoc. This solution effectively undercuts any genuine worship of God, however. For we will not – in fact, we *cannot* – give our ultimate allegiance to an immoral being. Such a God is not worthy of worship.

A second response claims that there is no answer to the problem of evil and injustice. God and God's ways are absolutely mysterious. This answer -- that is, no answer -- abandons any viable theory of divine action. If God is ultimately a mystery, why believe that God desires justice or even that God is real, active, and living?

An adequate solution to the problem of evil suggests that God is not culpable for causing, allowing, or failing to prevent injustice. I suggest that God cannot entirely control evil-doers because God cannot entirely control free creatures. Free creatures who fail to respond to God's call to love are culpable for the evil and injustice we encounter.

Those who work for justice and endeavor to love should envision God as essentially related to others in love. In these necessary love relations, God provides freedom to creatures and calls them to promote well-being. God can neither withdraw nor fail to offer freedom to others, because God is necessarily related to them. Being in relation to others through love is part of God's nature. And, to quote a hymn from Charles Wesley, "God's name and nature is love."

AS A FELLOW-SUFFERER, GOD FEELS THE PAIN OF ALL VICTIMS

To say that God is essentially related to others in love implies that God intimately relates to all creation. As one who intimately relates, God knows *all* our joys and sorrows. God rejoices with those who rejoice and mourns with those who mourn. God is, as Alfred North Whitehead famously said, "the fellow-sufferer who understands."

Empathy is a necessary part of the love that does justice. We often forget that justice requires feeling the feelings of others. Good intentions are not enough; empathizing with victims provides us with the heart and head knowledge required for effective love responses.

My relationship with my wife illustrates the truth that empathy is a necessary part of the love that does justice. When she suffers from the effects of evil, I often want to offer advice or act to correct things. I want to fix things immediately. But her greatest need is often a sympathetic ear and a heart that feels what she feels. She wants to know that I feel her pain.

Until the twentieth century, most theologians envisioned God as unaffected by the world's suffering. God was, to use Aristotle's phrase, the "unmoved mover." But most theologians today agree with Clark Pinnock (and others) that God is the "most moved mover." As one who is moved through empathy, God knows all things as the omni-sensitive one.

Those who work for justice should imitate God by empathizing with others. Love cannot act with full and far-reaching justice if the experiences of those treated unjustly are ignored. Love requires co-feeling.

GOD CAN SQUEEZE SOMETHING GOOD FROM THE INJUSTICE GOD DEPLORES

Many in the present and past have unfortunately excused the God capable of entirely controlling others by claiming that all injustice is part of this God's mysterious plan to bring about greater good. With this excuse, they sanction the status quo and sanctify every evil ever committed – from holocausts, to rapes, from genocide, to child abuse, just to name a few.

This excuse gains a footing because it contains a partial truth. That is, it is true that some good often emerges from events that are genuinely evil and unjust. We all know that sometimes a little pain and suffering is required if a better future is to become actual. But this truth is unfortunately applied to genuinely evil occurrences, and the damaging claim is made that God caused or allowed genuine evil to bring about some good.

I suggest that we best understand God as not wanting genuinely evil events to occur. But, upon their occurrence, God works with those involved to bring whatever good can be squeezed from what God did not want to occur in the first place. Something good can come from evil, but this is not the amount of good that could have been secured if the evil had never occurred. God continually works to bring about the best good possible, even as God deplores evil.

GOD CALLS US TO WORK COOPERATIVELY TO PROMOTE WELL-BEING

Finally, a vision of the divine adequate to inspire the love that does justice is a vision that includes a necessary role for our cooperation with God. Martin Luther King's words are helpful in understanding this cooperative venture: "Neither God nor man will individually bring the world's salvation. Rather, both man and God, made one in a marvelous unity of purpose through an overflowing love as the free gift of himself on the part of God and by perfect obedience and receptivity on the part of man, can transform the old into the new and drive out the deadly cancer of sin" (*Strength to Love*, 134).

To cooperate with God is to act with God in loving ways to bring about justice. The Apostle Paul put it this way: "We know that God is working for the good in all things, together with those who are called according to that purpose." God, who is a spirit with no wholly divine body, calls upon us to act as God's hands and feet.

In working to secure overall well-being, the justice aspect of love emerges. To act justly is to avoid granting excessive goods to a few at the expense of the many. The justice of love also gives to the few the rights and privileges properly afforded the many. In both cases, it is overall well-being that justice seeks and love requires. And in both cases, God calls us to work in cooperation with divine activity and other like-minded lovers to promote overall well-being. King's words provide a fitting conclusion: "God has promised to cooperate with us when we seek to cast evil from our lives and become true children of the divine will" (136).

28
VALENTINO LASSITER, Ph.D.

Valentino Lassiter serves as Pastor in Residence and lecturer of Religious Studies at John Carroll University, located in University Heights, Ohio. His course topics include: African-American Christian Ethics; History of the African-American Church; Life and Theology of Martin Luther King; Survey of African-American Theology; Theology of African-American Sacred Music. He received the B. A. degree from Fisk University, the M. Div. from Boston University, and the D. Min. degree from Eden Theological Seminary. Lassiter is the author of "Martin Luther King in the African- American Preaching Experience." He is involved in a number of boards and organizations that address concerns of religion and justice—e.g., vice-chair, Board of Directors for the national Justice Witness Ministries of the United Church of Christ. He currently serves as President of the United Campus Protestant Ministries. Lassiter and his wife, Yvonne, are the parents of three sons.

Engaged spirituality is that force of spiritual awareness that is characterized by an intentional ardent involvement for collective goals of unified peace. Such goals are often directed toward the social and spiritual uplift of persons. The very nature of an engaged spirituality consists of varying *spontaneous* acts of love and unity. The ideal result of such engagement of common thinking and altruism has proven to effect positive world view and opinions. Hence, the very essence of engaged spirituality is very often an existential involvement, as opposed to an analytical exercise.

Spiritual engagement stems from authentic sources of concern, justice, and love. Consequently, various forms of spiritual engagement are found in organized protests for common good, unified labors to heighten political awareness, and a spiritual courage for community. From time to time, this same engagement may take form through multi-disciplinary academic postulations of justice and peace. Of course, the content of given religious assumptions and belief practices are a major source of life for the spiritual community. These important assumptions are often crucial in the involvement and informing of tacit assumptions of love and justice. As belief systems are put into action, spiritual engagement is in process. Moreover, these systems often maintain the latent spirituality of given communities.

The Civil Rights Movement in the United States stands as a lasting example of this phenomenon of engaged spirituality. The movement for equality during the 1960s was a very *spiritual* movement. Viewing this era as a merely political occurrence leaves much to be desired. Courageous activity to bring changes to oppressive systems in the country were fueled by deep understandings of spiritual sources of interlocking religious faith.

Engaged spirituality made possible the successes and victories that were attained by persons of good will. Such spiritual identity presented race as a very nominal issue for unified engagement.

Love, Compassion, and Justice Work

Concrete suppositions of love and human compassion are essential for the execution of any effectual work in the name of justice. "Justice," by its very definition, often supposes a nature of legality. *Justice* ethics and systems of morality have often been influenced by prescribed legal codes of conduct—e.g., Ten Commandments, Old Testament Law Codes, Bill of Rights, Acts of Congress, etc.).

From a spiritual ideal, it becomes difficult to engage in perspectives of justice that are not motivated by love and human compassion. Theologians argue that an "oppressor's" view of justice may be limited to merely legal implications. This type of justice summation becomes an end to a means. When justice originates from sources of human compassion, however, there is a potential of ongoing growth and extended altruism. Relationships become extended and solid when the such limitations are removed. The sincere work of justice must carry a "risk factor" of giving of one's inner spirit and concern. Martin Luther King, Jr. reminds us that when justice is motivated by love, there exists a depth of authentic possibility of preservation and growth. Moreover, African-American theologians of justice, such as James Cone, et. al., emphasize that justice awareness is raised in the context of the victims of injustice. We must be ready to "experience" the pain in order to grasp the ultimate feeling of loss and fear. The privileged thoughts of claims will not always support an inclusive notion of justice that reaches beyond all boundaries. It becomes necessary to "name" the boundaries of social thought that may prohibit the ongoing free thought of open support for all persons.

Love and *law* cannot be dissected. The end result of justice is an enlightened world view of humanity that is not colored by exclusive notions of charity toward the poor. Justice that stems from a spirit of love and unified effort can make a perpetual difference in assessing the divide of power/compasion, morality/direction, and spirituality/abstract theory. Justice work that is based primarily upon foundations of love has far reaching effects upon the quest for world harmony and peace.

Beliefs and Practices Giving Rise to and Sustaining Activism

Beliefs and practices that have the capacity to foster and intensify activism are those systems of thought that are primarily centered upon the sanctity of the human life.

When the sanctity of the individual is celebrated, activism that is focused upon human uplift becomes a natural action. Concern for the full well being of others is activated by a central source of spiritual dynamism. There must exist an authentic spiritual source that informs us of the obligations and rewards of becoming a dynamic of change. Unless there is such a source(religion, spirituality, etc.), the involvement in activism may have a void quality.

Spiritual assumptions of ethical thought often result in actions that initiate "movement." Movement results when a community uses common goals, experiences, and spiritual sources to determine that positive change can take place. Of course, such actions are not to be found only in the Christian-Judeo heritage. We cannot neglect the fact that roots of Hinduism were crucial in the summations and execution of the Civil Rights Movement. Traditions of Judaism and Islam also merged with Christian definitions of humanity to form a unified goal of justice. Common ethical assumptions that derived from monotheistic religious systems informed the activism that occurred during the 1960s. Central beliefs regarding life, human rights, peace, and a deity of justice empowered movement toward a greater world good.

Movement involves a universal understanding and ownership of given ambitions as they are related to change. Activism and movement are informed by spiritual beliefs and goals that center upon the human struggle for peace and equality. This activism is often guided by the adoration of given supreme beings, written traditions of religious teachings, and the sacred nature of a collective human race that recognizes a world of diversity, equality, and unity of creation.

DIRECTION OF THIS RESEARCH

The current research should indeed be directed toward persons involved in studies of ethical, moral, or theological interpretations of justice and love. It is crucial that dialogues that take place in given areas of ethical studies maintain clear and definitive directions. Moreover, in assessing moral concerns, we cannot overlook the important historical foundation upon which many of these assumptions stand. Research is to be focused upon a pedagogy of justice that supersedes prejudice.

The community to which this research is directed should include: students of ethics on all levels; professors of Religion/Philosophy; social activists; all persons concerned with the fair execution of justice with compassion. There are many current theories and constant axioms that remain vital to the understanding of the work of justice. In addition, the place of reconciliation is a necessary pedagogical factor in the knowledge and enhancement of the essence of love, compassion, love-empowered justice, and ongoing activism.

The process of reconciliation leads to a more defined way of thinking and actions for universal uplift. Effective movement takes place at this level of awareness and dedication.

RESEARCHERS AND ACTIVISTS

Both communities can be of benefit to each other. Researchers are in a position to provide activists with necessary historical data and backgrounds on given issues of concern. In the process, many questions are already addressed with clarity and direction. Activists are given a more secure ground of purpose and direction as a result of concrete answers that have been provided by ehticists, sociologist, and historians.

At the same time, researchers learn from activists who present experience of real involvement and actions. Such sharing of experiences provides an important basis for doing ongoing study and observations. Together, both sides of the inquiries make a dynamic contribution to the knowledge of ethical need, social strife, and impact of human compassion.

Trial and error approaches and conclusions are important tools for assessing ongoing needs of society and of human nature.

Researchers may have a tendency to rely upon concrete facts and findings. On the other hand, activists present an emotional and compassionate view from having "felt" the frustrations and concerns. Both sides are very essential.

29
DONALD MILLER, Ph.D.

Donald Miller is the Executive Director of the Center for Religion and Civic Culture at USC, as well as a professor of religion and sociology. He is the author/editor of seven books, including Armenia: Portraits of Survival and Hope (University of California Press, 2003), Survivors: An Oral History of the Armenian Genocide (University of California Press, 1993), GenX Religion (Routledge, 2000), Reinventing American Protestantism (University of California Press, 1997), Homeless Families: The Struggle for Dignity (University of Illinois Press, 1993), Writing and Research in Religious Studies (Prentice Hall, 1992), and The Case for Liberal Christianity (Harper & Row, 1981). With his wife, Lorna, he has partnered with an association of orphans in Rwanda on an oral history project documenting the 1994 genocide. He is currently writing a book on global Pentecostalism with Tetsunao Yamamori, based on interviews and observations in twenty developing countries (to be published by the University of California Press). Donald Miller is married to Lorna Miller, Director of the Office for Creative Connections at All Saints Episcopal Church in Pasadena. They have two children: Arpi, a graduate student in sociology at UCLA; Shont, an attorney practicing in Los Angeles.

Recently Greg Stanczak, a postdoctoral fellow at USC, and I did over 75 interviews with exemplary individuals who embody an "engaged spirituality." Some of the analytical categories mentioned below emerged from this research project, and are summarized in a report that is available on the website of the Center for Religion and Civic Culture[4]. There is a larger context, however, to my reflections on the role of unconditional love. During the past five years, I have traveled in twenty different developing countries studying the social ministries of growing Pentecostal churches. In the process of conducting interviews with hundreds of pastors and lay leaders, as well as visiting dozens of programs focused on poverty reduction, education, and medical intervention, I have become convinced that spirituality plays a profound role in motivating people to engage in heroic acts of compassion.

---

[4] This report, "Engaged Spirituality: Spirituality and Social Transformation in Mainstream American Religious Traditions," is available online at www.usc.edu/crcc. In addition, a more thorough discussion of the findings from this project will be published in a forthcoming book written by Gregory C. Stanczak and published by Rutgers University Press.

Any convictions that I have about "unconditional love" have been moderated, however, by years of dealing with the issue of genocide. My father-in-law lost seven of his eight family members in the genocide of Armenians in Turkey in 1915, and grew up as an orphan. My wife and I interviewed 100 elderly survivors of this genocide and came away from this experience with a deep conviction that gross evil needs to be countered by powerful intervention against nations that engage in "crimes against humanity." Very recently, we collaborated on an oral history project in Rwanda with an association of orphans, whose members survived the 1994 genocide that claimed the lives of over 800,000 people. Once again, I became aware of the need for intervention by outside forces, and was morally sickened by the failure of the United States and other countries to support the United Nations, which had troops in Rwanda and very likely could have modified the outcome of the attempt to eliminate the Tutsis in Rwanda.

Hence, I am very hesitant to talk about love and justice without including the concept of power. Love is a wonderfully humane ideal, representing the highest aspirations of the human species. It is a strong motivator and should be the basis for interpersonal relationships. I am not convinced, however, that unconditional love is the basis for political action. While I am deeply opposed to our military intervention in Iraq and participated in every major demonstration in Los Angeles against the war, there are times when justice can only be served by the exercise of power. Early in my graduate training I was influenced by Reinhold Niebuhr, who argued that individuals may strive for moral perfection, but collective groups inevitably act out of self interest, sometimes of demonic proportion. Applying this insight to genocide, the slaughter that occurred in Rwanda could have been stopped with outside military intervention. The US State Department refused to respond to the situation, fearing a repetition of the events in Somalia.

WHAT DOES "ENGAGED SPIRITUALITY" MEAN TO YOU?

In our report on "Engaged Spirituality," Greg Stanczak and I offer the following definitions:

Spiritual experience: personal or collective experience that is interpreted by the individual to connect him or her with a socially constructed yet subjectively meaningful ideal, entity, or higher power.

Spiritual practice: any act, ritual, or attempt at communication or communion with this socially constructed yet subjectively meaningful ideal, entity, or higher power.

Spirituality: a collective term for the experience, practice, interpretation, and implementation of this phenomenon.

Engaged Spirituality: action in society that is motivated by transcendent moral values and is supported by regular practices that seek some connection with God or the sacred.

In our interviews with social activists, we discovered many different roots of engaged spirituality. Some individuals indicated that their commitment to social justice was developed in childhood, after observing their parents' commitment to serving other people. Other individuals said that their commitment to social justice came through reading and various educational experiences (e.g. exposure to liberation theology). Another route to social engagement came from various encounters with individuals in need, especially dramatic encounters with poverty and injustice. And, finally, there were a few individuals who had spiritual epiphanies in which God or the Holy Spirit spoke directly to them about their moral obligations and life commitments.

Engaged spirituality, then, is the opposite of navel-gazing, narcissistic self actualization. Engaged spirituality results from people being motivated by a transcendent force or power that awakens their social conscience and motivates them to live for others, rather than simply for themselves. In the very act of serving others, these individuals often experience profound joy, a deep sense of purpose, and an overriding humility about not being self-sufficient. They attribute their personal energy and the good that may result from their actions to a transcendent power that, in many religions, is identified as God. The task of human existence, in their view, is to align themselves with this creative, transformative force within the universe. Typically, this force is not impersonal; it is experienced in highly personal encounters, sometimes alone and sometimes in corporate moments of worship.

HOW ARE LOVE AND COMPASSION INTEGRAL TO THE SUCCESS OF SOCIAL JUSTICE WORK?

I can best answer this question by giving an example. I met Maggie, an upper-class Coptic Christian, in Cairo, Egypt. Some years ago, she made a purchase from a street vendor and her daughter. The woman was barefoot in winter and selling vegetables she had grown. As Maggie looked into the eyes of this woman's daughter, she saw her own daughter staring back at her; when she looked at the woman, she saw herself, precariously trying to support her family as a street vendor. When she went home after this transaction, she realized that God was speaking to her through this encounter. Today, Maggie is the driving force behind a network of over thirty nursery schools that she has helped establish in the slums of Cairo. I interviewed many of the staff working with Maggie, and they all referred to their encounter with Jesus as they looked into the eyes of the children they are serving.

Compassion is integral to social justice work. It is putting oneself in the place of the other. It is doing unto others as you would want them to do to you. Compassion is motivated by empathy. Individuals such as Maggie and her staff connect with God by seeing him in the eyes of those whom they serve. They touch God as they hug and minister to children whose parents make their living by sorting garbage. Social justice workers are made whole through the act of healing the community of impoverished and exploited people that surrounds them. Compassion is the opposite of exploitation; it is the basis for all self-transcending action.

In our research on engaged spirituality, we have created a typology of five different types of social roles associated with religious motivations: 1) The Good Neighbor; 2) The Community Volunteer; 3) The Professional Service Provider; 4) The Moral Advocate; 5) The Visionary Prophet. Sometimes these roles overlap, but we have found this to be a helpful typology in classifying the expressions of social service that are spiritually motivated.

WHAT BELIEFS AND PRACTICES SUCCESSFULLY GIVE RISE TO OR SUSTAIN ACTIVISM?

Everyone we interviewed for our Engaged Spirituality project—and I also believe this is true for individuals I encountered in the Global Pentecostalism project—has regular moments when they withdraw from the pressures of everyday life and commune with God and/or reflected on their moral obligations. During these moments of reflection, they submit their own ego-driven impulses to a higher power; they seek guidance for their obligations that day, and are renewed by encountering the source of life, if even for a few minutes. Daily spiritual practice is their touchstone for engaging the world and submitting to the hard work of social transformation.

Spiritual practice does not come in one size or expression. For some individuals, it is done at a specific time every day and a specific routine is followed, such as prayer and reading of sacred texts. Other individuals follow what we have labeled "eclectic improvisation." They borrow from various religious traditions and sometimes find that rather "secular" activities, such as working out at a gym, provide a time when they move beyond their own self preoccupation. A number of people also said that nature (e.g. mountains, sea, deserts) is where they are renewed, feeling a certain oneness with the universe. And, finally, one cannot ignore the value of participation in organized worship, which for many people is the spiritual practice that sustains their social justice work.

For our Engaged Spirituality project, we conducted interviews with individuals from a variety of religious traditions—Christian, Jewish, Muslim, and Buddhist. While the symbols and practices varied, there was a surprising convergence of experiences. For example, one individual told us about his experience of making a pilgrimage to Mecca and the overwhelming emotional impact of this ritual event on his life. For other individuals, it was the daily routine of "sitting" in Buddhist meditation that was personally transformative. And several Pentecostals told us how the Holy Spirit had encountered them, quite literally speaking to them about a change in their life course.

If there is a universal "belief" shared by the individuals we interviewed, it was that they are not self-sufficient; they owe their life and energy and vision to forces outside of themselves. Egoist self-absorption gets in the way of being in the "flow" with this lifesource. Furthermore, they would have burned out on their social justice work a long time ago if they were sustained simply by their own ambitions and personal power.

WHERE SHOULD RESEARCH IN THIS FIELD BE DIRECTED AND FOCUSED?

There is a decided absence of research on the relationship between emotion and social change in the literature on social movements. In our Engaged Spirituality project, we identify three broad families of "feelings." The first has to do with "feelings of community," which relate to feelings of connection with family, friends, and congregation, as well as "imagined" communities that anchor one's identity within a nation, ethnic heritage, and/or religious tradition. Being part of a community implies specific social roles and obligations. A second emotional root for social activism has to do with "feelings of empowerment," that are associated with a divine source or self-transcendent force. This feeling gives one the strength to do things that one could not otherwise accomplish. A third emotional resource comes from "feelings of transcendence," that express themselves in dreams, visions, voices, and other moments when an idea or inspiration enters their consciousness.

Here is my short list of things that I would like to research in the future:

- I am very interested in "turning points" in people's lives, especially those moments when individuals turn their backs on personal ambition and set a life course that involves them in addressing significant moral challenges. This project would involve in-depth conversations with a highly-skilled interviewer, and would include individuals from a broad cross-section of different faith traditions and geographical locations. Questions about religion and spirituality would not be asked initially; rather, the goal would be to see how individuals frame their experiences, with some individuals undoubtedly referencing transcendent realities while other individuals would not.

- Based on my Pentecostalism research, I am convinced that worship is what sustains social ministries. For many theorists, worship is viewed in purely functional terms (i.e., maintaining the collective values of the group), with scarcely a nod to the role of worship in inspiring heroic, self-transcending, and group-transcending social action. Therefore, I would like to research the connection between collective worship—including the role of music, dance, and ritual—and social justice work, because I suspect the failure to make this connection leads to very short-lived social movements.

- I am impressed by the role of "visionary prophets" and moral leaders, but I suspect that these individuals are always sustained by their relationship to a community of fellow travelers. It is this connection between leaders and co-conspirators that I would like to investigate. This research would require substantial periods of observation within a social movement in order to understand the ways in which leaders are nurtured by their followers and vice-versa.

Finally, I have two qualifications regarding how and where I would like to see research on these topics take place. First, I believe we should utilize the new digital technology of visual and sound documentation so that we do not privilege the written word or reduce human speech to the flat medium of transcribed interviews. If emotion and feeling have any role in motivating action, and if spirituality is at any level a sensate experience, then we need to capture this reality utilizing the best technology available. Secondly, my international research has convinced me that we must shed our Eurocentric and Western bias by engaging in global and cross-cultural research. Americans are a very privileged population, and spirituality is experienced in very deep and profound ways in a number of developing countries.

30
DAVID L. COOPERRIDER, Ph.D.

David L. Cooperrider is Professor and Chairman of the Department of Organizational Behavior at the Weatherhead School of Management, Case Western Reserve University. Professor Cooperrider is past President of the National Academy of Management's OD Division. He has lectured and taught at Stanford, University of Chicago, Katholieke University in Belgium, MIT, University of Michigan, Cambridge and others.

David has served as researcher and advisor to a wide variety of organizations, includingYellow Roadway Corp., Green Mountain Coffee Roasters, McCann-Erickson, Nutrimental Foods, World Vision, Cleveland Clinic, American Red Cross, and United Way of America. Most of the projects are inspired by the Appreciative Inquiry (AI) methodology for which Professor Cooperrider is best known. His founding work in this area is creating a positive revolution in the leadership of change; it is helping companies all over the world discover the power of strength-based approaches to planning and multi-stakeholder cooperations. Admiral Clark, the CNO of the Navy, for example, recently met with David to bring AI into the Navy for a multi-year project on "Bold and Enlightened Naval Leadership. In June 2004, Cooperrider was asked by the United Nations Global Compact to design and facilitate a historic, unprecedented, Summit meeting between Kofi Annan and 500 business leaders to "unite the strengths of markets with the authority of universal ideals to make globalization work for everyone." Cooperrider's work is especially important because of its ability to enable positive change in very large and complex systems.

In 1937, about ten years before his assassination, Mohandas K. Gandhi made a plea for a new mode of relationship between people of diverse faiths. It was a radical plea. Sitting in the turbulent vortex of ethnic and religious conflict that was often perpetuated in the name of God, Gandhi called not just for non-violence or tolerance, but for a much more radical kind of appreciative interchange. He called for a stance of openness, learning, and inquiry whereby people would actively seek to know the deepest and best in each other's religious wisdom, knowledge, and spiritual practice. He called it a "reverence for other faiths"-- something that with simple humility recognizes how all faiths are imperfect ("as they pass through the human medium") and that all have something to teach and share. He went even further, however. He proposed that we might, in our active exploration and appreciation of the Other, discover surprising things that are so good in the Other's tradition that *"we would not only not hesitate, but would think it our duty, to bring into our faith every acceptable feature of other faiths."*

Engaged spirituality? Radical for Gandhi's times? The answer is obviously "yes," as Gandhi himself was shot for such views. But the real question is this: What about these times? Still radical? How about Catholics and Protestants sitting down together in this Gandhian-like way in Ireland? Or Palestinian Muslims and Israeli Jews in Jerusalem searching for the deepest and best in each other and each other's religious and spiritual traditions? Impossible?

ARE LOVE AND COMPASSION INTEGRAL TO THE SUCCESS OF SOCIAL JUSTICE WORK?

I want to use the previous short opening to introduce several ideas.

1. That spirituality in social justice terms is a call to engaged *interspirituality*[5] --that is, a process of :(1) drawing upon the transformational strength of direct experience of the divine or ultimate mystery and allowing that experience to flow into our "horizontal" relationships with others; (2) connecting with all that is best and good in ourselves and others and using that *experience* to strengthen our capacity to link "vertically" with the divine or realization of vast awareness, as in Buddhism. At the heart of engaged interspirituality, as it is in most discussions of spirituality, is the mystical experience of awe, wonder, gratitude, and love. It involves the ability to connect to the non-material, invisible world, the world of spirit, as well as the capacity to sense, feel, or experience the vastness of the *appreciable world*—that is, the miracle of life on this planet and all that is valuable and possible. All of us in some degree are mystics—vertically, horizontally, or both simultaneously, every time we are in dialogue and communion with everything of value. Some, like Gandhi, are able to hold in one hand the invisible world and in the other hand the visible, and create such a powerful yoga/link/union that everything around them changes. It is a generative and special moment wherein "the radical brokenness of all existence" is suspended and eclipsed. Creative good emerges. An abundance of energy flows. New resources for change are unleashed—relational resources, shared material resources, and vision. The impossible becomes possible. But how? And can this kind of creative event be cultivated in everyday life—let's say by labor and

---

5 "Interspirituality" and "intermysticism" are terms coined by Wayne Teasdale to designate the increasingly familiar phenomenon of cross-religious sharing of interior resources, the spiritual treasures of each tradition. We live in an age of interspirituality, says Teasdale, which is making more possible direct contact with the divine, or ultimate mystery, and its profound transformative capacity. This spirituality is in dialogue and communion "with everything of value." This kind of spirituality, he demonstrates further, is always practical: its experience is eminently beneficial to relationships. I am in agreement with Teasdale, and want only to extend his argument. Interspirituality is possible not just on occasions of inter-religious coming together across boundaries, but whenever isolated groups, alone and fractured, transcend their separation and begin to connect to the deepest and best in each other's traditions or ways. For more, see: Teasdale, W. (1999) The Mystic Heart New World Library: Novato, California.

management adversaries in the unionized plant? Does the creative event have something to do with the key theme of this conference—that is, the interplay between the elevation of love as *a way of knowing* and extension of compassion as *a way of relating?*

2. In our own work with Appreciative Inquiry (Cooperrider and Srivastva,1987; Cooperrider, Sorenson, Whitney, and Yeager 2002; Cooperrider and Avital, 2004)[6], we have been surprised by what might be called *the cognitive power of love as a way of knowing*—something that draws us together to see the true, the good, the better, and the possible in every human being, *and the relational power of the experience of wholeness*—something that happens when the whole system is focused on the simple act of human conversation—i.e., people talking, across boundaries, about what they care about. In more practical terms, what has emerged in our own work is a large group methodology for bringing hundreds and sometimes thousands of "stakeholders" into the room interactively for 3-4 days to plan, learn, and enable/inspire one another to create a better future. The Appreciative Inquiry or "AI" Summit, as it has been termed, has for example, been used to bring Buddhists, Muslims, Christians, Jews, Hindus, and peoples of many indigenous spiritual traditions together, across boundaries, to end religiously-motivated violence and to create new cultures of peace and justice. In one effort that involved five global AI Summits at Stanford University, a new organization was born. The United Religions Initiative now has over 250 "co-operation circles" on every continent constituting an ever-expanding worldwide alliance. In another effort, a socially responsible business executive closed the entire factory and brought all 1,000 employees together to collectively co-create the company's business plan; it was the first time the machine operators had ever sat together, in dialogue and joint planning, with senior leaders, mid-managers, customers, union officials, and other community stakeholders. In the most recent example, the AI Summit was called upon by Kofi Annan and the UN's Global Compact to bring 500 CEOs of many of the largest corporations in the world to "unite the strengths of markets with the authority of universal ideals" and to open new paths to a moral economy that works for the world's poor, our shared biosphere, and the well-being of future generations. Every one of these events was inter-spiritual, as defined earlier. While each was explicitly task-focused, somehow a sacred space emerged, evoking the energy needed to create a new situation. That energy, as Rollo May so carefully writes, is the dynamic of love—"*the drive toward union with what we belong to—union with our own*

---

6   Cooperrider, D. L., & Srivastva, S. (1987). Appreciative inquiry in organizational life. In R. Wood-man & W. Pasmore (Vol. Eds.), Research in organizational change and development: Vol. 1: 129-169. Greenwich, CT: JAI Press Inc.
Cooperrider, D.L & Whitney, D. (2000). A positive revolution in change: Appreciative inquiry. In D. L. Cooperrider, P. F. Sorensen Jr., D. Whitney, & T. F. Yaeger (Eds.), Appreciative inquiry: Rethinking human organization toward a positive theory of change (pp. 3-27). Champaign, IL: Stipes Publishing.

possibilities, union with significant other persons...when we are able to open ourselves and participate, via imagination and emotional and spiritual sensitivity, in forms and meanings beyond ourselves in the interpersonal world and the world of nature around us." He then makes the idea as succinct as possible: "we are drawn to life by love."

3. While it is beyond the scope of this paper to describe all the outcomes and explain the dynamics of change, two observations can be shared. The first is that when people are connected across boundaries through open inquiry and deep exploration of the best in the other—"center to center unions," hope grows and community expands. The second has to do with the interspiritual nature of the experience of wholeness. Somehow, when large group events are designed to have all stakeholders in the room, the very best in human beings seems to come out, much like the awesome shift reported by astronauts when seeing the planet from a distance for the first time—i.e., "instant global consciousness."Something similar happens, often in surprisingly powerful ways, in each of the summits we have witnessed. The real question is why? Is it because, as Martin Buber put it, "in the beginning is the relationship" and therefore methods that respond to this understanding will have a special capacity associated with them? Is it because love and compassion are in fact not individual phenomena but about plurality— i.e., they thrive in the connective act of getting people into the same room? Perhaps it is what Meg Wheatley was recently speaking about when she wrote: *"I've seen that there is no more powerful way to initiate significant change than to convene a conversation...there is no power equal to a community discovering what it cares about."*

WHERE SHOULD RESEARCH IN THIS FIELD BE DIRECTED AND FOCUSED? HOW CAN RESEARCHERS HELP ACTIVIST? HOW CAN ACTIVISTS HELP RESEARCHERS?

The yearning for community and wholeness is worldwide. And the cultivation of love/compassion is essential, we believe, to tapping the transformational energies and omnipresent strengths that lie all around us—often dormant, fragmented, and separated.

As it relates specifically to appreciative inquiry and the large group "whole systems" approach, it is clear that we are infants when it comes to our understanding of appreciative processes of interchange and knowing, and the conscious co-construction of better worlds. We need a new vocabulary of change, especially the kind of change that is propelled by the positive energies of love. Questions for research include:

*   *Positive emotions:* what is the role of positive emotion—expressions of love, inspiration, hope, joy, in generating the magnitudes of social energy needed to create and sustain the action that enables transformation in oppressive political and institutional structures? How do we take findings in positive psychology, such as Barbara Fredrickson's "broaden-and-build" [7] model of the transfor-

---

7   Fredrickson, B. L. (2001). The role of positive emotions in positive psychology: The broaden-and-build theory of positive emotions. *American Psychologist,* 56(3), 218-226.

mational power of positive emotions at the individual level, and move it to the arena of large group dynamics?

- *Love and institutions:* if it is true that institutions often grow rigid and refract the worst in human capacity and intention, then what kinds of institutions do the opposite—that is, serve to refract and amplify our most valued qualities of love and compassion? Can we talk about compassion-amplifying organizations? Can we talk about a "compassionate economy" or "business as an agent of love" just like we talk, for example, about "learning organizations?" Is it true that, as Bellah and others have reminded us in <u>The Good Society,</u> that we are our institutions?[8] High on the agenda for research are the *integrative forms of scholarship* that connect the languages and concepts of love and compassion to institutions. While some early work in this area is beginning under the rubric of "positive organizational scholarship," we need to begin empirically designing studies to capture the idea of an institution as not just restraining but enabling us—i.e., an institution not as an area of constraint within which phenomena such as love is tested, but as an indispensable source from which love, compassion, and justice is amplified.

- *Stages in Large Group Dynamics:* We have numerous theories and empirical studies focused on the stages of development of small groups of 6-8 people, but virtually nothing theoretically or empirically on the stages of large group development in which the potentials of love and compassion are perhaps magnified through "contagion" effects and "tipping point" dynamics. An important set of studies could be initiated through a comparative analysis of large group approaches—such as appreciative inquiry in contrast to more deficit-based change approaches—that empirically examines love's intensity and extensivity and impacts (see Sorokin's theory and framework), as well as Bronfrebrenner's framework and set of hypotheses about "the ecology of human development."

- *Reflexivity in Knowledge and Implications for Love and Compassion?* Another important question has to do with the idea that inquiry (research) and change (action) are not separate moments; rather, they are simultaneous and human systems might in fact move in the direction of our most rigorous, persistent, and active inquiries. For our purposes here, constructionism is an approach to human science and practice that replaces the *individual* (or any "single" entity) with the relationship as the locus of knowledge. Philosophically, it involves a decisive shift in western intellectual tradition from *cogito ergo sum*—to *communicamus ergo sum.* The common thread in most constructionist writing is a concern with the processes by which human beings, their values, and commonsense and scientific knowledge are both produced in, and reproduce, human communities. In practice, constructionism replaces absolutist claims or the final word with the never-ending collaborative quest to understand and construct options for better

---

8   Bellah et al (1991) The Good Society New York: Vintage Books

living (for the major statement in this area see Kenneth J. Gergen's <u>Realities and Relationships</u> Harvard University Press, 1994). For purposes of our conference, it may be that constructionism's commitment to relational approaches to knowledge might provide a useful backdrop to bridging theorists and practioners, not only through its social epistemology but through methods such as collaborative action-research and grounded forms of theory building in participatory ways. *A key issue in human science is one of linking the means and ends of knowledge—that is, are there more loving, compassionate, and just ways of generating knowledge of love, compassion, and activism?*

31
MICHAEL A. EDWARDS

Michael Edwards is the Director of the Governance and Civil Society Program at the Ford Foundation in New York, one of the world's largest philanthropies with assets exceeding $10 billion. Prior to joining the Foundatio,n he was a Senior Civil Society Specialist at the World Bank in Washington, D.C. Before moving to the Bank, Michael spent 15 years as a senior manager in international relief and development NGOs, including periods with Oxfam-UK (as Regional Director for Southern Africa), and Save the Children-UK (as Director of Research, Evaluationm, and Advocacy). His many books and articles have helped to shape our thinking about NGOs, civil society, and international cooperation. Michael is the author (most recently) of "Civil Society" (Polity Press/Blackwell 2004), "The Earthscan Reader on NGO Management" (Earthscan/Stylus 2002), "Global Citizen Action" (Lynne Rienner 2001), and "NGO Rights and Responsibilities: A New Deal for Global Governance" (Foreign Policy Center 2000). A revised edition of his award-winning "Future Positive," dubbed "the book that revolutionized international cooperation," has just been published by Earthscan/Stylus. Michael was awarded a congratulatory double-first from the University of Oxford and a PhD by the University of London for his work on low-income housing markets in Colombia.

Over the last few years I have become fascinated by what one might call the "social science of love." By this I mean a set of theories, models, methods, and empirical cases that show how politics, economics, organizational development, social and international relations can be transformed through a radically-different form of rationality, a rationality of "love into action," so to speak, applied in and through the systems that are essential to the functioning of all successful societies. This, I think, is what Martin Luther King meant when he wrote about the "love that does justice," signifying the deliberate cultivation of mutually-reinforcing cycles of personal and systemic change.

How have I come to this conclusion? Two reasons. First, I have spent the last 20 years as a funder of social change for charities like Oxfam and Save the Children, and now at the Ford Foundation, constantly looking for and evaluating individuals and organizations that work for peace and social justice. This experience has convinced me that there is a missing link in many of these efforts that holds back their effectiveness and achievements; this missing link is love, or, more precisely, the failure to use love as the basis for the functioning of the organization and its work. The result is often burnout, over-competition, an inability or unwillingness to learn lessons or collaborate with others, and a failure to build the necessary alliances that could lead to sustained change on a significant scale.

Second, I was trained as a social scientist in the United Kingdom, and have spent a lifetime studying the conditions under which communities succeed or fail in realizing their visions of the good society. These explorations led me to focus on civil society as a critical element in such efforts, but also to a nagging sense of disappointment about the achievements of citizen groups, social movements, and faith-based organizations in the cold light of day. Although many see civil society as the natural home of virtue, even love, we have to remind ourselves that it is simply an arena – even a battlefield – for competing interests—the good, the bad and the ugly. So the core task, it seems to me, is not to fixate on civil society as a solution to social problems, but to ask how institutions across society can be transformed by altering their individual behaviors and interactions with each other through love.

These experiences led me to formulate a simple conceptual framework to describe what I and my co-writer Gita Sen have called "integrated social change." From the perspective of change, all social systems rest on three bases: a set of principles that form an axiomatic basis of ethics and values; a set of processes – the functioning mechanisms and institutions that undergird the system; the subjective states that constitute our inner being – our personal feelings and intuitions in the deepest sense. When we explore any episode of change, we can identify how these three dimensions work together to promote a particular set of outcomes. For example, the evolution of capitalism was built on the axiomatic basis that individual self-interest leads, by and large, to collective welfare. Its institutional structures are rooted in private property relations and market-based incentives. The subjective state of being most compatible with capitalism is a commitment to individual advancement and competitive interaction.

However, the linkages that develop between these three bases of change are not immutable. They can be altered to produce a different set of outcomes—for example, by rebelling against the subjective state that is promoted by a particular set of institutions, or experimenting with new institutions that operate from a different subjective or axiomatic base. This is why love, as the most powerful subjective state we can conceive, may have such a transformative effect when injected like a virus into economic, political, and social institutions. These institutions are not simply floating somewhere out there in space. They constitute and are constituted by each of us as conscious human beings or active citizens, to use a phrase currently much in vogue. So when we talk of engaging with these systems and structures, we are really talking about engaging with ourselves and with each other.

Many would argue that faith-based organizations are the logical place in which to locate this struggle, but faith is usually particularistic, attached to defined sub-sectors of humankind and agendas that are privileged. Love and loving kindness are universal and unconditional, attached only, as the definition offered by our conference organizers tells us, to the equal and general welfare of the whole. "The essence of love," they say, "is to affectively affirm as well as unselfishly delight in the well being of others, and to engage in acts of care and service on their behalf, without exception, in an enduring and constant way." There is nothing loving about the prejudice that one finds in some faith communities – the consistent attacks on women's rights, the homophobia, the narrow-mindedness and reluctance to enter into community-wide activities and concerns rather than intra-congregational commitments, and the substitution of individual acts of charity or service for a full and complete understanding of the structural factors that lead to oppression. "Pillar of the community, soccer coach, wife beater" reads a sign on the New York subway. Social conservatism is rarely more dangerous than when it cloaks itself in religious garb that cannot adequately be challenged by rationalist arguments for social justice because it assumes an other-worldly authority.

If faith-based organizations vary so much in their characteristics, it is clear that faith cannot be the deciding factor in determining these patterns. So what is it that really makes the difference? I think it is the presence or absence of the "love that does justice." Because of its unconditionality and its rigor, this kind of love provides an answer to these secular concerns, recognizing the importance of our inner experiences and the values-based motivations they bring to public policy, but separating them from the limitations of religion or even spirituality. This is a love that respects the necessary self-empowerment of others, eschewing paternalism and romanticism for relationships of truth and authenticity, even where they move through phases of conflict and disagreement, as all do. Elsewhere I have called this kind of love "critical friendship," meaning relationships that encourage us to live up to our social obligations as well our individual moral values, connect our interior life worlds to public spaces, encourage collective judgments, and create open networks of self-reflective and critical communication – all the things that are necessary for a healthy democracy and democratic public policy making.

Critical friendship signifies a willingness to care for the common good and address the structural barriers that stand in its way. But the moving force in this process must be love; without it, we may never make the necessary commitments on an enduring basis, or if we do we are likely to carry with us the "thieves of the heart" - the greed, ego, anger, fear, and insecurities that will likely pollute or erode the success of our efforts to be a positive force for change in the world. This why the transformation of the Self is so vital. Great inner strength is required to confront the structures of power in the world unselfishly, without demonizing one's enemies, alienating potential allies, or holding on too tightly to a particular vision of ends and means that can eventually become a prison. In the "love that does justice," personal and structural change are self-reinforcing. Only by operating from the space where we are joined together in some deep sense are we likely to find true common ground in facing up to the collective problems that confront us.

Confronting common problems in this way is, I think, the essence of the "love that does justice." As the song says, "don't hide your love away" by restricting it to your familiars or privatizing it to the sphere of family, friends, and faith. Take it out into the world wherever you go, at work, through the associations you belong to, in politics and government, education and social service delivery, foreign policy and international development. Sounds attractive, no? But can public policies motivated by love really "deliver the goods" in social, economic, and political terms? Can they generate enough jobs and an economic surplus large enough to satisfy human needs at lower cost to producers and consumers in globally-integrated markets, the environment, and the underlying values that hold societies together? Can they facilitate political decision making that is fair and effective in mediating competing claims and interests without falling prey to the "dictatorship of the majority" or the perils of special interest politics? Can they address problems of discrimination and exclusion in the social realm, which often require enforcement and coercion by state authorities, not just voluntary action? And can they resolve global conflicts and differences peacefully, but more effectively than at present, even in the most difficult of circumstances, such as the task of unseating tyrants?

The simple answer is: we don't know, and we won't know until we try to make these connections on a much larger and more systematic basis. This is why social activism is so important, especially among those pioneers who have already recognized that social change organizations can achieve significant improvements in performance when they integrate contemplative practices into their work and deliberately cultivate structures and forms of leadership informed by a non-denominational, spiritual awareness. Many of these pioneers will be with us for this conference, so we should be able to make a lot of progress during the time we will be spending together.

I think the interaction between action and reflection, or activism and scholarship, is essential here because each needs the other to be truly accurate, authentic, and effective. Activists know the on-the-ground realities of what it means to struggle with the "love that does justice," realities that scholars must also understand if they are to build up models, theories, or even empirical generalizations and explanations that hold water. But scholars usually bring a greater sense of rigor to the discussion, a depth of engagement in a particular set of issues and their history that few activists can match. Scholars also posess the skill of making connections across time and place that only comes through long, comparative study. They can help us to take a problem apart and put it back together again – for example, the differences and linkages between love, altruism, spirituality, theology, and religion that are often commingled, at least in my own mind! Unless we are clear on these differences, it is difficult to talk sensibly about the transmission mechanisms between love and justice. So I'm convinced we can help each other along the way. The marriage of action and research is never easy, and a perfect union is probably out of reach. But there is no reason why it should forever be dysfunctional! Perhaps in a conference on love and justice we can expect that some of the things that normally get in the way of collaboration will be left outside the door. I certainly hope so.

In conclusion, marrying a rich inner life dedicated to the cultivation of loving kindness and compassion with the practice of new forms of politics, economics, and public policy is, I believe, the key to social transformation. We are, to be sure, only at the beginning of our journey of love into action, a journey that will take many generations to reach the more humane world that lies in waiting at its destination. The power of this conference, it seems to me, is that it provides a safe space in which to legitimize a conversation about matters that are profoundly sensitive, complicated, and difficult, or that are often simply dismissed by their critics as wacky, new age, reactionary, or juvenile. On the contrary, it is my conviction that we are placed on the earth to love and be loved, not as an exercise in narcissism but as the wellspring of motivations that enable us to co-create a different and better world. This is our collective responsibility for the future.

A longer version of this paper and the paper to which I refer that was co-authored with Gita Sen are available for free download from my website at www.futurepositive.org (click on my photo and scroll down the list of publications to "spirituality").

32
ATWOOD GAINES, Ph.D.

Atwood D. Gaines is Professor of Anthropology, Bioethics, Nursing, Psychiatry and Professor in the College Scholars Program at Case Western Reserve University and its Schools of Medicine and Nursing. He is a cultural and medical anthropologist with public health training. After receiving his BA from San Francisco State University, he took his MA, C.Phil., and Ph.D. in Cultural Anthropology from the University of California at Berkeley (1978). His MPH is from UC Berkeley's School of Public Health (1978). Dr. Gaines' research interests include the cultural analysis of Western biomedical theory and practice, including psychiatry, dementia, comparative religion, cultural studies of science, cultural bioethics, social identity (ethnic, religious, gender, age), and health care. He has conducted research in Western Europe (France, England) and the US on the sciences of dementia. He has published two books with Robert Hahn on cultural studies of Western Biomedicine (1982, 1985), in addition to his noted work, "Ethnopsychiatry" (1992). He has also published nearly 60 articles in journals and books. Among others, he contributed articles on "race" and mental illness, to the Encyclopedia of Bioethics (2nd and 3rd editions, 1995, 2004, respectively), and co-wrote the Outline for Cultural Formulation and Culture-Bound Syndromes (Appendix I) of the American Psychiatric Association's "Diagnostic and Statistical Manual" (DSM IV) (1994). He has published in JAMA, the American Anthropologist, and the Lancet, as well as Culture, Medicine and Psychiatry, and Social Science and Medicine. He is currently completing manuscripts on US Psychiatry, Cultural Studies of Science and Medicine, Local Biology, and Millennial Medical Anthropology and Cultural Bioethics.

For an anthropologist, this question raises a number of issues. As an anthropologist concerned with cross-cultural studies of what in the West is defined as "religion," as well as other related phenomena that are not so defined, the question raises concerns about clarification, specification, and the problem of relativity. It also opens many topics for discussion.

We may take the notion of engaged spirituality as a positive form of engagement, but we should not assume this is a "natural" connection or relationship. It is important to ascertain the local meaning of both "spirituality" and "engagement." These are not universally evident terms or processes. Some examples will clarify the complexity of the notion of engaged spirituality when viewed in the context of the cross-cultural record.

To begin thinking about these issues, it is useful to recognize an implicit notion of a division between the spiritual and non-spiritual domains. Such a division may then suggest that there is a higher and, by implication, lower moral stance or universe. This is especially true in the context of that which is called religion in the West. This hierarchy, in and of itself, may pose a problem for a spirituality that is engaged in a fashion participants might view as beneficial and aimed at the general public good. For example, the notion of a higher calling may be used as a charter for acts of violence, where an end justifies any means. We see this today among the Taliban, Hamas, al Qaeda, and a variety of radical Islamic clerics. One should also recall the warrior popes of the early Middle Ages in Europe, and the contemporary terrorist acts against pregnancy termination facilities. The engagement of the spirituality of individuals in these groups is surely not what participants think of as spiritual engagement; in their local contexts, however, it is. We must consider the nature of the spirituality, as well as the nature of the engagement and its end(s) in our thinking.

Absent the hierarchy in views, as noted above, we may be yet concerned with the implications of spiritual preoccupation. Such preoccupation may actually disengage individuals from the body social and the quotidian life. For example, one may lead a contemplative life, preoccupied with soterological concerns, rather than an active life focused on concerns of the workaday world of injustice.

Spirituality may also be a means to avoid the disadvantages of a social system, as in India. There, one sees that the apotheosis to a religious role may be a key means for the extraction of the self from a system of caste stratification in which life chances are determined at and by birth and are immutable. One means of escaping this once rigid prisonhouse of social distinction is the assumption of a religious role that puts one outside that social system. However, the assumption of the spiritual religious role leaves the inequities of that social system unchallenged.

Our conversations center around a spirituality that tries to apply the lessons and or morals of the There to the Here and Now; it applies the transcendent to the mundane. Such a spirituality appears in many guises, including some that are outside of the context of an eastern or western religion. That is, we may speak of an engaged spirituality that derives from a civil or disciplinary ethos or ethic, and not a theology.

How are love and compassion integral to the success of social justice work?

In terms of cross-cultural issues, we are again set to think of the relativity of the central concepts as concepts. Love, for example, has a particular cultural history in the West, one that is not duplicated in other parts of the world. The central social tie that binds in most of the world is not love but duty—and, indeed, the love of duty. For example, a majority of the world's people do not marry for love, a personal good as we in the West see it; rather, they marry as a result of parental arrangements, a social good. The basis for the marriage is not love, especially since the prospective couple may never have met, but rather duty and a love of that marital duty.

For the West, it appears that love and compassion may be integral elements of social justice action, though they are not alone as motivating forces. That is, social justice work may be motivated by a desire for change, retribution, retaliation, and even anger. In other cultural contexts, motivating forces may be very different and include honor, acceptance, and duty and tradition (or its reinstatement).

WHAT BELIEFS AND PRACTICES SUCCESSFULLY GIVE RISE TO OR SUSTAIN ACTIVISM?

It would seen that communitarian values, whether transcendent or not, are essential to sustained activism. But, there must also be hope, for action aimed at salutary change is unlikely where there is no hope.

An important question is whether activism is in itself positive, negative, or neutral. Here we must consider hope and the nature of the changes that are sought.

WHERE SHOULD RESEARCH IN THIS FIELD BE DIRECTED AND FOCUSED?

An important area of research would be a focus on the personal as well as ascribed motives of individuals engaged in social activism. Earlier research, whether on student protests of the 1960s in the US or the Hungarian Freedom fighters in the 1960s, shows the often personal motivations of protest that may be distinct from ascribed motive (i.e., patriotism, nationalism).

HOW CAN RESEARCHERS HELP ACTIVISTS IN THEIR WORK, AND HOW CAN ACTIVISTS HELP RESEARCHERS?

One might say that one should become the other, a merging of identities such that activism is knowledgeable and measured. As an anthropologist, I would suggest long-term participant observational research as a key tool to understanding activism. If research data are better reflections of local knowledge, they can thus inform other activists in other places advocating other causes.

33
JULIE JUOLA EXLINE, Ph.D.

Julia Exline received her Ph.D. in Clinical Psychology from Stony Brook University in 1997. Since Fall 2000, she has been an Assistant Professor of Psychology at Case Western Reserve University. While in graduate school, she collaborated with another student to begin studying spiritual issues—particularly the struggles often associated with religious and spiritual life. She has published papers on anger toward God and sources of strain in religious life, both of which have been major areas of ongoing research. While doing postdoctoral research at Case Western Reserve University, Roy Baumeister invited Dr. Exline to collaborate with him on a grant from the John Templeton Foundation entitled, "Humility, Egotism, Forgiveness, and the Victim Role." Over twenty studies on forgiveness and repentance have stemmed from this grant, including personal narratives, writing interventions, and laboratory experiments. One pivotal finding from this forgiveness grant was that a prideful, entitled attitude is a major barrier to forgiveness. Dr. Exline has received funding from the Institute for Research in Unlimited Love to evaluate a conduit model of love: the notion that receiving love will help people pass on love to others.

REPENTANCE AND FORGIVENESS:
HOW CAN THEY PROMOTE THE "LOVE THAT DOES JUSTICE"?

At a fundamental level, social justice involves identifying wrongs and trying to make things right again. For example, social justice may entail correction of unfair practices, punishment of offenders, compensation for offended parties, or helping to restore relationships that have been damaged by offense. Over the past 7 years, I've been delighted to have the opportunity to conduct research on forgiveness, repentance, humility, spiritual and religious life, and altruistic love. I believe that these topics are centrally relevant to social justice issues, as I will describe below. Also, I am very eager to learn more about how these topics are viewed—pro and con—in the world of activism and social justice.

My goals for this brief essay are modest. My main aim is to introduce a few ideas about how repentance and forgiveness are relevant in social justice contexts. I would also like to suggest that forgiveness and repentance can be powerful manifestations of unselfish love.

REPENTANCE AND APOLOGY: STEPS TOWARD RESTORING JUSTICE AND COMMUNITY

As a recent text on the dark side of forgiveness reminds us (Lamb & Murphy, 2002), one problem among forgiveness activists is that they often seem to put a double burden on the offended party: This person who has already been badly mistreated is now being pressured to forgive as well. What about the offender, the person who committed the wrong? Before moving to forgiveness, then, let's start with the other side: cases in which people commit crimes or, in more everyday contexts, in which we hurt others.

First, let's start with how offenders should ideally act. When people realize that they have hurt others, they should feel remorse that naturally prompts a desire to repent—that is, to apologize, make amends, and commit not to repeat the misdeed. From a moral or spiritual perspective, it is easy to see how sincere repentance could facilitate growth and character development. Furthermore, when offered from sincere and upright motives, attempts at relational repair can be potent manifestations of love. As described by Everett Worthington, a pioneer of forgiveness research, apologies and amends reduce the size of the "injustice gap" that arises in the wake of offense (Worthington, 2003). As such, sincere apologies make forgiveness much easier—and reconciliation much more likely.

Within social justice contexts, then, it seems reasonable to propose that if we can set up situations to open the door for apologies by offenders, we should do so. This is already happening in some restorative justice settings, which seems like a major step forward from our traditional retributive system of justice. Granted, some apologies do seem forced or manipulative. And there is no question that apologies cannot repay the debt in the case of major damage or loss. Nonetheless, research suggests that apologies are almost always a step in the right direction in terms of restoring relationships.

Even young children know that apologizing is the right thing to do. Yet in the wake of offense, the natural instinct is not always to apologize; the more natural instinct is to hide. I've seen this phenomenon among certain 6-year-olds of my acquaintance. Once children are developmentally able to understand that they can be held responsible for wrongdoing, panicked protests such as, "It wasn't my fault!" or, "He made me do it!" seem to be learned almost instantaneously. Ducking responsibility seems to be part of human nature.

Typically, anything that reminds people of their dark sides makes them want to run for cover. For example, in a recent study of altruistic giving (Exline & Fisher; presented at the Compassionate Love Research Conference in May 2004), we asked people to recall times in which they received unwarranted acts of kindness from others. We then gave them an opportunity to donate to charity. Our notion was that reflecting on unearned kindnesses would inspire people to give. After all, if people think about love that they didn't earn, shouldn't the resulting feelings of gratitude motive them to pass on the love? Yet the experiment backfired, in a sense, because recollections of unearned kindness often prompted feelings of guilt or shame (e.g., "I beat up a kid next door, and then he was nice to me later."). And to the extent that people's recollections brought up feelings of shame or guilt, they gave *less* money to charity. Some of our forgiveness studies have yielded similar results: If you show people their dark sides, they often become moody and defensive—both of which translate into being less giving and more harsh toward others.

So how can we give people the courage to look at their dark sides without causing them to immediately back away or point a finger at someone else? This is an important applied question, whether in a jail cell, a confessional, or a marital counseling room. Granted, some people are so skilled at externalizing blame that it may require nothing short of a miracle for them to acknowledge their wrongs. But to maximize the odds that people can face their wrongdoings, I suggest that we need to provide a certain type of environment: one that conveys a sense of safety, respect, and (of course) love.

By way of example, I'd like to share one of the most practical clinical tools that I have ever encountered. Many people use this technique already, whether by instinct or by training. It's called the "sandwich technique." The basic notion is that when you need to correct someone, you need to start by saying something positive that conveys caring and respect for the person. Next, you offer the correction in a constructive way. You end by giving more positives. In this way, you "sandwich" the correction between positive statements. There may be a more technical term for this phenomenon, and there is probably research on the topic in some other guise. Anecdotally, however, I must say that the sandwich technique works. It works really well. Why? It conveys a sense of safety, affirmation, and positivity that makes the person more able to tolerate the correction.

Within justice contexts, can we increase the odds of helping offenders apologize by helping them to feel safe and loved? As we have written elsewhere in a chapter on humility (Exline, et al., 2004), people may only be able to humble themselves—a crucial step in apologizing—if they feel safe enough to do so. By conveying love and respect, we give them the safety to humble themselves and admit their wrongs. So we can see how an environment of love can lead to humility, which in turn leads to more love (now in the form of repentance).

Forgiveness: Can It Complement Justice in Some Cases?

From a justice perspective, it's quite easy to talk about the need for offenders to repent and apologize. Talking about forgiveness is a much thornier issue. Elsewhere, my colleagues and I have written about many controversies surrounding the interface between forgiveness and justice (Exline, Worthington, Hill, & McCullough, 2003). These controversies cannot be addressed in depth in this brief space. However, a few points seem crucial to make here.

The term "forgiveness" has many potential meanings. In most current psychological circles, forgiveness refers to an internal, personal process in which the offended party lets go of feelings of vengefulness and bitterness toward the offender. Forgiveness does not imply condoning or excusing offenses, nor does it imply that offenders should not be held accountable in legal cases. People can also forgive without trusting their offenders or wanting to have close relationships with them.

There is no question that forgiving serious offenses can be extremely difficult. But if we consider forgiveness as a form of emotional release or transcendence, it
becomes interesting to consider how forgiveness might be beneficial, even in the case
of serious injustices. In emotional and physical terms, relief from grudges and angry
rumination will usually be beneficial. In spiritual terms, people may feel strong or close
to God when they forgive. In interpersonal terms, forgiveness will help to stop conflicts
from escalating into cycles of retaliation and revenge. Furthermore, forgivers who cultivate a compassionate stance toward their offenders may be willing to provide the kind of
"safe environment" discussed above, in which they show kindness to those who have hurt
them. They may even be able to confront their offenders in constructive ways, thereby increasing the odds of getting the apology or explanation that they often desperately desire.
This will not always happen, of course. In cases with absent or unrepentant offenders,
emotional relief or spiritual growth may be the main benefits of forgiveness. Yet it seems
important to consider that, in some cases, forgiveness will actually lead to apologies and
other attempts by offenders to restore justice.

I would like to suggest, then, that although the term forgiveness is often taboo
in justice settings, the concepts behind forgiveness may nonetheless have a place there.
Often there is no way that offended parties can be adequately repaid. Their losses are too
great. But if they can find a way to forgive (independent of the processes of legal justice),
they may help themselves to heal and to grow spiritually. Of course, one might do harm
by thoughtlessly pressuring people to forgive. But there do seem to be situations in which
the costs of bitterness and vengefulness seem to outweigh the costs of principled resent-
ment. In those situations, the true pursuit of justice may entail gently helping people
along the road to forgiveness.

Here again, a supportive and positive environment seems key. Forgiveness, like
repentance, often requires a humble attitude. And people need to feel safe and valuable
in order to humble themselves. Thus, if we can position ourselves to show love to both
victims and offenders, we can help give them the courage to make steps toward healing
and restored community. Perhaps love gives us the courage to be humble, which in turn
makes us willing to reach out in love.

REFERENCES

Exline, J. J., Campbell, W. K., Baumeister, R. F., Joiner, T., Krueger, J., & Kachorek, L. V.
(2004). Humility and modesty. In C. Peterson & M. Seligman (Eds.), *Character
strengths and virtues: A handbook and classification* (pp. 461-475). New York: Oxford.

Exline, J. J., & Fisher, M. (2004, May). *The self as a conduit of love: Oh-so-preliminary findings.*
Presentation at the Compassionate Love Research Conference, Washington, DC.

Exline, J. J. Worthington, E. L., Jr., Hill, P., & McCullough, M. E. (2003).

Forgiveness and justice: A research agenda for social and personality psychology. *Personality and Social Psychology Review*, 7, 337-348.

Lamb, S., & Murphy, J. G. (Eds.). (2002). *Before forgiving: Cautionary views of forgiveness in psychotherapy.* New York: Oxford.

Worthington, E. L., Jr. (2003). *Forgiving and reconciling: Bridges to wholeness and hope.* Downers Grove, IL: InterVarsity Press.

34
BYRON R. JOHNSON, Ph.D.

Byron Johnson is Professor of Sociology and Director of the Baylor Institute for Stud-
ies in Religion, at Baylor University. He is also a Senior Fellow at the Witherspoon Institute in
Princeton, New Jersey. He formerly directed the Center for Research on Religion and Urban Civil
Society (CRRUCS) at the University of Pennsylvania, and most recently was a lecturer in the Poli-
tics Department at Princeton University. Professor Johnson's research focuses on quantifying the
effectiveness of faith-based organizations to confront various social problems. Recent publications
have examined the efficacy of the "faith factor" in reducing crime and delinquency among at-risk
youth in urban communities, and several studies examining the impact of faith-based programs on
recidivism reduction and prisoner reentry. He is currently conducting a study of Teen Challenge, a
faith-based drug treatment program.

Johnson has been the subject of numerous media interviews for radio, television, and
newspapers including The New York Times, USA Today, The Los Angeles Times, The Dallas
Morning News, The San Francisco Chronicle, The Miami Herald, The Philadelphia Inquirer, The
Washington Times, The Washington Post, Wall Street Journal, U.S. News and World Report, World,
The National Review, The Weekly Standard, Policy Review, The Chronicle of Higher Education,
National Public Radio, CBS News, Fox News, and ABC World News Tonight.

WHAT DOES "ENGAGED SPIRITUALITY" MEAN TO YOU?

For me, "engaged spirituality" refers to the extent to which an individual's religious beliefs or commitments are consistent with the way they actually live and behave
on a daily basis, no matter the setting or circumstance. A person who exhibits engaged
spirituality, might be said to unswervingly "practice what they preach" or truly live-out
their faith in everyday life. Conversely, someone that is not spiritually engaged could be
deemed a hypocrite. A social scientist interested in trying to study engaged spirituality,
might try to determine whether attitudinal or self-reported measures of spirituality are
highly correlated with behavioral measures of spirituality. This approach would help determine if the level or degree of one's internal spirituality or religiosity, resembles one's
external actions in real life situations.

George Gallup and I recently conducted a nationally representative public opinion poll to help answer this very question and the results were released at a press event called the Spiritual State of the Union (2003). Through a lengthy and methodologically rigorous process we developed a series of items designed to measure what we called Inner Commitment and Outer Commitment. By inner commitment we were hoping to tap into the spiritual relationship between the individual and God (i.e. love of God). By outer commitment we were hoping to measure the relationship between the individual and their neighbor (i.e. love of neighbor). The final list of items used in each of these two scales are listed below:

Inner Commitment
- I exist to know, love and serve God.
- I believe that God is actively involved in my life.
- have an inner peace from God.
- When facing a crisis, I find hope from my faith in God as I understand God.
- Because of my faith, I have meaning and purpose in life.
- I am a person who is spiritually committed.
- I feel the need to experience spiritual growth in my daily life.

Outer Commitment
- God calls me to be involved in the lives of the poor and suffering.
- I give my time to serve and help others in my community.
- My first priority in spending money is to support the work of God.
- I know my spiritual gifts and use them in helping others.
- My faith is involved in every aspect of my life.
- I am active in a church of faith community.
- My friends and neighbors would say that I love God.

Consistent with decades of previous survey work, we found that Americans report very high levels of spirituality or inner commitment (80%). As expected, reported levels of inner commitment were significantly higher than levels of outer commitment.[9] For example, respondents were much more likely to report being spiritually committed (inner commitment) than they were to indicate they were called to be involved in the lives of the poor and suffering. Our assessment of the spiritual state of the union confirmed what we expected, namely, Americans are highly spiritual, but their spirituality is not necessarily engaged.

We found that levels of spirituality (both inner and outer) were influenced by key demographic factors like gender, race, age, income, and education. Higher levels of inner and outer commitment were linked to being female, older, lower income, and lower education. Interestingly, the factor most highly associated with either higher inner or out-

---

9   However, reported levels of outer commitment were also quite high (70%).

er commitment was frequent church attendance. Indeed, the effects of gender, race, age, income, and education are neutralized when we control for church attendance. Stated differently, frequent participation in religious activities seems to be the great equalizer, and might well be a key to deeper levels of spirituality and engaged spirituality. At the same time, it is important to note that measures of religious commitment or spirituality are far from perfect. Standard religiosity measures do not account for all the possible social networks or personal mentoring and other beneficial support mechanisms that may be fostered within congregations, all of which may influence engaged spirituality.

How are love and compassion integral to the success of social justice work?

This is a difficult question to answer, because it depends, among other things, on what one means when referring to social justice work. For many, the phrase social justice has come to represent efforts to eliminate poverty, hunger, discrimination, persecution, or to protect the environment. Very few would argue that these are not honorable goals. Nonetheless, the term social justice conjures up very different meanings for different people. For example, there are many people engaged in activities that might broadly be deemed "social justice" in orientation, who would greatly resist any attempt to label their work as social justice. For some, social justice is code for secular approaches to addressing various ills confronting society.

Among those who spend a great deal of time doing volunteer work in a variety of different areas where there is great social need, it would be interesting to know what percentage would consider their efforts to be social justice work. Perhaps some would claim they are simply answering a call and might be more likely to call their volunteer work a ministry or mission -- something they are compelled to do and almost certainly would not do otherwise. Would Mother Theresa's work for the poor in India qualify as social justice work? Would she have described her own work in this way?

The obvious answer to the above question is that love and compassion are foundational to the success of social justice work. But just exactly where do love and compassion come from? It is hard to answer this question without addressing a variety of theological or spiritual perspectives on justice. For example, in the Sermon on the Mount, Jesus taught followers not to seek justice in this world, but at the same time, to never cease giving it. In other words, to be about seeking justice could be construed as a self-serving function that ultimately distracts one from God. In Micah 6:8 we are told that God requires us to do justice. If one truly seeks God rather justice, they will be more likely to give justice in everything they do.

What beliefs and practices successfully give rise to or sustain activism?

As a sociologist who does a great deal of work in the field of criminology, I will try to answer this question by drawing from my own experiences within this field.

Since 1980 the American prison population has grown dramatically from 300,000 to more than two million today. The enormous growth of the prison population over the last two decades has given birth to a new problem -- more than 600,000 prisoners returning to American communities each year. This unprecedented prisoner reentry problem has many within local, state, and federal government scrambling for solutions that will promote public safety.

Though most Americans would agree that we will never be able to build our way out of the crime problem, people have very different ideas about how we should deal with the problem of crime and punishment. Some social justice proponents would argue two million prisoners is ample and clear evidence of widespread social injustice. Some would go so far as to argue that the problem is not with those who violate the law, but the criminal justice system itself. The current system, they would argue, is punitive, racist, and does more harm than good.

Though most would agree that the system has flaws, even serious flaws, many still contend that crime, in essence, remains largely a moral problem that requires a spiritual solution. Both groups are engaged, but both have very different ideas about what to do given the current predicament.

Over the last twenty years I have invested a great deal of time studying the American criminal justice system and have focused a great deal of my research on prisons, prisoners, offender treatment, and prisoner reentry. In particular, I have studied the role of religion in helping inmates adjust or cope with being in prison. I have also studied the conversion experiences of prisoners and the process of spiritual transformation and how these spiritual interventions may or may not reduce the likelihood of recidivism. As a part of this research, I have also had the opportunity to observe and interview thousands of volunteers. These volunteers come into prison at all hours of the day and night and donate their time to work with prisoners. They help inmates with reading, writing, arithmetic, GED tutoring, computer skills, and life skills. They lead victim-offender reconciliation groups, preach sermons, and teach Bible studies. In a number of published studies I have documented the beneficial role of faith-based interventions on outcomes like recidivism.

One of the questions I am always asked is this, what if you were to study a comparable program that was not faith-based or not Christian. What if you were to study a program that was similar, but was completely secular? What do you think the results would look like. My response is always the same -- this is an empirical question that we are not able to study due to the fact that virtually all of the volunteers in prisons all across the country have been and continue to be people motivated by faith. The intriguing question for me – where are the secular volunteers? Is it possible that the spiritually engaged are more likely to respond to this particular form of social justice activism.

It 2002, I released a study that reviewed the results of well over 700 studies that examined religious beliefs and practices and various social, physical and mental health outcomes. Around 85 percent of these found increasing religiosity to be associated with decreases in depression, drug use, crime, delinquency, suicide, and increases in longevity. In other words, religious commitment clearly had a protective feature for diverse samples of subjects. Also, religious beliefs and practices were positively associated with educational attainment, hope, meaning, and purpose in life. Thus, increasing religiosity seems to have both a pro-social (i.e., helping people to engage in positive behavior) as well as a protective influence (i.e., buffering people from harmful outcomes). Can we assume, therefore, that strong religious beliefs and practices give rise to or sustain behavior activism.

A current experiment may shed light on this question. In 2001, Amachi, a partnership between Public/Private Ventures in Philadelphia and Big Brothers and Big Sister of America was launched. The program sought to increase the number of Big Brother and Big Sister "matches" in Philadelphia by intentionally reaching out to churches, synagogues and mosques. The historic partnership was unique for two reasons: (1) it brought together religious congregations and a secular mentoring program, (2) the Amachi program was specifically designed to attract mentors for children of prisoners, by all counts, the most disadvantaged children in America. The Amachi motto: "People of faith, mentoring children of promise." In the course of one year, the amount of matches in Philadelphia doubled – something that had not happened in the previous 85 years. Amachi has now spread to cities all across the country. Some would argue that this enormous growth is simply to due to the fact that churches are simply volunteer rich. But interviews with Amachi mentors indicate that their initial motivation and indeed their sustained participation, well beyond the suggested one year commitment, is largely driven by spiritual factors.

WHERE SHOULD RESEARCH IN THIS FIELD BE DIRECTED AND FOCUSED?

We need focused research on volunteers of all types with a view to understanding the roots of their motivation for doing social justice work. Is there work simply a response to an obvious need or is it a distinct calling? Do they do this work because they enjoy it or because they feel good about themselves after helping others, or do they do it because they are compelled to do it? What sacrifices do people make in order to do volunteer work?

We need research to test, for example, Robert Putnam's assertion that much of the nation's social capital (i.e., community connections of trust and reciprocity) is actually spiritual capital produced by community-serving religious leaders, volunteers, and institutions. Does living in a poor urban neighborhood that is rich in spiritual capital have any independent effect on one's present well-being or future life prospects? Can spiritual capital prevent teenage pregnancies, reduce public health problems, combat illiteracy, and achieve many other vital social goals?

HOW CAN RESEARCHERS HELP ACTIVISTS IN THEIR WORK, AND HOW CAN ACTIVISTS HELP RESEARCHERS?

Those who are engaged do not believe that research is needed to validate their work and for this reason have often been hostile to researchers. Activists from the left to the right need to be open to research since research can help shed light on the efficacy of their efforts. Researchers can help activists improve their efforts by documenting what works best, or perhaps, what does not work at all. Similarly, researchers can learn from activists by simply listening to them. By hearing the voices of those who are engaged will help researchers better understand the not-so-obvious nuances that might otherwise be overlooked.

35
SOLOMON KATZ, Ph.D.

Katz has written, presented, and organized symposia resulting in over 200 major papers, books, and chapters on a wide range of topics, including molecular biology and genetics, cybernetics and biocultural evolution, field studies on diet and physical and mental health in children and adults in many regions of the world, neuroendocrinology, epidemiology of health problems in children, and the evolution of cuisine and nutrition practices. Katz is an elected fellow, officer, and president of many professional organizations, and is the recipient of many awards and grants. From 2001 to September, 2004, Katz served as president of the Metanexus Institute on Religion and Science. During this three-year period, Metanexus grew from a small regional discussion group and an online web-based information network to the largest science and religion organization in the world. Its scholarly exchange and funded research involves over 130 local societies in over thirty countries and 23 research projects; over fifty active world class scholars have served on its board of directors.

While participating in the MacArthur "behavior and health network," Katz developed a concept of secular morality and health in a pluralistic society. He used a series of derivations of the revitalization theory developed by Wallace to predict prospectively the outcomes of the anti-smoking revolution. The MacArthur Foundation funded a series of five workshops and symposia to develop and discuss the significance of this model. A book entitled "Morality and Health" was a direct product of this work, and may be used/adapted to model the successes and failures of various social activists.

Katz has also served to redefine the biological concept of race. He chaired the task force that redefined the UNESCO statement on race for the American Association of Physical Anthropologists and the International Union of Anthropological and Ethnological Sciences, a division of UNESCO that led the NIH and the US Census Bureau to change their definitions of race.

WHAT DOES "ENGAGED SPIRITUALITY" MEAN TO YOU?

As a concept to be used in research on activism, I would further develop the meaning of engaged spirituality (ES) in stages that begin with a definition that fits the meaning of the words "engaged spirituality," and then move on to clarify it in terms of activist exemplars whose actions and life histories provide added depth to the concept. However, as I examine the phenomenon further by careful analysis of the exemplars and the meaning of the terms, I would go back to the initial definition and further refine it by asking a series of questions about how the "activist exemplars" either fit and/or vary from the initial meaning/definition. In other words, my definition would try to develop an initial model of "engaged spirituality" and then see how various exemplars fit the model. From a wide range of experience with this kind of work, I would imagine that this process would lead to a very active Socratic dialog that would result in a working model that could serve as an initial step for addressing research on the topic.

Whether or not ES is the right term is a question that is also open for debate. For example, one of the close meanings of "engaged" is affectionately or lovingly pledged to another, as in engagement before marriage. When the concept implied in engaged is connected to the spiritual, does spiritual always imply a love of God that drives the activist to be so dedicated to his/her goals? In some cases, it is probably perfectly appropriate to make this assumption and there is validity in studying these individuals. However, if the goal for the use of the term is to account for a more generalized phenomenon, there also may be some kind of 'centeredness' that comes with a deep secularized sense of spirituality. This sense is associated with, but may not fully account for, the level of commitment implied by the enormous contribution that many social activists make.

Furthermore, it is important to point out that the process of selecting the questions to develop further will shape much of the research that follows. For example, if the process of questioning and model building stops too soon, we may be tempted to conclude that "engaged spirituality" is the only significant factor that accounts for activism; any competing explanation of activist behavior might be left out or diminished in importance. Moreover, there may be more than one type of ES. Thus, one concern I would have at the outset would be to leave the door open to alternative explanations and models of the behavior that are proposed for study. My suggestion to overcome this problem is to ask all of the questions without limiting the outcomes. We can then shape them and the terms we use, such as ES, from the perspective of having conducted the empirical research.

HOW ARE LOVE AND COMPASSION INTEGRAL TO THE SUCCESS OF SOCIAL JUSTICE WORK?

Love in the altruistic compassionate sense is connected to the social justice worker by the self sacrifice of kindness and sympathy. My colleague, Joan Koss (1), has suggested that radical empathy, in which the person, often a physical and spiritual healer, becomes so deeply involved that the pain of the afflicted is actually experienced by the radical empathic healer. In other words, there may be other dimensions to this phenomenon that are not included in the more western conceptualizations of love and compassion. Social justice work (and/or its types) could be scaled on a level of compassion and love. People involved in social justice work (SJW) may vary from high to low on such a scale, and as in most other activities, there would be considerable variance. My point is that we should test the hypothesis about the degree to which love and compassion are associated with (or integral to) SJW, and then account for the remaining correlates/ factors of SJW. Also, there may be some differences among areas or types of SJW that may be associated with differing degrees and/or types of love and compassion. Once again, even among SJW leaders, we should not necessarily make the conclusion without testing the hypothesis objectively. By determining the conditions when love and compassion are (or are not) integral, we will be in a much better position to understand the roles (relatively speaking) of love and compassion in these areas of SJW.

WHAT BELIEFS AND PRACTICES SUCCESSFULLY GIVE RISE TO OR SUSTAIN ACTIVISM?

Since one source of knowledge in this realm is self experiential, I will speak in the first person. My sources are listed in my bio statement. Having spent my life trying to make contributions to human understanding for purposes of peace and betterment, I will suggest that I did what I could all the way along my career. Rather than wait until someone else did something, I have always been willing to volunteer to get a job done that in areas in which I thought that I could do well. During the 60s protest periods, I learned very quickly that I could fight injustice with my body and/or my mind. While it was nice to be self sacrificial for some cause, as many of my friends were, I thought that I could have more of an impact by carefully using my talents and physical efforts to make a difference in any of the injustices that I saw and/or realistically had an opportunity to impact. For example, in 1966 and 1967, I stopped writing my PhD dissertation to work for the Japanese-American amicus curiae brief/ statement for the Lovings v. Commonwealth of Virginia case in the US Supreme Court. I conducted extensive research and concluded that the biological concept of race could not be used for legal purposes. As a young predoctoral student, my arguments and analyses were actually made through the kindness, understanding, and insight of a legal team that I worked with. As the "professional expert" to the Earl Warren Court, nearly all of the justices queried/ discussed the arguments and analyses that I made. These points were presented in the brief in front of the court and actually became a part of the decision to throw out the anti-miscegenation laws. Later this activist experience served me well when I became chair of the Task Force to revise and update the UNESCO Statement on Race, which I used in its original form in the amicus curiae brief.

More generally, my experience was that many people became experts in a particular field of specialization, but very few knew a couple of fields really well; even fewer had expertise in several fields. My thought was that real contributions to the collective human endeavor could be made if I made it my life work to know a number of fields really well and make contributions that combined their integration in novel ways. Furthermore, I knew (or I thought I knew) that by becoming an academic anthropologist most of my material interests would be put aside (not completely, but certainly relegated to a much lesser status at every turning point in my career), and this would allow me to devote all of my attention to what really mattered at a humanistic level. Over the years since then, I have made it my business to make contributions where and whenever I could; some of the major contributions are listed in my bio statement. For example, instead of carrying out theoretical research at the Krogman Growth Center, where I have served as director since 1971, I chose to be sure that we focused every opportunity for over thirty years of research on investigations that would also benefit disadvantaged children throughout our region and the world. Other examples include issues involving: aging ("meals on wheels," Senator Claude Pepper); environmental issues (lead paint - Senator Richard Schwieker and PA Department of Environment Governor Milton Shapp); the first Governor's (Shapp) Commission on Health and the Status of Women. My sustenance comes from knowing that these labors of love, as I have come to call them, are a very satisfying source of gratification that I have derived from quietly and humbly seeing them through from beginning to end. My time and effort are my contribution, and I have also learned that this can multiply with age instead of diminishing—as I thought it would when I was much younger!

WHERE SHOULD RESEARCH IN THIS FIELD BE DIRECTED? AND WHAT CAN WE LEARN FROM SPIRITUAL ACTIVISTS?

For the past several years, I have been forming and conducting a large interdisciplinary program on Spiritual Transformation, funded with the generous support of the John Templeton Foundation (see booklet that describes the entire program) (2). However, my interest in this concept actually started about thirty years ago, when I first became active in the religion and science dialog. At the time I was working with Anthony Wallace, who had formulated and presented a model for the origins and development of religious movements that he called revitalization movements (RM) (3). Although I was very interested in doing research on the details and implications of Wallace's model, in those days there was virtually no chance of receiving any funding to move forward. So I developed, presented, and published a paper in Zygon (4), and it became the basis of much of my thinking about religion and science thereafter. In fact, it became the basis of a "secular morality" and health model (5) that I developed in the later 1980s and early 90s with the generous help of the MacArthur Foundation.

AFC Wallace described a term "revitalization movement" (RM), that appears to relate closely to the roles and potentials that various social activists play in most societies. In describing RMs, Wallace emphasized that these movements always have a charismatic leader who provides a new vision to lead the society out of a widely experienced loss of purpose and meaning and increasing anomie, that may come about from a variety of reasons. At the core of every revitalization movement is a spiritual transformation (Wallace calls this a "mazeway resynthesis") of an individual who becomes the charismatic leader of the RM. Most often the charismatic leader shares and spread his/her spiritual transformation to a disciple group that further differentiates and interprets the new vision as it is carried forward to the entire society.

If we step back and analyze two of our questions, about the direction of research and what can we learn from activists, I believe that the answers could be enhanced by understanding the nature of revitalization movements, their spiritual journeys, and transformation of their charismatic and visionary leadership. My testable, working hypothesis is that the presence of a "spiritual transformation" (ST) is a significant predictor of the success of the activists who become leaders of great movements. In other words, most of these leaders have undergone a powerful ST that provides a critical basis for their roles as leaders.

In order for any model to work and for research to go on, we need to engage the assistance and active cooperation of the people who might serve as subjects of the research, and who could serve to verify and critique models that emerge from the research sector. Another vital area for cooperation is putting the research that emerges to use. Often, research done in the academic realm has to slowly trickle down into the public sector, where it might be used to improve conditions that provide effective compassionate support of activists. Of course, the results need peer review and further verification, but often the time between a new discovery in the social sciences and its effective integration into public understanding and use is prolonged. A part of any program that emerges should pay attention to this inadequacy.

REFERENCES

(1) Joan Chiono-Koss Spiritual Transformation and Radical Empathy: Essential Ingredients of Healing? abstract of paper presented at the Society for the Study of Psychiatry & Culture Annual Meeting, Montreal, Hotel Omni, October 2-6, 2003.

(2) The Spiritual Transformation Scientific Research Program see Prospectus Booklet at http://www.metanexus.net/spiritual%5Ftransformation/

(3) Wallace, Anthony F.C., Religion: An Anthropological View (Random House, New York; 1966).
(4) Katz, S.H. 1974 The Dehumanization and Rehumanization of Science and Society. Zygon, 9:126-138.

(5) Katz, SH "Secular Morality and Health" in Allan M. Brandt and Paul Rozin eds."Morality and Health" Routledge; (June 1, 1997) ISBN: 0415915821 pp 297- 331.

36
SAMUEL P. OLINER, Ph.D.

Dr. Samuel P. Oliner (Ph.D., University of California at Berkeley) is Professor of Sociology at Humboldt State University, and Founder and Director of the Altruistic Personality and Prosocial Behavior Institute. He is the author and co-author of several dozen publications on the Holocaust, altruism, prosocial behavior, and national and international race relations. He has appeared on numerous national television shows, presented scholarly papers at professional conferences, and has lectured widely in the U.S. and several other countries on the topics of rescuers of Jews in Nazi-occupied Europe, racism and anti-Semitism, war and genocide, and heroic altruism.

WITHOUT LOVE WHAT HAVE WE GOT? A WORLD WITHOUT A HEART

The title of this paper is taken from a heroic rescuer of *Jews in Nazi-Occupied Europe,* whom we interviewed and who had an important impact on my thinking and academic life.

This recent statement by a group of Jewish, Christian, and Muslim women who live in Jerusalem and who participated at a conference has particular relevance to my current research, "Unless we understand that one life is lived in the other, our attachment to our identities, national and religious, is superficial, presumptuous and meaningless". [10]

Psychologists, theologians, philosophers, marriage counselors, psychiatrists, and other healing professionals have informed us convincingly that human beings do not flourish without love. I believe that it is also true for animals. Harry Harlow's famous experiments with the baby monkeys, in which he separated infant monkeys from their mother and raised them in separate cages with two substitute "mothers" demonstrate this theory. The wired "mother" had a bottle for the infant, the cloth "mother" did not. As soon as the infants finished feeding they went for the cloth "mother" for comfort. Mary Carlson, an associate professor of neuroscience in psychology at Harvard's medical school, was influenced by Harlow's earlier study, and recognized its relevance to human deprivation and lack of loving contact between mothers and their infants. [11] When the infant monkeys were raised in a cage, from which they could see, smell, and hear -- but

10   From NAAMAT magazine, Summer 2004: 6.
11   For an elaboration of Dr. Carlson's research interests please see http://whyfiles.org/087mother/4.html

could not touch the mother monkeys, the baby monkeys developed what Carlson called "autistic-like syndrome," characterized by grooming, self-clasping, social withdrawal, and rocking.

Carlson reported on a study she did on orphanages in Romania, where children were devoid of human contact and their institutionalized care was not sufficient to maintain the human baby's social capacity. In Romania, the dictator Nicolae Ceausescu was a strong believer in technological progress, and was highly skeptical of all things "touchy-feely." He clamped down on psychology and social work, and preferred engineering and science. He greatly favored policies to raise the birth rate and establish institutions for orphans and children whose parents could not care for them. Carlson's observations have many implications for our society, where she sees a consistent relationship between poor care and increase in cortisol. Her research raises the question of what happens to American children in poor day care centers.

LOVE AND RESTORATIVE JUSTICE

Addressing the importance of love, Thomas Lewis, et al., in their major work *A General Theory of Love*, ask the questions: "What is love, and why are some people unable to find it?"and "What is loneliness, and why does it hurt?" The authors raise the question of the importance of attractors, which are patterns that are more or less imprinted in the limbic system from infant and childhood limbic connections. While looking at *A General Theory of Love*, Lynn E. O'Connor of the Wright Institute says that, "Less than optimal limbic connecting in whatever manner it fails to do the job, tends to get repeated throughout life, in terms of choice of love partners and other close relationships."[12] The authors explain that people who have experienced dysfunctional and unloving parents tend to select and continue to select partners that essentially match the parents in some limbic way, and that in the end are not good for them. Psychotherapy, when it works, helps to change the limbic patterns just enough to allow the person to begin to select more comfort-inducing partners and friends."

The Agape Love Ministries maintain that, "Love is the language that can be heard by the deaf seen by the blind and felt by the loneliest of hearts." They further enumerate that "Love is being happy for another person when they are happy, being sad for the other person when they are sad, being together in good times, and being together in bad times. Love is the source of strength...love is the source of life". [13]

There is of course faith-induced love. For Christianity, the notion of love means unconditional love, acceptance, forgiveness, openness, oneness with all, and treating others as you deserve to be treated. In Buddhism, especially Tibetan Buddhism, the concept of "Bodhicitta" means selfless or unselfish altruism, aspiration to relieve the sufferings of all, compassion, and service—meaning also love and forgiveness. There are a number

---

12   From Book review of Thomas Lewis, Fari Amini, and Richard Lannon A General Theory of Love (NY: Vintage Books, 2001) by Lynn E. O'Connor in the Human Nature Review, 10 March 2002, (2): 89-91, found on the web at http://human-nature.com/nibbs/02/leo.html on August 10, 2004.

13   See Agape Love Ministries on the web at http://www.ourchurch.com/member/r/ronlor777/, downloaded on August 4, 2004.

of examples in real life where unlimited love and loving kindness is exhibited—e.g., the hospice system and L'Arche, which consists of communities of people living with those who have developmental disabilities.

There are different kinds of love, developed by Anders Nygrens in his book called *Agape and Eros*.[14] The essentials of agape are love that is: 1) spontaneous and unmotivated; 2) indifferent to value; 3) creative; 4) the initiator of the fellowship with God. Divine love is spontaneous in that it does not look for reward. Divine love seeks those who do not deserve it, and can lay no claim to it. *Agape* love, then, is God's creative activity and it initiates fellowship with God. Stephen Post (2003) says, "In essence, unlimited love is abiding in an other-regarding perspective and emotional attunement that affirms and serves all of humanity unselfishly and unconditionally, without any exception whatsoever." Others such as John Templeton say that, "Unlimited love is a form of love that arises from every conceivable limit to embrace all of humanity in joy, creativity, compassion, care, and generativity; it lies at the heart at of all valid and worthwhile, spiritual, religious, and derivative philosophical traditions. It is often associated with a divine presence that underlies the cosmos and makes life a meaningful gift. Indeed the life of unlimited love probably begins with the sense that every life is a gift." These explanations are the heart of agape.

At a conference at Villanova University held May 31-June 5, 2003, the statement that encapsulated the conference was, "Unselfish love for all humanity is the most important point of convergence shared by the world's great spiritual traditions. We marvel at the power of love, and find in it the best hope for a far better human future. People from all walks of life, often those disadvantaged themselves, excel in love and kindness, not just for the nearest and dearest but also as volunteers and advocates on behalf of all the strangers."

Drawing on my own personal experience, in which I had been left at the age of twelve in a dangerous world without parents or loved ones in WWII, I felt lost and alone until compassionate people had taken an interest in me after the war ended and showed me not only that they loved and cared but also respected me. From this personal experience, and from having reviewed the research on the topic of love, young infants or even human beings throughout life who are deprived of love suffer the greatest negative consequences through much of their adult lives.

Next I want to turn to restorative justice. Just as we see currently a "culture of apology and forgiveness" in this country, as well as around the world, so do we discern centers for the study of restorative justice. Some say that there are over forty-five centers of restorative justice in the U.S.A. Restorative justice has also developed in other parts of the world, including the European Union, Australia, New Zealand, South Africa, Canada, and so forth. Restorative justice research and applications have come about as a result of victims and offender satisfaction with the process and outcome. Those who have experienced restorative justice say there is greater likelihood of resolution of conflict,

---

14   NY: Harper and Row, 1930.

reduced fear among victims, and reduced frequency and severity of further criminal behavior. Mark S. Umbrei, who focuses on the harm of wrongdoing more than rules that have been broken, shows equal concern for both victims and offenders, involving both in the process of justice.[15] The practice also works towards the restoration of victims' empowerment and responds to their needs. Additionally, there is support for offenders by encouraging to understand, accept, and carry out their obligations. Molly Ryan Strehorn, of the University of Massachusetts Center of Public Policy and Administration, says that countries around the world use restorative justice to heal the relationships damaged by crime. The philosophy is based upon four key values: encounter; amends; reintegration; inclusion. The holistic process brings justice back into the community and offers remediation for both the victim and the offender.[16] Gordon Bazemore (1998) provides a discussion of the roots of the new integrative and restorative justice theories, as well as the success of current preliminary applications of these theories. [17] Arguing that the traditional and opposing theories of the retributive justice and treatment model offer only a simplistic choice between helping or hurting offenders, the author contends that these symptoms fail to address adequately the needs of the community victims. The victims' active participation is needed in defining the harm of the crime and shaping the obligation placed on the offender. Then there is the role of the community, which is responsible for supporting and assisting victims, holding offenders accountable, and ensuring opportunities for offenders to make amends. The offender actively participates in competency development. Over all, the purpose of restorative justice is to enable and develop rehabilitation for the offender and some sort of reconciliation between the offender and the victim. In order for restorative justice to take place, good will needs to be accompanied by other-regarding, perspective taking, empathy, apology and forgiveness. Marilyn R. McNamara, in her research on the role of apology in restorative justice, maintains that "apology has to be commensurate with a particular hurt or offense, and it should be an expression of responsibility, remorse, reparation, and forbearance." She goes on to say that the role of empathy is important in an apology. McNamara concludes that the restorative justice process offers the offender the opportunity to accept responsibility, feel remorse, make amends, recover his or her self esteem, and encourage a desire to forebear from such anti-social action in the future. The offender also may integrate into society with a restored social identity.[18]

---

15   Mark S. Umbrei works with the Center for Restorative Justice and Peacemaking, in the School of Social Work, at University of Minnesota, for a further elaboration see Mark S. Umbreit. and William Bradshaw. "Assessing Victim Satisfaction with Victim Offender Mediation And Dialogue Services: The Development and Use of the Victim Satisfaction with Offender Dialogue Scale (VSODS)," found on the web at http://2ssw.che. umn.edu/rip/Resources/Documents/V-Scale.MON.pdf, downloaded on August 6, 2004.
16   Strehorn, Molly Ryan. Restorative Probation in Franklin County, Massachusetts. University of Massachusetts Center for Public Policy and Administration. 7/01/04. Thesis. http://www.sfu.ca/cfrj/fulltext/ strehorn.pdf.
17   Gordon Bazemore. 1998. "Restorative Justice and Earned Redemption: Communities, Victims, and Offender Reintegration," American Behavioral Scientist (41)6: 768-813.
18   Marilyn McNamara and Dhami, Mandeep, "The Role of Apology in Restorative Justice from Victims' and Offenders' Perspectives," paper presented at the International Conference on Restorative Justice held at Simon Fraser University, B. C., Canada June 1-4, 2003.

Julie J. Exline, et al., addressed the question of the relationship between forgiveness and justice. Why are individuals motivated to do restorative justice? Forgiveness and restorative justice is a "warm-based" virtue, similar to compassion, empathy, and altruism. Others assign higher values to the so-called conscientiousness-based virtues, such as responsibility, honesty, accountability, and duty. In many situations, the authors say that warm-based virtues and conscientious-based virtues should complement each other. It is possible that individuals who are more altruistic and empathic perceive the notion of restorative justice as being important for reconciliation. The authors conclude that the time has arrived for psychologists, and perhaps other social scientists, to understand the interface between forgiveness and justice.[19]

What role does love/*agape* play in altruistic behavior, caring, and compassion for diverse others, apology/forgiveness, and restorative justice? The current research in progress in the United States and Poland deals with the role of altruism and love, religiosity and spirituality, and apology and forgiveness.

---

19   Julie J. Exline, Everett L. Worthington, Jr., Peter Hill, and Michael E. McCullough, "Forgiveness and Jusitice: A Research Agenda for Social and Personality Psychology," *Personality and Social Psychology Review* in press.

37
MARGARET M. POLOMA, Ph.D.

After completing her Ph.D. at Case Western Reserve University (1970), Margaret M. Po-loma began her tenure as an assistant professor of sociology at The University of Akron, where she was on full-time faculty until 1995. Although retaining academic residence in the sociology depart-ment and sometimes teaching at The University of Akron, she has accepted visiting professorships in sociology of religion and related courses at the following seminaries and universities: Fuller Theological Seminary (Pasadena) 1996; Ashland Theological Seminary (Ashland, OH), 1996; Northeast Ohio College of Medicine, 1997; Oberlin College (Oberlin, OH). 1998, 2000; Vanguard University of Southern California (Costa Mesa) 1997-2000. Early retirement has permitted Poloma to focus her research efforts on her long-standing interest in the integration of spirituality and social science (including the topics of prayer, divine healing, religious revival, and Pentecostalism). Her current projects include a study of an inner-city ministry in Atlanta (funded by the Institute for Research on Unlimited Love) and of charisma and institutionalization in Pentecostalism (funded by the Louisville Institute).

LOVE THAT DOES JUSTICE: AN EXERCISE IN REFLEXIVE SOCIOLOGY

As a sociologist who has sought to allow her faith to inform her sociology and sociology to inform her faith, Alvin Gouldner's work on "reflexive sociology" has provided me with insights that have impacted my work. In calling for sociological self-reflection some 30 years ago, Gouldner saw the need for scholars to be involved in a certain amount of soul searching – lest we sell our souls. This posture has forced me to "demystify" not only sociology, but also aspects of my Christian faith. The ongoing dia-lectic between my faith (especially the experiential dimension) and social psychological theory has been foundational to my formulation of research questions, research methodol-ogy, and data interpretation over the years. Recent funding from the Institute of Research on Unlimited Love afforded me the opportunity to build on some of my earlier research findings and to explore unexplored terrain. The focus is on the relationship between spiritual empowerment and love within the context of a particular ministry that I will call "Atlanta Church of the Poor" (ACP). Participant observation at ACP, complemented by interview and survey data, provided a unique vantage point to explore the general question provided by Dr. Stephen Post (letter of 3/17/04) that guides this conference: "What is the link between spiritual practice, unselfish love, and the rigorous pursuit of social and distributive justice?" What follows is a brief discussion of each of the five key issues recommended for inclusion in our discussion.

WHAT IS "ENGAGED SPIRITUALITY"?

Spirituality, although usually intertwined with aspects of beliefs and practices that make up religion, is distinct from religion in that the latter involves self-transcendence – mysticism, if you will. Although mysticism comes in varying types and intensities, anyone who experiences the supranatural is a mystic in the broadest sense of the term. My ongoing research fits well with other work that suggests that mysticism is "normal" – that humans are "hardwired" for such experiences. "Engaged spirituality" implies that many are moved by a sense of a relationship with God and what they interpret as "divine direction" to engage in loving behavior.

George H. Gallup and Timothy Jones' groundbreaking work on *The Saints Among Us* provides statistical information and anecdotal examples of "engaged spirituality." They advance a simple proposition that appears to exist between spirituality and engagement: "The greater the 'spiritual commitment,' in other words, the greater the expressed concern for others; the less the spiritual commitment, the less involvement in helping others" (pp.22-23). Their work suggests that for the "saints," "God seemed not to be just an article of belief, but a living reality." They sought God's will, experienced God's comfort and support, and often experienced an "insight" or an "awakening" that motivated them for service. Our survey results from ACP confirm the Gallup-Jones hypothesis. "Spiritual commitment" (perhaps better termed "mystical or religious experiences") explained a significant part of the variance in altruism scores for both the homeless clients and the volunteer providers.

This "engagement" takes on different forms and degrees of intensity– even in a single social context such as ACP. For some in leadership of ACP, and for the Board of Directors, it involves minimal relational involvement with the poor; for intermittent part-time volunteers, relationships may be more transactional than interpersonal as they go about providing a specified service; for most full-time volunteers who provide daily service to the poor, relationships often assume more personal relational qualities; for the homeless, especially those who have made the shelter a temporary home, there is more of a "live-in engagement," complete with more intense interpersonal relationships that provide opportunities for loving service.

It is of interest that the poor/homeless demonstrated spirituality—as measured by Hood's mysticism scale and Poloma's charismata scale, that is indistinguishable from that of the volunteers/providers. Respondents in both groups were likely to report having a direct relationship with a God who spoke to them, guided them, and provided for them. No statistically significant differences were found for the mean scores reporting altruistic behaviors for the two groups. A major difference, however, was found in the relationship between the spirituality measures and empathy (a strong predictor of altruism). When a model was tested for the role spirituality and empathy (compassion) played in altruistic behavior, the results were significant for both the providers and the homeless with one important difference: the model accounted for nearly twice the amount of explained variance in the homeless group. We wish to suggest that altruism may be more of a "way of the life" for the poor than it is for their providers. This interpretation fits well with Gallup and Jones' finding of a greater concentration of "saints" being found among poor, Southern, African Americans than any other group.

HOW ARE LOVE AND COMPASSION INTEGRAL TO THE SUCCESS OF SOCIAL JUSTICE WORK?

Much depends on our definition of terms, but my observation is that "love and compassion" and "social justice work" do not necessarily demonstrate a direct relationship. There is evidence in my research (and in personal observations) that compassion may be present but may not translate into social justice work. It is also possible to do social justice work (as a job or vocation) without feeling much compassion.

The comments made by a 29-year-old homeless man I encountered during a recent trip to ACP were particularly insightful on this issue. I met Omar outside the church and we exchanged perfunctory greetings. He then said to me (seemingly out of the blue): "We are in a circle – an unbroken circle that is ongoing. There are those who make their living off our homelessness. Whether they know it or not, if they didn't have these jobs, they themselves might find themselves where we are. Others earn recognition as well as income for the 'help' they give to us. No one is really interested in breaking the circle. Maybe it can't be broken."

I would suggest that compassion motivates many workers, but their assistance can be part of an "unbroken circle" that can be devoid of justice. The leader of ACP has said on more than one occasion, "We have learned a little about compassion, but we don't have a clue about how to do justice." Much of the literature tends to blur compassion and altruism with justice issues – an issue worth discussing at this conference.

A reading of a recent article in *The New Yorker* (8/2/04—"The Gift") reminded me of the complexities involved in wrestling with the nature of justice. Zell Kravinsky, a philanthropist who had given nearly his entire $45 million dollar fortune to charity and then donated one of his kidneys to a stranger, is driven to do more and more. Despite his altruism, this husband and father of four seems obsessed and joyless. When asked by his good friend why he did not experience more joy if he were really on a path to enlightenment, Kravinsky replied, "It's not enlightenment. It's the start of a moral life."

There are undoubtedly many cases where love and compassion are the prime motivators of this "moral life." There are other cases where narcissism or seeming obsession will produce leaders who work effectively to bring about justice. I am struck by the cases of great leaders for justice who seemed to love humanity but showed much less compassion for those close to them.

The relationship between compassion ("sympathy for the suffering of others") and justice ("to deal with somebody fairly") is one between affect and cognition. It has long been known in the social sciences that "sentiments" and "acts" can be dissonant. What people "say" ("say they feel") is not necessarily correlated with what they "do". What we say we feel (empathy, compassion, love) often fails to translate into "fairness." Most of our research on social activism has focused on love, compassion, and empathy, rather than on the thorny issue of justice in an unjust world.

WHAT BELIEFS AND PRACTICES SUCCESSFULLY GIVE RISE TO OR SUSTAIN ACTIVISM?

I would like to tackle the issue through the lenses of what Pitirim Sorokin describes as the "five dimensional universe of psychosocial love" – intensity, extensity, duration, purity, and adequacy. Love involves relationships (with God and with neighbor), but love (and relationships) differs in intensity. I would suggest that there may be an inverse relationship between intensity and extensity—i.e., the more one loves "all people" the more difficult it may be to maintain intense interpersonal relationships with close family and friends. Purity of love is assessed in terms of motivation, and there are many examples of how less than "pure" motives (utilitarian) can paradoxically bring about justice. Although it is often discussed in studies of social activism, motivation takes on subjective qualities that are difficult or impossible to assess. Perhaps the most important two dimensions for the question at hand are duration (sustaining activism) and adequacy (discrepancy between objective outcome and subjective disposition).

Adequate love requires a cognitive sense of justice for assessment – define a "fair" outcome. In our longitudinal study of ACP, it soon became apparent that the service offered was good "charity," but it fell far short in meeting its self-proclaimed goal of being a "family" in which the poor were valued members. The homeless felt the dissonance – but most providers seemed blind to the discrepancy between what was being said and what was being done. Although the ministry was given high marks by the homeless for being "the safest shelter in Atlanta" and for the quality of food served at the public meals, the process of transformation through loving relationships has been far less successful than what was proposed. The dimension of duration was quickly raised in the interviews with the homeless. ACP was there for them today, but few were counting on tomorrow. Many dealt with this dissonance by noting that God – not ACP – was their Provider. While grateful for the assistance, most of the poor knew that it was folly to rely on any benevolence group. This posture became even more apparent in interviews with the homeless when a schism occurred within ACP leadership.

Based on our ongoing study of ACP (and in accord with earlier theorizing), beliefs and practices are only the tip of the activism iceberg. What appears to be a prime motivator is what Sorokin has termed "love energy" (defined as "the supraconsciouness in man's (sic) mental structure, creativity, and cognition"). Love energy can be produced by the interaction of human beings and/or "an intangible little-studied supraempirical source called 'God,' 'the Godhead,' 'the Soul of the Universe,' 'the Heavenly Father,' 'Truth,' and so on." Our findings at ACP confirm those reported by Gallup and Jones (The Saints Among Us) and Robert Wuthnow (Acts of Compassion) as to the importance of spiritual experiences as motivators of altruistic behavior.

WHERE SHOULD RESEARCH IN THIS FIELD BE DIRECTED AND FOCUSED?

Perhaps the first order of business is conceptual clarity, similar to the efforts taken to clarify the concepts of "spirituality" (in relation to "religion") and "compassion" (in relation to "empathy"). I am particularly interested in discussing types of "social activism" and the nature of "justice" in this seemingly "unjust world." In such work, social justice needs to be differentiated from social activism (two concepts that are interrelated yet distinct).

I would like to see more research efforts directed toward understanding the motivators of social activism/social justice. Among those commonly listed are: (1) sense of duty (normatively stimulated—e.g., by sacred writings or parental socialization, and experientially stimulated—e.g., a sense of profound gratitude); (2) intrinsic rewards (e.g., a sense of fulfillment; feelings of joy); (3) spiritual experiences (e.g., divine prompting, leading or other mystical encounter).

Although some have done research demonstrating the relationship between religious variables and social activism, less has been done on "spirituality." I would like to see more research focused on mystical experiences and empowerment (with beliefs and practices as a minor chord). There are men and women involved in social action/justice who are empowered by a sense of divine destiny that is fed by ongoing experiences of the divine. We have found such people at ACP among the providers, as well as among the homeless – people who are empowered by what Sorokin has called "love energy."
This research will need to be done in specific social contexts, as we are doing at ACP. Historically, it is evident that approaches to "engaged spirituality" can and do differ. The approach of George Fox (Quaker) is not the same as that of Katherine and William Booth (Salvation Army) and is not the same as Dorothy Day (Catholic Workers) or Mother Teresa (Sisters of Charity). Whatever the context and whatever the specific focus, the experiential (mystical) appears to be an important source of motivation and empowerment. Indicators need to be developed that will tap into this spiritual phenomenon for different religious groups and in different social contexts. There is evidence that Hood's general mysticism scale does work in varying settings, but other more specific descriptors are also needed (analogous to Poloma's charismata scale for Pentecostal/charismatic believers).

HOW CAN RESEARCHERS HELP ACTIVISTS IN THEIR WORK, AND HOW CAN ACTIVISTS HELP RESEARCHERS?

We worked together with ACP to develop a research problem that was of interest to both the investigators and the subject group. Such collaboration right from the start of the project promises to be mutually rewarding. In the last analysis, however, the researcher can only do the work, request input, and offer the results to the activist. There is the ever-present possibility that the researcher/messenger's news may not be what the activist wishes to hear. Even in such cases, collaborative efforts do pay off. Even if the results are not utilized by the research subjects, they promise to provide quality information for dissemination among scholars and activists alike.

38
ADAM B. SELIGMAN, PH.D.

Adam B. Seligman is Professor of Religion at Boston University and Research Associate at the Institute for Culture, Religion and World Affairs. He has lived and taught at universities in this country, Israel, and in Hungary, where he was a Fulbright Fellow from 1990-1992. He lived in Israel for close to twenty years, where he was a member of Kibbutz Kerem Shalom in the early 1970s. His books include The Idea of Civil Society (Free Press, 1992), Inner-worldly Individualism (Transaction Press, 1994), The Problem of Trust (Princeton University Press, 1997), Modernity's Wager: Authority, the Self and Transcendence (Princeton University Press, 2000), and with Mark Lichbach Market and Community (Penn State University Press, 2000). His work has been translated into over a dozen languages. At present, with the help of major grants from The Ford Foundation and Pew Charitable Trusts, he is working on the problem of religion and toleration. Part of this work is devoted to establishing school curricula for teaching tolerance from a religious perspective. In this endeavor, he is working with colleagues in Berlin, Sarajevo, and Jerusalem. With them, he has established the International Summer School on Religion and Public Life, which leads seminars on religion and the public square in different parts of the world. His latest book is Modest Claims, Dialogues and Essays on Tolerance and Tradition (Notre Dame University Press, 2004).

THE TOLERANCE PROJECT

One of the major changes in the past twenty years has been the increased saliency of Public Religion—that is, religion that has not allowed itself to be retired to the "private sphere" of individual belief and practice, but has insisted that it take a role in political and social ordering. This effort has taken a number of forms that reflect the contrasting tendencies of modernity. It has taken totalizing forms, which are identified with the so-called fundamentalist movements that aim to create totalistic political and social regimes that conform to some overriding religious vision or normative order. At the same time, it has taken forms that accept and advance pluralism. One salient example of this pluralistic form of public religion has been the role of the Catholic Church in Poland and Spain. Another example would be the role played by the Franciscan order in many parts of Bosnia during the 1992-1995 wars in former Yugoslavia.

Thus, one of the major issues concerning religion and public life is the relationship of religion to democracy and pluralism. This is a very complex topic because the issue is many sided. Democracy itself has both totalizing and pluralistic aspects, and fundamentalist religion may have a strong link to Jacobin or nationalist democracy. At the same time, pluralistic orientations in both politics and religion may not necessarily br linked to democratic ones. One must also ask to what extent and under what conditions pluralistic orientations in religion and politics develop out of totalizing democratic religious and political practices.

This question is not only important in regard to the nature of life within religious groups and states, but also to relations between religious groups. While religious and ethnic/national conflict has existed independently of the "input" of totalizing fundamentalist religion, as in the cases of Israel-Palestine, India, Bosnia, and other places, it is apparent that they exacerbate existing conflict—and in some places, are responsible for conflict itself.

THE TOLERANCE PROJECT

The Tolerance Project at Boston University was established in 1998 to explore and contribute to specifically religious resources for tolerance and pluralism. It combines a global perspective on religious thought with social scientific research into tolerance, civil society, and a pluralistic approach to pedagogic practice. Its goal is to transform both the theoretical models and concrete practices through which religious orientations and secular models of politics and society engage one another in the school environment. Its guiding principle is that the perceived barrier between secular, modern, and more traditional religious values must be broken down in order to build relations of tolerance and understanding between groups and to shape a civil society. Political orientations, social practices, and pedagogic techniques must be developed that will draw on both religious sources and the insights of secular modernity in new and creative ways.

The Tolerance Project has focused on the preparation of school curricula to teach religious tolerance and values of democracy and civic belonging to religious students in religious schools; these curricula are based on religious texts and orientations. We have drawn on local regional resources in the Balkans and the Middle East, as well as on international resources in Europe, North America, and elsewhere.

The Project's goals are to increase students' critical and complex thinking, develop the ability to understand others' perspectives, and, ultimately, to enhance the social capital of a significant multi-ethnic, multi-religious, and multi-cultural partnership in a common country.

SINCERITY, RITUAL, AND THE STRUCTURES OF MODERN DISSONANCE

Moving beyond the realm of pedagogy, the Tolerance Project has begun a careful exploration of different religious practices that may have their own unique, and, for some, counterintuitive structures, of tolerance that are not immediately apparent to those schooled in Western, secular, and (what are so often) post-Protestant ways of thinking. Thus, for example, and quite unexpectedly, ritual and ritualized activities (both formally religious and more secular) have re-emerged as forms of social practice in many parts of the world. These present new or renewed forms of spiritual practice or "engaged spirituality," and it is our hypothesis that they also present new forms of what may be termed "spiritual capital." More specifically, we wish to test the hypothesis that ritual, as a spiritual practice, may provide an important resource for tolerance and openness (indeed, of compassion) to others; it may also provide a critical component for social progress at the dawning of the 21st century.

We posit an ideal typical distinction between sincerity and ritual as two modes of being in the world, which we suggest has important implications for how people deal with ambiguity and difference (and hence the existence of the other, who is by definition different). Whatever else may determine social progress in this new century, the ability to live together in a world of radically deconstructed and changing boundaries will certainly be one of its core aspects. Our work so far suggests that ritual acts provide a critical and necessary tool in this attempt (however counterintuitive this may be to regnant ideas of self and society). Given this renewed importance of ritual in so many different contexts, we propose a research project dedicated to one key question in the study of both sincerity and ritual: *To what extent do sincerity and ritual present alternative models of spiritual practice with different implications for social interaction and civil order?*

Framing our query is the somewhat counterintuitive notion that, in certain circumstances and certain societies, it is ritual rather than sincerity that allows individuals to deal in a more creative manner with ambiguity and contradiction. This idea questions the governing assumptions of modernity on the importance of sincerity and honesty as the only or best ways to navigate successfully the shoals of those contradictions that define the human condition. We believe that sustained inquiry into this problem will help sharpen our understanding of aspects of religious renewal and the growth of new spiritual practices in different societies, worldwide.

Our proposal grows from a theoretical distinction between two fundamental modes of thought that we term the "ritual" and the "sincere." In ritual, we subject ourselves to externally given categories of order, whose source can be anything from a transcendent deity (as in Judaism) to the natural ordering of the physical and social world (as in Confucianism). Ritual concentrates on the performative nature of the act, rather than on its denotative meaning. By using multiple non-linguistic media such as dance, incense, music, and breath control, ritual insists on the importance of doing rather than saying. Many of its words will not even reduce to proper language: the speech is archaic and difficult, or mantric and incomprehensible. Formally, it tends to be repetitive and anti-discursive. For us, ritual includes religious practice, but also etiquette, forms of music, dance, and some aspects of play. Pure ritual puts questions of belief or truth aside in favor of the shared social world its action creates and requires

Sincerity, by contrast, grows out of internally-generated categories, looking to substitute a genuine and thoughtful state of internal conviction for mere social convention. Each individual thus takes on an enormous responsibility. To many sincere critics, one problem with ritual is that it does not proclaim its inner states in so many words. Ritual is "merely" prescribed action, and therefore subject to dismissal from those whose focus on sincerity sees ritual as either hypocrisy (a kind of lie) or foolishness (a kind of play). Unthinking repetition of such acts appears as hypocrisy to those who insist that they should instead reflect internal conviction.

A life of pure ritual or pure sincerity would be absurd. Both modes of thought coexist in all of us, though not without tension. From the point of view of sincerity, ritual is mere hypocrisy and convention. Viewed from the point of view of ritual, however, sincerity – with its stress on internal, individualized processes - can be a threat to the very existence of society. Though the tension between the two is usually kept under control, it does have a tendency to break out, as we can see in the world's religious traditions—e.g., the Buddhist critique of Hinduism; Christian critique of Judaism; Reformation critique of the Catholic Church; Wang Yangming's critique of neo-Confucianism, etc. Reform movements based on sincerity tend, however, to be "tamed" over time, with new creations of ritual. Of course, extreme forms of sincerity discourage all ritual-like behavior – not just ritualized religious practice, but music, play (for adults), dance, and even humor.

These considerations lead us to query whether the balance between ritual and sincerity in a given context may have powerful effects on social and civil life, particularly on the ability to deal with difference. For example, it is quite clear in contemporary Israel that there is no chance of peace without engaging the religious communities, and perhaps no chance of a continued democracy either. (Remember that the assassin of Prime Minister Rabin was from the orthodox religious community.) We can, moreover, easily isolate varied Jewish religious communities in Israel whose differential positioning on a ritual/sincerity scale correlates with different attitudes towards democratic values and a culture of civic and political rights. Examples of this would be the attitudes presented by the former Chief Rabbi of Tel Aviv, R. Haim David HaLevy (who developed a position predicated on a universal natural law) towards rights of non-Jews, and those racist and incendiary opinions voiced by Rabbis such as R. Ginzburg of Yeshiva Kever Yosef. In Israel, too, we can see the growth of Islamicist movements that have, to a great extent, replaced the Israeli Communist Party as the political organ of Palestinian social and national demands (within the Jewish state). Yet these movements are far from being all of a piece, and the differences between such seminaries as those at Um El Fahem and Bak-al-Ghrabia exemplify religious differences and different attitudes toward spiritual and ritual practice that are mirrored by different political orientations as well. We could as easily expand this with other examples, such as the varying and competing Islamic practices in Central Asia or the Balkans, where different attitudes towards ritual also correlate with different political orientations. Variations in attitudes toward ritual and sincerity exist even closer to home—e.g., in the disagreements within the Episcopal Church about the ordination of an openly gay bishop.

Our research explores one aspect of the following general hypothesis:
The ways in which the tension between ritual and sincerity is played out in various reli-
gious groups in different parts of the modern world have important effects on the plural-
istic structuring and fundamental rules of justice in civil life.

More specifically, we test the counterintuitive idea that ritual, as a form of spiritual practice, may in fact provide critical tools for tolerance and pluralism, enabling progress towards a less violent and more civil world. We thus examine the possibility that ritual and sincerity offer alternative modes of social action and interaction, and that the "balance" between and differentiation among realms addressed by each in society have critical consequences for the civil order. These are very relevant considerations in countries where the national form of religion is at stake.

Both empirical research into the social orientations of ritual communities and a sustained scholarly engagement with the phenomena will, we believe, uncover hitherto unrecognized resources of practical spirituality. It is our hypothesis that ritual, precisely in its performative and, we would claim, subjunctive meanings, provides unique resources for tolerance, pluralism, and acceptance of an ambiguous world, in which the other remains other. Its role as an "untapped" resource for social justice and, indeed, social activism needs to be addressed if we are to engage the vast majority of the world's population, for whom ritual practice is the very core of spiritual life.

39
JUDITH SMETANA, Ph.D.

Judith Smetana is professor of psychology and pediatrics at the University of Rochester (Rochester, NY). She obtained her A. B. degree with Highest Honors in Psychology at the University of California at Berkeley, and her M.S. and Ph.D. in Psychology at the University of California at Santa Cruz. She completed an NICHD post-doctoral fellowship in the Department of Psychology at the University of Michigan before moving to the University of Rochester as an Assistant Professor. From 1995 to 1998, she held the Frederica Warner Chair of Education and Human Development; since 1998, she has been the head of the Developmental Psychology Ph.D. Program in the Department of Clinical and Social Sciences in Psychology.

Dr. Smetana's research focuses on children's moral and social reasoning, parenting beliefs, and adolescent-parent relationships, and cultural influences on development; she has written numerous articles on these topics. She is the author of "Concepts of Self and Society: Women's Reasoning about Abortion" (Praeger), the editor of "Parental beliefs: Causes and Consequences for Development," (Jossey-Bass), and editor (with Melanie Killen) of the forthcoming "Handbook of Moral Development" (Erlbaum). She is currently conducting longitudinal research on middle class African-American families with adolescents, and on adolescent-parent relationships in different cultural contexts. Her research has been funded by the National Institute of Mental Health, the National Science Foundation, the William T. Grant Foundation, and the Institute for Research on Unlimited Love. Dr. Smetana has been Associate Editor of Child Development and has served on the Editorial Boards of several journals, including Developmental Psychology, Human Development, Social Development, and Journal of Adolescent Research.

PSYCHOLOGICAL RESEARCH ON MORAL DEVELOPMENT:
RELATIONSHIPS TO SOCIAL JUSTICE AND SOCIAL ACTIVISM

I will respond to the questions posed by Dr. Post through the lens of research in developmental psychology and, more specifically, psychological research on children's moral development. Because Dr. Youniss' statement focused extensively on the research on volunteering and service, I will address other aspects of the moral development research that might contribute fruitfully to our dialogue. First, I will discuss research on moral reasoning development, focusing on Kohlberg's well-known approach to moral judgment development and then on more recent research from the social-cognitive domain approach, including recent research on adolescents' understanding of civil liberties. Finally, I will discuss findings from my recent research on African-American adolescents' civic engagement.

STAGES OF MORAL JUDGMENT DEVELOPMENT

For many years, the dominant paradigm for research on adolescents' and young adults' moral development was Kohlberg's theory of moral judgment development (Colby & Kohlberg, 1987; Kohlberg, 1971, 1984). From responses to hypothetical dilemmas that opposed conflicting concerns with law, life, interpersonal obligations, trust, and authority, Kohlberg proposed that children's and adolescents' moral judgments develop through a series of six universal, sequential, and hierarchical stages of progressively more differentiated and integrated concepts of justice. His theory focused on the underlying structure of individuals' moral judgments, rather than on the content or particular decisions that individuals made.

> *According to Kohlberg, moral judgments in middle and late childhood are structured by concerns with obedience, punishment avoidance, and instrumental needs (labeled "preconventional" reasoning and divided into two stages). Increased perspective-taking abilities were seen as liberating children from this external focus on obedience to authority and authority sanctions, leading to the development of broader interpersonal and societal perspectives on morality. At this next level, labeled "conventional" morality and consisting of two stages, moral judgments were seen as structured by an understanding of role obligations, interpersonal needs, and respect for societal rules and authority. Kohlberg described a further developmental level of "post-conventional" or principled moral judgments, which he asserted were structured by concerns about mutual respect, contractual arrangements among individuals and their rights and duties, and differentiated concepts of justice and rights.*

In Kohlberg's scheme, the highest stage of morality, which was labeled as *Stage 6, postconventional reasoning*, involves a systematic application of universal ethical principles, as articulated within Kantian ethics and drawing on Rawls' (1971) theory of justice. More specifically, Kohlberg proposed that Stage 6 reasoning entails following self-chosen ethical principles pertaining to the equality of human rights and the respect for the dignity of human beings as individuals (Colby & Kohlberg, 1987). Kohlberg illustrated Stage 6 reasoning in terms of moral exemplars such as Martin Luther King, Jr. and Mahatma Gandhi, and in terms of individuals who engaged in acts of civil disobedience, such as helping slaves escape before the Civil War (Kohlberg, 1971). Kohlberg's theory focused primarily on the process by which children, adolescents, and adults make moral judgments; with development, however, judgments and actions are increasingly coordinated so that at the highest stages, individuals (such as Gandhi or Martin Luther

King, Jr.) would be compelled to act on their self-chosen ethical principles.

Unfortunately, the research does not provide compelling evidence that individuals (in the US or elsewhere) normatively develop principled moral reasoning. Because it was observed so infrequently, Stage 6 was described in Colby and Kohlberg's (1987) later formulations as a meta-ethical stance rather than as a normative developmental stage; longitudinal research has found little evidence that late adolescents' or young adults' reasoning progresses beyond a conventional understanding of morality. Furthermore, in their analysis of moral exemplars (*Some Do Care*), Damon and Colby did not find evidence that moral exemplars were necessarily post-conventional in their moral orientations.

BEYOND KOHLBERG: DOMAIN SPECIFICITY APPROACHES

Kohlberg's theory (Colby & Kohlberg, 1987; Kohlberg, 1984) describes the process of moral development as entailing the gradual differentiation of principles of justice or rights from non-moral (e.g., conventional, pragmatic, and prudential) concerns. In his formulation, it is not until post-conventional stages of development (which research has shown, are rarely achieved) that individuals distinguish issues of justice, welfare, or rights from more arbitrary and consensually determined customs, conventions, and rules. In contrast, an extensive body of research from what has come to be known as a domain specificity approach has demonstrated that even young children have a (rudimentary) understanding of concepts of justice, welfare, and rights; these moral concepts are differentiated from their understanding of social convention and personal issues (see Smetana, 1995, 2002, in press; Turiel, 1983, 1998 for reviews of research supporting these claims). In this view, morality is seen as regulating the social interactions and social relationships of individuals within societies, and is defined as individuals' prescriptive understanding of how people ought to behave towards others. Children and adolescents across a broad age range have been found to evaluate moral issues as prescriptive, obligatory, generalizably or universally applicable, and permissible (or wrong) independent of concerns about authority sanctions or punishment. In contrast, they have been found to view conventions as arbitrary, contextually relative, and contingent on rules and authority.

A great deal of research indicates that young children make distinctions between moral and non-moral (e.g., conventional, personal, and prudential) issues and apply moral criteria, such as generalizability and authority independence, to moral events. In other words, the research shows that young children judge that simple moral acts (such as hitting another child) as wrong on the basis of the act's intrinsic consequences (such as its harmful effect on others), rather than the presence or absence of a rule. During the pre-school years, children have a clearer moral understanding of issues pertaining to concrete harm and welfare than they have of fairness and psychological harm. During middle childhood, children are increasingly able to apply moral criteria to unfamiliar moral events and to a broader range of moral concepts (such as psychological harm). Moral concerns in middle childhood about strict equality and equal treatment between persons are transformed in pre-adolescence into a concern with equity—i.e., an understanding that fair treatment may entail unequal treatment when considering individual differences in needs and statuses. Early adolescents continue to consolidate their moral understanding of equity and equality; combined with the prescriptive and universalizable element of morality, they are more readily able to extend their moral concepts of fairness and welfare to abstract others and beyond their own group. During middle adolescence, concepts of fairness become more broadly comprehensive – that is, they become more generalizable across situations and more able to take situational variations into account.

APPLYING MORAL CONCEPTS IN COMPLEX SITUATIONS

This research indicates that children's moral thinking about prototypical moral situations becomes increasingly sophisticated from early childhood through adolescence. But situations that involve moral decision making or moral actions may be complex, and may entail overlaps or conflicts between competing moral considerations (as in Kohlberg's famous Heinz dilemma, where the choice is between valuing property and preserving life – two conflicting moral concerns), or between moral and non-moral considerations.

Moral decisions may become problematic in situations where the moral status of the situation is ambiguous or contested, or where moral concerns come into conflict with other types of concerns. In some situational contexts, moral concerns may predominate, and adolescents may demonstrate autonomous moral thinking. For instance, Helwig (1995) has proposed that there may be a general developmental pattern where increasingly more abstract and complex moral concepts are applied first in straightforward moral situations, and then in complex or multifaceted situations entailing conflicts between moral and conventional concerns. This can be illustrated through recent research on adolescents' understanding of civil liberties.

Previous survey research on Americans' attitudes towards civil liberties (discussed extensively in Turiel, Killen, & Helwig, 1987) indicates that individuals support freedoms and rights when questions about these issues are posed abstractly; the same individuals express substantially less support when civil liberties are described in various situational contexts. For instance, survey research on large and representative samples of Americans has found that nearly all individuals strongly endorse "freedom of speech" when this liberty is described abstractly. However, much smaller proportions of Americans have been found to support freedom of speech when presented with concrete examples (freedom to express hate speech, high school students' freedom to express views contrary to their school's position or policy, freedom to criticize the Iraq war or support Al Qaeda, etc.). Such findings have been viewed as indicating individuals' lack of principled moral thinking. In contrast, Helwig (1995, 1997) has proposed that these findings reflect conflicts between various moral concepts and principles applied in complex situations.

To test this proposition, Helwig (1995) asked adolescents of different ages to reason and make judgments about two examples of civil liberties (freedom of speech and freedom of religion) presented in different types of situations. He found that when civil liberties were decontextualized and presented abstractly, or when they were presented in contextualized situations where there were no other competing moral concerns, early adolescents displayed sophisticated conceptions of them; they nearly unanimously endorsed civil liberties and judged them using moral criteria.

However, concepts of civil liberties were not fully applied when early adolescents judged situations in which freedom and rights were described as in conflict with laws and equality. In these multifaceted situations, freedom of speech and religion were less likely to be affirmed and more likely to be subordinated to other concerns. In general, older adolescents gave priority to civil liberties across a broader range of situations than did younger adolescents. Late adolescents were better able to integrate their evaluations of legal systems and acts. They were also able to evaluate both legal restrictions on rights and acts violating restrictive laws from the perspective of abstract rights. Furthermore, when judging multifaceted situations that depicted conflicts between concerns pertaining to rights versus equality (e.g., between competing moral concerns), older adolescents were better able to coordinate their notions of equality with differences in individuals, as would be predicted from the account of developmental changes in moral concepts described previously. Thus, these findings indicate that judgments that appear to entail exceptions to general principles may be explained in terms of conflicts in multifaceted situations. In this study, failures to endorse civil liberties in early adolescence were due to adolescents' difficulties in coordinating different principles and concerns in their social judgments, and these abilities increased from early to late adolescence. Similar age-related patterns have been found in recent research on children's and adolescents' judgments of inclusion and exclusion from peer social groups (Killen & Stangor, 2001).

In my view, this research provides some evidence of the developmental underpinnings of committed social activism and social justice (or at least, individuals' understanding of the need for social justice). The research suggests that the development of moral understanding (including individuals' ability to coordinate different moral and non-moral concerns) may be involved in thinking about social justice, although it is likely that moral understanding alone is not sufficient for social action. Once individuals are able to make generalizable and universalizable moral judgments, what factors might move them forward to committed moral action? In his essay, Dr. Youniss discusses several programs of research that provide some clues. In their research on adolescent moral exemplars in Camden, New Jersey, Hart and Fegley (1987) assert the importance of moral identity and the merging of moral identity into broader conceptions of self and identity. Their research does not examine the processes, however, that lead to the differences observed between moral exemplars engaged in community activism and service and comparison youth who are not. (Likewise, Damon and Colby's book, Some Do Care, provides useful examples of moral exemplars' experiential narratives about committed moral action. It should be noted, however, that a great deal of research on autobiographical memory indicates that we organize – and reconstruct - our life stories to provide a coherent narrative, and that the psychological processes that motivate us may not always be transparent to ourselves.)

SPIRITUALITY AND CIVIC ENGAGEMENT

On a separate note, as part of a longitudinal research project on middle class African-American adolescents' development in family contexts, I have conducted research (Smetana & Metzger, in press) on the family and religious antecedents of adolescents' civic involvement. In our research, we have distinguished both conceptually and empirically between three forms of civic involvement: church; community; political involvement (Metzger & Smetana, 2004). We have examined the longitudinal influence of family interactions, religiosity, and spirituality on these different forms of current and future (intended) civic involvement. Adolescents' spirituality (assessed 3 years prior) and mothers' current community involvement were found to predict adolescents' involvement in their community; adolescents' current religiosity/spirituality and mothers' current church involvement influenced current church involvement. Interestingly, family (including parents' current level of political involvement) and religious factors were poor predictors of adolescents' current political involvement. Intended church and community involvement were predicted by parents' more positive communication in family interactions observed 3 years earlier. We have hypothesized that parents who communicate more effectively and with greater clarity may be better at expressing their values and ideas; they also encourage more discussion and negotiation of ideas. Intended church and community involvement also were influenced by earlier spirituality, but the influence of earlier spirituality on intended church and community involvement was mediated by current religiosity/spirituality. Again, the psychological variables were poor predictors of intended political involvement, although lower income adolescents expressed greater intentions to become politically involved in the future (perhaps because lower income youth are more disenfranchised from society and therefore more motivated to change it). This research suggests the importance of family and spiritual factors in community involvement, at least for African-American middle class youth.

FUTURE RESEARCH NEEDS

In terms of future research needs, a great deal of current theory and research has focused (separately) on children's and adolescents' moral and affective development. Howver, there is little developmental psychology research that examines how children's moral understanding connects with positive moral concerns of beneficence and kindness toward others and leads to committed moral action. Research is especially needed on the relationship among children and adolescents' concepts of "negative morality"— those actions that are wrong, "positive morality"—those actions that promote the well being of others, and moral action.

40
PAUL LAURITZEN, Ph.D.

Paul Lauritzen is the Director of the Program in Applied Ethics at John Carroll University in Cleveland. He has written extensively on issues in bioethics, as well as on the use of appeals to personal experience as a form of moral argument. For example, he has published work on how experientially-based arguments have been used in debates about capital punishment, assisted suicide, and human rights policies. Thus, his research has often focused on the stories that activists tell about their work. He is currently overseeing John Carroll University's collaboration with Sr. Helen Prejean and Tim Robbins to present Robbins' draft stage adaptation of Dead Man Walking on campus. Part of the collaboration involves a year-long focus on the death penalty as a topic of sustained discussion on campus. The project on the death penalty continues Lauritzen's long-standing interest in the way forgiveness and restorative justice may be sustained by particular spiritual commitments.

My interest in the themes of this conference goes back to my dissertation work, which explored the way religious narratives may work to shape (and sustain) a believer's emotional life. The burden of that work was to argue that the dichotomy traditionally posited between reason and emotion is incorrect, and that we should not ignore the role emotions play in the moral life. I suggested that attending to the role of emotions in the moral life is particularly important for religious ethicists, because a religious vision of human life and history may bring about significant moral changes in the life of the believer. I tried to illustrate this point by showing how a religious conception of the nature of moral relations may have an effect on the emotion of anger—and thus on the possibility of forgiveness. This work on the role of the emotions in the moral life dovetails nicely with the themes of the conference, especially with the importance of emotions such as love and compassion to the work of social justice.

In addition to intersecting with my past work on the role of the emotions in the moral life, the conference engages current research and writing interests. I will spend the bulk of my statement articulating those interests as they bear on the conference themes. Given that one of the purposes of the conference is to promote dialogue among activists and scholars "through dialogue and sharing," permit me to begin with a story that will explain my research interests.

Almost fifteen years ago, I published an article in which I drew upon my experience of being infertile and seeking to become a father in order to discuss a range of ethical issues raised by reproductive technology. I had been convinced by critics of traditional moral philosophy that ethical reflection is impoverished when we fail to attend to both fictional and experiential narratives. Therefore, I discussed in detail the nature of my infertility, the tests and procedures my wife and I tried, and other generally private matters. I suggested that all serious moral reflection must involve a dialectical movement between general principles and concrete cases. As a result, proper moral deliberation involves attending both to rules and to the affective responses of particular moral agents facing particular decisions. I thus appealed to my own experiences as part of a project to assess various objections to reproductive technology that had been raised in the literature of medical ethics.

I did not develop a defense of my use of personal experience or seek to elaborate a critical apparatus for mobilizing experience in the debates about reproductive technology. Nonetheless, my appeal to experience as a touchstone of moral analysis was not so different from what a growing number of writers were and are doing when addressing issues of applied ethics.

My article was well received; one reason was surely that readers conceded to me a kind of authority that comes from first-hand experience. If I spoke of feeling a sense of coercion in the mere offer of various reproductive interventions, this feeling could be cited as corroborating feminist objections that reproductive technology is coercive to women, and apparently men as well. Who would know better than someone who had been through the ordeal of infertility treatment? Because of my experience in dealing with infertility, many readers found my analysis of reproductive technology both compelling and persuasive.

Then a curious thing happened. Colleagues who read and commented favorably on my article were annoyed to discover that my wife and I had been successful in our efforts to conceive a child. Although my article indicated that we had about exhausted the range of medical interventions available to us, our first child had been born by the time the article actually made it into print. Instead of eliciting expressions of congratulations or happiness at our good fortune, news of our son's birth was frequently met with anger and dismay by those who had read the article. What could account for this response?

The answer to this question is instructive in helping us to clearly understand the importance of providing a framework for assessing appeals to personal experience, including an appeal to the sort of engaged spirituality that this conference wishes to explore. The most obvious answer is that news of my son's birth, following so quickly upon the publication of the article, could lead readers to believe that I had lied. Perhaps I had simply imagined what it might be like to undergo infertility treatment, and then reported these imaginary feelings as actual ones. If so, my article relinquished any privileged access to truth. Worse still, if the events I narrated had not happened, then I had betrayed the reader's trust. Neither the narrative nor the conclusions, reached partly through appeal to the narrative, could be trusted.

Although this is a plausible explanation of why some readers responded to the news of our success as they did, it is important to point out that this explanation rests upon a certain (questionable) understanding about the nature of "experience" and the role an appeal to experience plays in moral deliberation. On this account, experience is understood to be largely unmediated, a sort of brute fact upon which one can build an argument. So the appeal to experience functions as an effort to reach moral bedrock. This is why the possibility that the experience is not factual is so threatening. If the experience is fictional, there is no foundation upon which the arguments finally rest.

Although this explanation is plausible, appealing to experience is a much more complicated matter than this picture suggests; this fact is revealed by attending more carefully to why my article should be thought to be persuasive if the events I narrated "really happened"—but not if they didn't. One reason has to do with the fact that we usually draw a very sharp distinction between fact and fiction, and we usually think about "experience" as falling on the factual side of this divide. Notice, however, that the contrast between "really happened" and "imagined," or between "fact" and "fiction," will not be as easy to sustain as might initially be supposed. To be sure, either I was treated for infertility or I was not. But in describing my infertility treatment, I was not merely providing a chronicle of events at a clinic. What value would a catalog of procedures, along with the dates and times they were undertaken, provide to the project of assessing the morality of assisted reproduction? I was recounting the lived reality of these events; I was relating the meaning these events had for me. Yet, seen in this light, the contrast between actually happened/imagined appears problematic. In what sense can the meaning of these events be said to have actually happened?

The difficulty of answering this question highlights the general difficulty of thinking of experience as foundational. Experience is simply not transparent in the way required by the foundationalist account, at least not in a way that is useful for moral reasoning. To be useful to moral deliberation, the appeal to experience must be more than a mere cataloguing of events in the life of the agent; the events must be drawn together in a meaningful pattern. Yet, to acknowledge this point is to acknowledge that an experiential report does not map reality in an uncomplicated way; indeed, it might be better to say that an appeal to experience provides an interpretation of reality. So whatever persuasive force an appeal to experience has cannot be accounted for by thinking of experience as an unimpeachable record of what actually happened.

At the same time, however, if an appeal to experience is to function as a kind of moral argument, the distinction between what actually happened and what was imagined, or between fact and fiction, must be maintained.

With this as background, I suggest that there are a number of important questions that our conversation may wish to engage. For example:

- Does the personal experience of activists in pursuing social justice give them a special authority in reflecting on issues of social justice? If so, what is the nature of that authority and can it be misused?
- What does it mean to narrate the experiences of social activism truthfully?
- What responsibilities do activists have to narrate their experiences truthfully? (Think of the controversy regarding Rigoberta Menchú.)
- If different activists have conflicting experiences in working for social justice, how do we adjudicate the differences?

41
RAMEZ ISLAMBOULI

Ramez Islambouli, a native of Lebanon, moved to the USA in 1985 to pursue his academic studies. He holds an undergarduate degree in biomedical engineering and a Master's degree in Bioethics, both from Case Western Reserve University. He teaches Islamic law at the law school at Case. He also teaches Islamic studies at both John Carroll University and Cuyahoga Community College. He serve as a Muslim Chaplain at University Hospitals and the Cleveland Clinic. He also serves as a Muslim Chaplain at the Richland Correctional Institution and the Cuyahoga Hills Juvenile Correctional Facility. Currently, he is a member of University Hospitals' IRB.

ISLAMIC PERSPECTIVES ON LOVE AND JUSTICE

Love is a great and important factor in life. Any person whose nature is normal is attracted by tenderness, a show of love, affection, and sympathy. No one can seriously claim that he/she does not need to love or be loved. We all have feelings of love and hatred, likes and dislikes. We may, for instance, love a book or beautiful scenery; a man may love a woman to the extent of worshipping her. The child, the teenager, the lover, the wife, the husband, the elderly man, the weak, the oppressed, and even the criminal feel the need of love. But it is a love bound by limits and constraints, like any other human love. We feel attached to the good we derive from anything we love or from the pleasure and joy we feel by being near the person we love. But this love may not continue in the same degree of intensity, or it may even turn into antipathy if anything untoward happens to the person or object of love—or if the beloved's figure becomes maimed due to an accident, the food becomes stale and putrid, or the climatic conditions change the beauty of the natural scenery.

In Islamic creed, the love the believer has for God is absolute love; it is not subjected to any constraints or limitations. Indeed, the love we have for persons and objects in this world is in reality our love for God through His creations—i.e., the persons and objects that He has created and placed at our disposal so that we may make use of them or enjoy by seeing them or feeling them.

Many creations are sources of fear for us: a blazing fire, a wild beast, a deadly poison, or a ruthless tyrant may frighten us out of our wits. But such a fear is bound by the extent of danger we visualize or that may result from the source of our fear. If the danger is over, our fear will vanish. But the fear of God is unlimited and not subjected to any checks and restraints. The belief in God is based on the love and fear of Him. They form the spirit of worship. Fear of God should neither cause panic in us nor anxiety, which may make us lose our mental equilibrium. It should, on the other hand, induce in us the love of God through obedience to Him. It should make us lead a life of purity in both conduct and character that are acceptable to God. The Holy Quran says: "Say O Prophet: if you love God, follow me." (3:31). Thus, the true gauges of love and fear are adherence to the path of guidance and abstinence from all that has been forbidden by God. Such obedience is the fruit as well the proof of true love for God. In Islamic traditions, Prophet Muhammad used to teach Muslims to say:

"O Lord, grant us Your Love, and the love of those whom You Love, and the love of those who would bring us closer to Your Love. And make Your Love dearer to us than cool fresh water in a very hot day."

"Justice" is a comprehensive term, and may include all the virtues of good behavior. But the religion of Islam asks for something warmer and more human, the doing of good deeds even where perhaps they are not strictly demanded by justice—such as returning good for ill, or obligating those who in worldly language "have no claim" on you, and, of course, fulfilling of the claims of those whose claims are not recognized in social life. "*God enjoins justice and kindness, and giving charity to kinsfolk, and forbids indecency and abomination and wickedness: He instructs you, that you may receive admonition.*" Quran (16:90)

The central notion of justice in Islam is based on the mutual respect of one human being by another. The just society in Islam means the society that secures and maintains respect for persons through various social arrangements that are common interests of all members. Every human being must be treated as an end in himself or herself and never merely as a means, since he or she is the cream of God's Creation. The requirement is the equal integrity of each person in the society and his or her loyalty to the country concerned, which in turn will make it the duty of the society to provide equally for each person's pursuit of happiness.

Justice must be done equally to all and sundry, even if it is to be done against one's self, one's parent, or relatives or friends. There must be no difference between rich and poor.

"O you who believe: Stand out firmly for justice, as witnesses to God, even as against yourselves, or your parents, or your kin, and whether it be against rich or poor. For God can best protect both. Follow not the lusts of your hearts, lest you swerve, and if you distort justice or decline to do justice, verily God is well-acquainted with all that you do."
Quran (4:135)

234

Justice is God's attribute. To stand for justice is to be a witness to God, even if it is detrimental to our own interests, as we conceive them, or the interests of those who are near and dear to us. According to the Latin saying, "Let justice be done though the sky should fall." But Islamic justice is something higher than the formal justice of Roman law or any other human law. It is even more penetrative than the subtler justice in the speculations of the Greek philosophers. It searches out the innermost motives, because we are to act in the presence of God, to whom all things, acts, and motives are known.